GW01278828

NEIL CROMPTON
BEST SEAT
IN THE HOUSE

NEIL CROMPTON
BEST SEAT IN THE HOUSE

WITH
AARON NOONAN

HarperCollinsPublishers

HarperCollins*Publishers*
Australia • Brazil • Canada • France • Germany • Holland • Hungary
India • Italy • Japan • Mexico • New Zealand • Poland • Spain • Sweden
Switzerland • United Kingdom • United States of America

First published in Australia in 2021
by HarperCollins*Publishers* Australia Pty Limited
Level 13, 201 Elizabeth Street, Sydney NSW 2000
ABN 36 009 913 517
harpercollins.com.au

Copyright © Navaction Investments Pty Ltd 2021

The right of Neil Crompton to be identified as the author of this work has been asserted by him in accordance with the *Copyright Amendment (Moral Rights) Act 2000*.

This work is copyright. Apart from any use as permitted under the *Copyright Act 1968*, no part may be reproduced, copied, scanned, stored in a retrieval system, recorded, or transmitted, in any form or by any means, without the prior written permission of the publisher.

A catalogue record for this book is available from the National Library of Australia

ISBN 978 1 4607 6045 1 (hardback)
ISBN 978 1 4607 1382 2 (ebook)
ISBN 978 1 4607 8931 5 (audiobook)

Cover design: Design by Committee
Front cover images: Mark Horsburgh (top); Graeme Neander/AN1 Images.com (bottom)
Spine image: Justin Deeley/AN1 Images.com
Back cover images: Roderick Eime (top); Crompton Family Collection (bottom)
Typeset in Sabon LT Std by Kirby Jones
Printed and bound in Australia by McPherson's Printing Group

This book is dedicated to my true love, Sarah, and my wonderful children, Emma and Sienna.

Thank you also to my fellow motorsport enthusiasts for their incredible support over the journey and especially in the recent past.

Special thanks to Aaron Noonan for his undying commitment to the creation of this book.

CONTENTS

Foreword by Roger Penske — 1

Prologue — 3
1. The Early Years — 7
2. My Hero — 19
3. My Own Wheels — 25
4. Forging the Path — 30
5. On the Air — 39
6. Get Your Backside Trackside — 50
7. Not in the Lucky Sperm Club — 63
8. Two Corners at Calder — 71
9. Bathurst 1987 — 81
10. The King of Bankstown — 86
11. My Friend Brock — 97
12. Lion Tales — 105
13. Skaife and the Karma Bus — 126
14. A Bitter Podium — 138
15. The Rough Diamond from Albury — 147
16. The Wollongong Wiz — 158
17. Larrikin Larry — 171
18. The Toilet on Wheels — 175
19. A Date with the Dame — 178
20. The Amazing Allan Moffat — 185
21. A Mountain Win — 193
22. Setting Up Supercars — 201
23. The American Dream — 209
24. Racing in America — 219

25. Wheeling and Dealing	232
26. Cool Race Cars	237
27. Racing for the Blue Oval	256
28. Sliding Doors	268
29. Giving Back	272
30. The Kid and Green-Eyed Monsters	278
31. If, Buts and Maybes	291
32. The Home of Motorsport	298
33. 8 September 2006	308
34. Farewell, PB	312
35. The Tightrope of TV	320
36. The Take Off for AirTime	330
37. The Greatest Great Race	340
38. Sidetracked	347

FOREWORD

NEIL CROMPTON IS ONE of the brightest minds and most trusted voices in motorsports. His diverse experience and his knowledge of the sport provide great perspective, and I have always admired his work and his passion for racing. Neil has the unique ability to look at our sport through different lenses and still focus on the big picture.

From his years of experience behind the wheel as a driver to his legendary career as a broadcaster and someone who is still a true race fan at heart, Neil has a great appreciation for what makes motorsports so unique and special.

I got to know Neil well a few years ago when he and his company produced a documentary on Team Penske, and I was so impressed by his professionalism, his creativity, and his drive to tell our story in the most complete and entertaining way possible.

I am proud to call Neil a good friend, and I look forward to reading the book and enjoying some more of his great stories and exploits on and off the race track.

Roger Penske – Chairman, Penske Corporation

Roger Penske

PROLOGUE

IT WAS LOVE AT first sight – and sound. A life-changing epiphany.

The prelude was a bone-jarring ten-hour ride from Ballarat, in western Victoria, in the back seat of a family friend's Holden Torana XU-1. For added fun, the interstate journey was followed by a sleepless night camping under the stars surrounded by drunken goons, too many of them armed with firecrackers, and all seemingly with access to an endless supply of grog.

Welcome to the top of the mountain at Bathurst, 1977 style.

And then, the following morning, it happened. Winding up the hill, on a trailing throttle, it sounded like a car repeatedly speaking Aussie – 'Mate, mate, mate, mate, mate ...' On a wide-open throttle, the exhaust note declared war on your eardrums. The Mazda RX-3 was heard long before it was seen, and then it appeared, dancing, bouncing, sliding over the crest of the hill at Reid Park, slipping past the 'metal grate' and vanishing into the distance in a blaze of raspy glory.

I thought I was witnessing a NASA rocket launch. The car was so fast that it took my breath away. After years of pre-dawn, pre-race television-tweaking of the brightness, the contrast and eventually, in 1975, the colour settings, actually seeing and hearing a racing car in the flesh as it tackled the magical winding ribbon of road at Bathurst was a moment of pure joy. I was 17 years old and I was hooked.

Compared to the faster V8 Ford Falcons and Holden Toranas that appeared seconds later, the little Japanese rotary-powered coupe was hardly the rocket I conjured in my mind at first blush, but I thought it was brilliant nonetheless, and the image remains vivid in my memory today. Throughout practice and qualifying, I was awe-struck by the passing parade of superstars and their cars at this holy place, and it all led to the Great Race on Sunday.

In those days, self-preservation meant adopting neutral colours. Although I was a devoted Peter Brock fan, it became obvious very quickly that not wearing a Holden or Ford T-shirt meant you could enjoy a form of peace, and dodge the abuse handed out to those who dared to support either brand. My Suzuki motocross T-shirt was the perfect attire – except after day three ...

The naive teenager's guide to Mount Panorama survival in 1977 began with finding a good location from which to watch the race. My chosen position was in the fork of a tree next to the Shell Tower at Skyline. My bladder was full

PROLOGUE

and my stomach empty. I did not move all day, staring and studying every piece of racing information I could capture. Braking, lines, turn-in points, downshifts – all with a totally uninterrupted view. Here they all were, the legends, my heroes and their iconic cars, all day long. It was heaven.

It was the best (if most uncomfortable) seat in the house.

As a Brock fan, I was frustrated that his Holden Torana A9X and ambitious three-car team assault, backed by Holden dealer Bill Patterson, was struggling, unable to repel the mighty Moffat Ford Dealers Falcons of Allan Moffat and Colin Bond, who stormed to a crushing one-two finish in that year's Bathurst 1000.

Thinking about it later, the impression made on me by that Mazda RX-3, and then by Moffat, Bond, Brock and co., was profound. It left me with a fixation: I had to find a way to get to the other side of the fence.

I had wanted to race cars from as far back as I could remember, and that first Bathurst trip sealed the idea in my mind. The problem was that I had no idea how on earth I was going to do it. In that period of my life, sage grown-ups, teachers and other wise souls all liked to ask what you wanted to 'do' in life. But I knew what I wanted to 'be'.

Despite the dismissive smiles and disengaged chuckles, my matter-of-fact response was always the same: I wanted to be a racing driver.

My brother, Glen, and me in the driveway of our family home in Ballarat.
Crompton collection

1

THE EARLY YEARS

AS A TODDLER, I would stand and lean in between my parents from the back of the car across the gigantic bench seat while we were driving along, and call out all the various brands and models of the cars rattling towards us. At the age of three I could spot a Hillman Hunter from a Hillman Imp a mile away. Already I was perfecting one of the most useless skills known to mankind.

Clearly, almost six decades later, I've made zero progress in life. I'm still shouting at cars from afar.

Back then there was no such thing as a compulsory seatbelt. By modern standards, this was crazy dangerous. And can you imagine the boring monologue my parents had to endure from the gibbering kid in the back? Urgh. But ever since then, my imagination has been overstimulated by anything on wheels, and anything to do with engines, automation and performance.

I was born in July 1960 in Ballarat, about an hour from Melbourne. It's a town that can be bitterly cold for large chunks of the year; I often say I was born, bred and snap-frozen there! My love of all things automotive kicked in early. The catalyst for my lifelong obsession was probably my dad, Colin.

In fact, the whole Crompton household had an automotive vibe. Dad and my mum, Olwyn, detailed cars for various local dealers and, in a wonderfully 1960s Australian phrase, 'did up' cars, buying and selling them in their spare time. That was how they made a bit of cash on the side to pay for the extra trimmings they desired in life. My family didn't come from wealth, so Mum and Dad had to be resourceful, like many people in the 1960s.

Dad worked as an electrician for the State Electricity Commission, and jammed in a bunch of other part-time activities, including working after hours at a friend's engine reconditioning shop. He was technically gifted, annoyingly detailed and frequently displayed a shocking temper.

Mum was a stay-at-home mother who added to the family bank balance by doing some bookkeeping work on a part-time basis for an automotive reconditioning, parts and accessories business. Before my younger brother Glen and I arrived on the scene, she had worked for many years in the office at the Beaurepaires tyre centre in Ballarat.

We lived in Hawthorn Grove in Wendouree, a northern suburb of Ballarat, not far from Lake Wendouree. Our upbringing was typical of a lower-middle-class Aussie family in the 1960s.

THE EARLY YEARS

In primary school I towered over most other kids. Early in the game of life I was five-foot-ten. Living in that rare air up there meant I had some horsepower to exercise burn, and I ended up being captain of the Wendouree Primary School football team. I played centre half-forward and ruck rover and loved it. I had an unfair advantage and could muscle my way around the miniature paddock, snatching the footy with ease – which was all fine and dandy until the other kids had their own growth spurts, and pretty quickly my swagger vanished. My interest in the game slowed further when I broke a finger battling for a mark. Plus I really hated how damn cold and miserable it was crawling around in the midwinter Ballarat mud.

Cars and motorbikes and anything else with an engine were my magnet, and soon enough ball sports fell to the wayside. Drawing, reading, talking about and dreaming of driving cars consumed me.

As a kid, the allure of even seeing a race car with a racing number or a driver's name painted on the side of it was a major thrill. So imagine my excitement when Donald Campbell, the British speed record chaser, visited Ballarat with his Bluebird K7 speedboat and Bluebird land speed car in 1963. Even though I was only a toddler, I was captivated by those deep blue machines, parked on the back of a pair of open trucks in Ballarat's main street. They captivated many others in Ballarat too, and throngs swarmed to Sturt Street to take a look.

The Bluebird CN7, with Campbell at the helm, broke the land speed record at Lake Eyre, in South Australia, in July the following year, setting a mark of 403.1 miles per hour, a shade under 650 kilometres per hour.

To me, motorsport was a dazzling show with larger-than-life characters and extraordinary machines doing amazing things. Those deep blue Bluebirds completely fitted the bill. There were cars and automotive books everywhere in our house when I was growing up. Everything in my world was about cars and racing. And nothing has changed: my love of motorsport today still feeds off that childhood passion.

I have a distinct memory of riding with Dad in his Fiat 125. With apologies to Fiat fans, it was a boxy little rust-prone sedan with just one redeeming feature, but it was a good one: a sweet exhaust note. When Dad blipped the accelerator pedal as he down-changed a gear, I thought he was a magician. I loved that sound, and I was intrigued by the technique. Dad positioned his right foot to nudge the throttle with the side of his right heel, while he kept the ball of his foot on the brake pedal. For an impressionable brat like me, this was high art.

Most downshifts in a Supercar or race car are done this way. It's a bit of a black art called 'heel and toe', and its purpose is to smoothly harmonise the engine, the transmission and the road speed, so as to avoid the car lurching forward on the downshift and hammering the valve springs or other breakable internal parts.

The sound of that car, as Dad drove us around Lake Wendouree, was like a symphony to me. I made him accelerate and downshift repeatedly, just so I could hear that music!

There were all sorts of cars in our family's driveway when I was a kid. For some obscure reason, Dad had a fleet of Goggomobil Darts – they were everywhere! At various

THE EARLY YEARS

stages, the driveway would be littered with them. White, red, black, blue – it was like they were in a sixpack!

Because of that, it was a huge thrill decades later for me to meet Bill Buckle, the man who created the famous Dart in the late 1950s and early 1960s. He'd decided to bring out a little chassis from Europe with a two-stroke motorcycle engine tucked into it, and then fit a locally made two-door fibreglass body. They were weird toys, so light and tiny, with an even weirder 'sideways' H-pattern manual gear shift.

I still bear a scar on my right shin from an exhaust burn I copped from one of those little beasts when I got too close to the back of the car after one of Dad's hot laps of the block. I'm forever branded, like one of my TV mate Mark Larkham's cows on his farm! To this day, I don't know why Dad had so many of them. I should have found a way to hang on to one of them at least!

For me back then, driving past the Chrysler, Ford or Holden dealerships was a very big deal. The competition between the companies was fierce. They'd launch new cars regularly, or facelifts of existing models, fighting bitterly for market supremacy. Car lovers devoured every development. When Chrysler brought out the Valiant Charger, it was a breathtaking, groundbreaking update. Dad and I went to the Ballarat Showgrounds and peered through the cracks in the locked metal doors to catch a glimpse of the new model before its release.

*

I started driving on a farmstead owned by family friends near the tiny hamlet of Yaapeet, in far north-western Victoria, when I was seven or eight years old. The chosen weapon was a nasty old Ford utility we called 'Chitty Chitty Bang Bang', after the 1960s fantasy car movie starring Dick Van Dyke. I'd drive flat-out on the dirt roads between the two houses on the private farm property and pretend to be racing. The car boiled frequently, and one day it caught fire, so I traded up.

There were various models of Holdens and often Minis in our rotating fleet, including the very cool Cooper S models, which had more grunt. I'd drive on the disused southern end of the main runway at Ballarat Airport. I was about ten at the time, and Rallycross was becoming a big deal at the Calder Park Raceway, outside Melbourne. I'd invent a course that was part tarmac and part dirt and imagine I was a Rallycross driver.

The Mini was front-wheel drive, and the radiator was hanging to the side of the east-west mounted engine, so you couldn't drive it for too long on the wet dirt or grass before it would get clogged up with mud and overheat. I'd have to pull over and scrape the mud off the boiling radiator, then get going before it cooked itself again!

The Mini also had an electrical distributor mounted on the front of the engine. It seemed that if someone so much as spat on the road, moisture would find its way into the electrical system and disrupt the spark supply, and the Mini would grind to a silent halt.

There's a photo of me at the wheel of a white Holden Monaro at the ripe old age of 11 at Ballarat airport. It was one of Dad's cars, a six-cylinder 186-cubic-inch version, not the big 327- or 350-cubic-inch V8 versions that had won Bathurst in 1968 and 1969, respectively. In an open-face helmet, with the window open, my head on the tilt, yanking

Yours truly behind the wheel of our family Monaro at Ballarat Airport.
Crompton collection

away on the 'three on the tree' steering column mounted gearshift, I was channelling my heroes Colin Bond and Peter Brock, all the while killing another set of Dad's skinny crossply tyres and melting more drum brakes.

Back in the 1960s and early '70s, there was no quick way to get the latest information on motoring and motorsport. Television coverage of the sport was sketchy in an era long before 'via satellite' sports broadcasting became commonplace.

Magazines provided the racing fix we needed. The fortnightly specialist motorsport magazine *Auto Action* was my go-to. A newspaper-style publication, it started in 1971 and celebrated its 50th anniversary in early 2021. In the modern era, can you imagine waiting two weeks to unpack the detail about your favourite driver, team or event? The only way I knew motorsport events were being conducted in those days was either through the 'car people' connected to Dad (via the Light Car Club of Australia branch in Ballarat) or the pages of *Auto Action*.

Auto Action featured the latest news, event reports from tracks around the country, and I devoured every page. Whether it was the columns written by the top drivers of the period, their exploits in recent events or even the trade advertisements, I soaked it up and read each issue from front to back. I analysed every story, every photo and every advertisement, and tenderly stored every issue under my bed, to the point where I couldn't fit any more.

I went to as many Calder and Sandown race events in Victoria as possible. Calder Park Raceway is near the suburb of Keilor in western Melbourne, while Sandown is over the south-east side of Melbourne, around the suburb of Springvale. Very occasionally there was a trip to Phillip

Island as well, but that was rare, given it was a long way from Ballarat. Travelling interstate to car racing was way outside our family budget, and we didn't have the time in any case.

I always saw motor racing through romantic goggles. The smell, the BP start/finish sign, officials in white coats, crew in team uniforms, hero drivers in their suits, incredible engineering examples everywhere. Even more impressive was the sight and sound of machines being pushed to the limit.

The allure for me stems back to those formative years of my life, watching motorcycle racing in Victoria Park, local rallies in the bush around Ballarat, or a gymkhana out at the Light Car Club of Australia at the airport.

Kart racing was held out at a local track in Haddon, on the outskirts of Ballarat. It's the entry level of motorsport, where so many stars of Australian and world motorsport first cut their teeth before moving onto car racing, but it never had a strong presence around our family.

Dad had a background in motorcycles, so my taste for the racing bug was satisfied by a string of minibikes, that progressed into 125cc, 250cc and big-bore motocross bikes.

Dad and all his mates rode motorcycles, so I was excited to get my first machine, even if it was a pretty primitive one: a horrible old 90cc Yamaha model *something*. It had a chrome reverse-looking fuel tank and was red with a pressed-steel frame. It was a horrible-looking thing – we resurrected it from junk, which was what you did in those days.

My first brand-new bike was a much bigger deal. I was the proud owner (fully funded by the bank of Mum and Dad!) of a Honda SL70 minibike. The first thing we did was lop off the standard exhaust and muffler and fit a straight-through chrome exhaust, so it looked and sounded awesome.

Well, I thought so, anyway. In hindsight, I reckon perhaps our neighbours weren't such fans of the racket.

I have a vague memory that the Honda cost $275 and we somehow dodged the sales tax charge by using the exemption available to primary producers. We weren't farmers, but we knew someone who was! No dodgy declaration was off-limits to save a buck.

*

I'll never forget my first race. It was in 1972, the same year Peter Brock won the first of his nine Bathurst victories. The event was held at Wallan, north of Melbourne up the Hume Highway – and I won it. What started as a racing bug became an incurable disease.

I still have the photo of the presentation. We remained seated on our bikes, helmets on, trophies in hand and had our photo taken. One of the kids sharing the podium with me was Rob Urquhart. I still see Rob, who is a great bloke and works as a crew member for MW Motorsport in the Dunlop Super2 Series at Supercars events. He's a hardcore lover of motor racing. Fabulous. That little trophy is lurking around at home in a box somewhere, but for me the satisfaction of actually racing meant more than anything else. Winning was a pure bonus.

Mum hated the notion of me racing back then, and would continue to hate it throughout my racing years. Even now, when I goof off on a drive-day mission, she scowls. 'You be careful,' she still says.

Uh-huh, sure, Mum, that's my primary objective – to be careful.

THE EARLY YEARS

Dad was a perfectionist, and some might suggest that trait was handed down. Parental performance pressure is an awkward intruder for any young racer, and at the time when I went racing dirt bikes there were times that I didn't enjoy the racing and would clash with Dad – the expectation of performance from both of us could ruin the pleasure.

It's not uncommon in motorsport. I see it today administering the Toyota GAZOO Racing Australia 86 Series. I can smell the discomfort from kilometres away, and spot it in the eyes of young competitors.

Overwhelmingly, though, Dad did so much for me it now makes me emotional to reflect on it. At the time I didn't properly appreciate the sacrifices he made for me. Time, money, energy, effort. His commitment was enormous – something I only truly understood when I became a parent myself.

It was my parents' hard work and support that allowed me to go racing – and, as things turned out, that enabled me to channel my passion into a lifelong pursuit. I learned how to prepare and maintain machinery to go racing, and how to race. I broke a few bones along the way and captured some trophies, including becoming the 1975 Victorian Junior Motocross Champion.

But my eyes were always on something else: I wanted to race cars.

I vividly remember watching a car race on TV, then I went riding my motocross bike at Monza Park in Ballarat. Although I was riding this bike, in my head I was imagining I was in a race car. How I braked, how I cornered, the throttle treatment, the rhythm – I always visualised being in command of a race car. That was where I wanted to be.

Note the number 7 on the car – it's the number I raced under for many years. *Crompton collection*

2

MY HERO

I TENTATIVELY TOOK MY prized pencil, complete with its blue plastic golf club–shaped cap, from my well-worn pencil case and handed it over.

The recipient?

Peter Brock, my racing hero.

The first time I met him was as a schoolboy, aged 11, out at Calder Park in 1971 at a rallycross event. There's a photo of us standing together next to his supercharged rallycross Torana. What a weapon – and boy, did it sound good. It howled. The car started life as a GTR Torana and it was still road-registered. It was white and black in the early days, and painted yellow (quite poorly) later on.

My mission that day was to ask Holden's emerging superstar driver to write something for my school magazine, *Mixture Magazine*. My editorial contribution? To write 'Car

Corner' of course! I asked him to describe a flying lap of the Calder rallycross track in his supercharged Torana. Not only did he agree, but he also wrote it on a piece of paper there in the pits, leaning on the grubby matte-black Torana bonnet. That left a huge mark on me.

I've still got the original handwritten piece. It's getting a bit yellow and scruffy, but I treasure that sheet of paper – it's sealed in a plastic folder and safely tucked away in my office to this very day. Here's what Brock wrote:

> *A flying lap in the supercharged Torana, changing out of third gear at the starting line. The car accelerates up to nearly 110mph before negotiating the kink; a quick flick of the steering wheel sets it up and then it's on with the brakes and back to 2nd [gear] for a tight Repco corner.*
>
> *After the back straight and Esses, it's into 3rd [gear] for the fast right-hander and up to 80 before braking and putting it back to 2nd for Shell [Corner]. Once the car is pointed straight then it's full power to the jump – hang on for this one, then accelerate carefully through the mud and onto the straight, into 3rd and away we go for another lap.*

This was when the little kid with hardcore passion somehow connected with a special and popular racing driver in what was a life-changing encounter. The arc of our 35-year storyline is a bit special. Doting child fan becomes adult friend, becomes teammate, farewells his friend at nation-stopping state funeral. Writing this makes my hair stand on end.

MY HERO

Pre-dating the *Mixture Magazine* contribution, I remember writing a letter to Brock at the Diamond Valley Speed Shop, the family business his dad Geoff ran out in Hurstbridge. (If you look closely at the old photos of his career-starting Austin A30, you'll see 'Diamond Valley Speed Shop' on its flanks.) My fanboy ramble would have helped him sleep, yet he wrote back. It was a handwritten response, just brilliant.

Peter was incredibly engaging. The mere fact he took the time to look you in the eye, talk, share and engage was a really, really big deal. It was this, as well as his race results, that reinforced Peter's hero status to so many.

He was the all-Aussie boy who drove a Holden, smoked Marlboros, ate pies and barracked for Collingwood – he was about as Australian as they came in that era!

Rallycross was cool. Put simply, it was like rallying on steroids. Instead of one car disappearing into the bush at a time, competing against the clock, rallycross put the great aspects of rallying into an enclosed environment. I loved it. Man-made jumps, water crossings, cars going sideways, fierce battles, all positioned in such a way that a regular racetrack like Calder was transformed into a bullring of automotive action.

Racing was a simple caper back then. Brock's Holden Dealer Team 'transporter' was a Holden HK panel van, duck-egg blue in colour, hitched to a tandem trailer with one, maybe two crew members to look after it all. That was motor racing in those days, out in the open and not even a tent to shade the car and crew from the elements. No multimillion-dollar transporters or 'engineers' armed with multiple laptop computers. It was simple and straightforward, an era of motor racing that many deem the 'golden days' of Aussie motorsport.

I recall that Leonard Teale, a big-time actor of the day who starred in the *Homicide* TV series, always pitted alongside Peter at Calder as his 'paddock neighbour'. He also belted around Calder in a Toyota Corolla, and even finished as runner-up to Brock in one of those rallycross series.

As a little kid going to Calder – which, on any given day, meant you were frozen or sandblasted, or possibly both in the same day – you could see Brock the motor racing hero and alongside him a guy who arrested all the baddies on HSV-7 on TV the night before! That was living the big-time right there!

The thing about Brock that struck a chord with me, and no doubt thousands of others over the years, was that he hadn't been crafted by public relations spin. There was no media manager circling over his every move like they do these days. I know he was 'working the room' to a degree, but there was a natural flair to his personal engagement, and it literally made Peter a household name.

Clutching the galvanised-wire fencing at the circuit edge like Garfield in those days, I was always desperately trying to get a quarter of an inch closer to the action. For teenagers like me back then, Brock was a sporting god. I wanted to be him – everyone did – so it was a case of 'take a ticket and get in a very long queue'. If you could count up how many males under 50 years of age in 1972 wanted to be a Holden racing driver, I reckon it would have been in the hundreds of thousands, maybe more!

I came to see the characters of motorsport as heroes and villains. That's something racing trades on to this very

Peter Brock and Allan Moffat sharing a Coke at Calder, 1971.
AN1 Images/Terry Russell

day. It's the tribalism of the sport, and something we've done for over 50 years. Brock was the good guy, the wearer of the 'white hat', while his Ford rival Allan Moffat was the 'black hat'. In truth, this wasn't even close to accurate, but it brought the theatre of racing to life in the most wonderful way.

Never in my wildest dreams did I think I'd become close to both men.

3

MY OWN WHEELS

I GOT FAILED. MY first attempt at getting my driver's licence as a teenager didn't go well. That's a distinct difference from saying that I failed, because I know I did not. The testing officer failed me, and to this day it still riles me.

My first car was a light blue Chrysler Hillman Hunter, and that was the car I went for my licence in. The tyres were so crazily skinny they looked more like cross-ply rubber bands than vehicle tyres!

One of the requirements during the test was to perform a handbrake stop on a left turn. I still remember the exact location: on the left turn out of Cobden Street into Barkly Street on the east side of Ballarat.

Being an old goldrush town, Ballarat has plenty of bluestone gutters lining its roads. I was mindful I didn't go too close to the edge of the road, where there was mud and slop and dirt that would undoubtedly get onto my lovely little Hunter. I've always been into 'clean', and I didn't want to get my car dirty unnecessarily.

I came to a stop and pulled on the handbrake to bring the car to a complete standstill. The indicator blinked away, informing the world of my next move: a left turn into Barkly Street. I reached down and released the handbrake, slipped the clutch and smoothly eased Chrysler's finest away in first gear.

None of this was a big deal. After all, I had been driving cars for ten years or more up to this point. I was on the road to getting my driver's licence and winning the freedom to go wherever I liked whenever I wanted to.

But then we got back to the office. I was full of positive vibes, but what the instructor said next floored me: 'You failed the test.'

I thought it was a joke. 'What? Why?'

He said when I was making the left turn into Barkly Street, I wasn't close enough to the left edge of the road, and was too near the middle line.

Between the edge of the sealed road and the bluestone gutters, there was mud, water and potholes, and I just didn't want to drive my car though that stuff. And anyway, regardless of my clean-freak gene, it was illogical to make the turn from off the sealed road.

But that didn't matter. It was a single-lane street, and this bloke thought I should be turning left from the dirt. He had failed me.

I thought he was a halfwit, and made sure he knew it. It's fair to say that didn't help my cause. My outburst didn't change anything, of course, and I had to go back later and do another driving test to get my licence. When I did, I got my licence with zero drama – this time with a different testing officer.

These days, whenever I head back to Ballarat to visit Mum, I often pass through that intersection – and it still grinds my gears and I mildly heat up!

*

I certainly wasn't a hoon on the road as a youngster, although I went through the same phase as most in my P-plate days. Mistakes are made as a result of poor judgement and/or putting yourself in dumb positions. It was a thrill to be 'off the leash', and teenage males often incorrectly believe they're both skilled and invincibile.

My history of car ownership as a young bloke is littered with all sorts of cars. I had a tiny Renault 12 for a time, before I ran into the back of someone in it. That was nothing compared to what happened to my beloved Holden Torana.

It was a lime green 'Plus 4' model Torana, a pretty weird-looking thing. A four-door, this four-cylinder Holden had 'Plus 4' decals in the same way its sister six-cylinder version had 'G Pack' decals on the side. Those stickers did nothing for the speed or the styling of either car!

My Torana was always immaculate. Dad was always fastidious about car preparation. The tyres were always blacked, the lettering on them gleaming in white or gold. Every car in our driveway was cleaned on a weekly basis to within an inch of its life.

Back in my motocross days, I was familiar with the dirt roads to and from the Monza Park track between the suburbs of Buninyong and Sebastopol in Ballarat, and one day I thought I'd add some spice to the trip. These roads were always nicely graded, wide gravel roads, compacted with very hard, fine material. A wannabe rally driver's paradise. I had a mate onboard, and my show-off 'devil horns' came out for a fleeting moment in a desire to generate a little sideways action.

I threw the Torana into a corner, fully expecting to be flying around the turn in a controlled slide like the best rally drivers of the day. Instead, I pitched it straight off the road and into a ditch.

'Uh-oh ...' I thought.

Dad had fitted the SL/R 5000 front lip spoiler onto the car not long after purchase, so it looked just like the Toranas that Peter Brock and Colin Bond raced at the time. It turned out that it lacked frontal ride height ground clearance when I needed it most, and the earth bank ripped the bottom off the spoiler.

There was no hiding the damage when I sheepishly made it back to Crompton family HQ. But I didn't own up straightaway to what had happened, and instead started cleaning the car, hoping I could wash the damage away. It didn't polish out!

There was no chance I could hide the fact I had stuffed up, and Dad went berserk at me for being a complete moron.

'If you do that again, I'll kick your arse until your nose bleeds!' he told me.

I learned my lesson.

I had a Lancia Beta Coupe later on, a lovely little two-door Italian car that had a great exhaust note. It was burgundy and I had it for a long time, but the bloody thing nearly killed me once.

I was driving it to Sydney and somehow the battery started smouldering, and I got a massive toxic headache from the acid fumes. It was bad enough that I had to pull over near Mittagong in New South Wales. It's never good when your enduring memory of a car is that it delivered the worst toxic headache you've ever had!

There was a succession of panel vans for my business, Navajo Action Sports & Cycles. I remember driving a HJ Holden panel van for a time and also a red XA Ford van. I would sometimes drive these rotten devices on all-night trips to Sydney when I was in the early years of my commentary career. On one trip I fell asleep and woke up driving sideways across the saplings in the middle of the divided road.

That certainly gave me a big wake-up call. Finding yourself oversteering through weeds at 100 kilometres per hour tends to do that.

After a few near misses, the messages from the universe will penetrate a thick skull – if you bother to listen …

4

FORGING THE PATH

THE SAME YEAR I saw my first Bathurst race in person, 1977, was also the year I figured that I had little interest in anything educational at school.

By that stage I was in Form 5 (these days called Year 11) at Ballarat High School. I was always a middle-of-the-road student, never at the bottom but never at the top. I was like a bowler in a cricket match, just trying to roll my arm over enough to make it to the end of a tedious innings. School just seemed like something that was getting in the way of what I needed to do.

And what I needed to do was race – or find a way to become involved in racing.

I completed my Leaving Certificate in 1977 and started my High School Certificate the following year, but made the decision to pull the pin in March 1978.

FORGING THE PATH

From a very early age I'd always loved to work. On weekends and school holidays, I had worked for a gentleman by the name of Tom Gill in a boat shed called Gill's Marine, on the edge of Lake Wendouree in Ballarat, and I went to work for him properly immediately after I left school.

I did everything. I sold boats, outboard motors and boating accessories, restocked shelves, ordered bits and worked in the workshop, repairing and servicing Evinrude outboard motors. It was a great introduction to life in the 'real world', and Tom was the most placid and wonderful man.

Boating had been a big part of my childhood. Ballarat was surrounded by good freshwater skiing locations, Lake Burrumbeet and Lake Learmonth, and I'd started water skiing at six years of age. Six decades later, I still frequently slalom ski.

Done with school, it was time to craft my own path. I didn't know it at the time, but an unlikely series of events, opportunities and meetings would take me from Ballarat to Bathurst and beyond, as I would fulfil my dream of becoming a racing driver.

I was a frustrated young man around this time, not really knowing exactly what to do. I spent time working for a local real estate agent, Benjamin's, and another division of their business, CHC Homes. My job was to guide prospective buyers through display homes – but I found, to my dismay, that I was expected to work on the weekend of the Bathurst 1000.

The display homes had only 'prop' furniture, intended to give customers an idea of how the home might look if they were to purchase it. But that didn't extend to including a television set. This was a large-scale disaster for a young rev head like me, desperate as I was to watch the biggest race of the year.

I'd been watching Bathurst for as long as I could remember. Race day morning was a TV ritual. Adjust the set, watch the test pattern and settle in for a non-eating, non-moving, non-normal-body-function all-day race fest! There was no way I was going to let work make me miss the Great Race.

Dismayed, I headed to the local TV shop and promptly bought a brand-new portable colour television, took it to the display home, plugged it in, adjusted the rabbit-ear aerials and promptly sat in front of it all afternoon, only begrudgingly getting off my stool when yet another annoying customer turned up.

Looking back on it, this was shockingly unprofessional, but at the time I figured the prospective buyers could figure out for themselves that there were three bedrooms and a bathroom – they didn't need me to tell them that! Clearly, I was the wrong guy for this job, and my time there didn't last much longer.

Next I sold motorcycle accessories on commission, which saw me travelling around western Victoria selling parts on behalf of my former sponsor, Clifton Hill Suzuki in Melbourne. But hot-lapping Victoria and begging motorcycle dealers to buy stuff was gruelling, tiresome and yielded little in the way of cash, so in the end I went to work for the source. Andy Findlay was the guy who owned the business, which was based in Thomastown, a northern suburb of Melbourne.

What started as Clifton Hill Suzuki, a pure retail operation, became Triple C, a wholesale import and distribution business. Triple C was an importer of motocross gear in the mid-1970s

Flying has always been a passion of mine. This is at Ballarat
Airport in 1984 with a Cessna 152, a plane I flew from 1980 to 1986.
Crompton collection

when motocross exploded. Andy was one of the first to spot this trend and frequently visited California to source the latest cool products, which he would then sell back in Australia.

Every day I drove back and forth to Melbourne, carving my own groove in the Western Highway. It was during this time that Dad and I had a talk.

'I think you should be in your own business,' Dad said to me. 'You can then fend for yourself.'

I was shy and not at all good at self-starting. Dad wasn't an entrepreneur but he had a wonderful entrepreneurial spirit. I have no doubt that same entrepreneurial thread was passed on to me. And that's why I started Navajo Sports Gear at 1 Creswick Road, Ballarat, in 1979 as a sole trader. Later we moved to a store in the main street of Ballarat, Sturt Street, and I changed the name to Navajo Action Sports & Cycles and at the same time created a company structure when I was 22 years of age. The setup of the business wouldn't have happened without Dad. He and a family friend, Doug Orr, rolled their sleeves up and helped make the shop a reality. Whether it was painting the walls or building shelves, their help was invaluable, and meant I saved some cash.

Navajo was a little retail shop that catered for action sports long before they became a 'thing'. It was *way* ahead of its time. I wasn't obsessed with football, cricket or tennis, like the rest of Victoria. I was into everything that wasn't those things: water skiing, surfing, roller skating, surfboards, skateboards, mountain bikes, BMX bikes, motocross and car racing. The business grew over the following years to become a great success.

Why the name 'Navajo'? As a teenager, my love of cars was matched by a serious interest in aeroplanes. In 1975 Dad scraped enough money together to hire a private aircraft to fly us (and my bike) from Ballarat to Hobart to enable me to compete in the Australian Motocross Championships at Sandford, near Hobart.

The aircraft, a twin-engine, pressurised Aero Commander 680, was owned by Geoff Robertson. He was the highly successful owner of Franklin Caravans, which at the time was a huge brand, one of the biggest local manufacturers of caravans.

Sitting alongside the pilot for the first time blew my mind and introduced me to an exciting new world. I loved, and still love, flying.

For a fair period of time I flirted with the notion of training to become a senior commercial pilot, as it was known then (now you go for your air transport pilot licence, or ATPL). I also had an interview in Melbourne to learn what it would take to train as an air traffic controller or flight service officer. In the end, I correctly reasoned that I was too dopey at maths and science to ever succeed. But I did begin training for a private pilot licence (or PPL) at 16 years of age.

Oddly, I would ride my bicycle to the airport, fly an aircraft and then ride back home. I was too young to drive but old enough to fly! Australia has some oddball rules, and now more than ever, the various states have their own wacky agendas.

As for the motocross championships in Tasmania – I led the majority of the Junior 125cc Australian Motocross race on my Clifton Hill Suzuki RM125, only to slam heavily into the loamy sand after I landed awkwardly on a tree root that began to appear late in the race. Racing has a sobering way of bringing you back to earth on occasion.

Even so, it was thrilling to be there. We were based in the Suzuki team tent throughout the weekend, alongside the reigning motocross world champion, Gaston Rahier, who was a pint-sized Belgian motocross superstar. It was an exciting period in motorcycling, and I knew that the racing environment was my natural habitat.

While training for my private pilot's licence in Ballarat, I came across an aircraft called the Piper Navajo. Piper, a US-based manufacturer in Vero Beach, Florida, named all their various aircraft models after Native American tribes. There was the Comanche, Cheyenne, Mojave, Cherokee, Navajo and others.

I thought the name had a pleasant mystique, and learned that the name 'Navajo' meant 'the wanderer'. It sounded cool to me, so I went with it.

I loved flying. I flew a tiny Cessna 150 Aerobat, a Cessna 152 and a bigger Cessna 172. (Amazingly, I still see the 150 and 152 in the air around Ballarat to this day.) I flew solo in just over five hours and earned a restricted PPL, which enabled me to fly within five miles of the reference point of the aerodrome and within the confines of the training area.

I learned alongside a good friend, Peter Terrill. He went on become a highly qualified senior airline pilot, and we still occasionally fly together now.

I obtained a limited aerobatic rating for loops, spins and barrel rolls in the Cessna 150. I'm not sure what possessed me to do 'aeros'. Having endured jammed throttles, broken steering and failed wings in racing cars later in life, I was putting ridiculous faith in the skills of people I did not know or trust when I tipped that little machine upside down.

To pay for all this adventuring, my business sold a range of other products, and I became both a wholesaler and importer of products from the United States, which was the home of all the things I loved.

I registered 'Trik Stix' as a business name and under that banner began buying, importing and repackaging decals and stickers from the United States, then selling them via mail order and wholesaling them to motorcycle and bicycle and BMX shops all over Australia.

The manufacturer I bought the stickers from was called 'Stick Em Up' and that business name got me into a bit of a sticky situation one day. 'Stick Em Up' was owned and run by Cliff Johnson and his family, who were based in Livermore, in northern California.

Now, that name sounds fine – it's a nice play on words for an organisation in the business of selling zillions of stickers – but it wasn't so funny when it came time for me to go to the local Commonwealth Bank to arrange a bank draft to send money to the United States to pay for them.

In those days, to pay for goods and services offshore you needed a bank draft, effectively the international version of a bank cheque. But the first time I wandered into the Sturt Street branch of the bank in Ballarat and muttered the words 'Stick Em Up', all hell broke loose! On subsequent visits to get further bank drafts, I'd take great care to preface what I was about to ask for. Very carefully I would explain the name of the business, step by step, and that I needed to send funds, and that I was most certainly not there to relieve the bank of its cash reserves.

Thankfully, the bank manager at that branch, Gus, was a member of the Light Car Club in Ballarat. He was able to smooth things out for me, but whenever there was a new teller at the bank, I had to approach them very cautiously!

The success of the business should have made me happy. At its peak, we held tens of thousands of dollars worth of sticker stock. It was a great little business on top of the other retail stuff we did. I was in my early twenties with a business that was making a solid dollar, and on the surface things looked great.

However, I have a strong recollection of standing at the shop counter on one of those cold, wet, dreary Ballarat winter days, watching the rain tumble down outside. It was the early 1980s and there was not a customer in sight. Not one of those positive things in my business life had moved me even fractionally closer to what I really wanted to do.

By this time I hadn't raced for what seemed like forever. I felt like I was surrendering to the miserable notion that car racing would never be more than a hollow dream.

Little did I know, wheels were about to turn.

5

ON THE AIR

FROM PARKING ROGUE TO being offered the motorsport television gig of a lifetime with one of the biggest networks in the land! It's beyond extraordinary as a story. How on earth could that occur?

'Would the owner of Holden panel van, registration ABC 123, please report to the tower ...'

I was certain I was in trouble. My car's registration details were heard all over the PA system of the Metro West BMX track at Liverpool Speedway in Sydney, and I, as the owner of that luxurious vehicle, had been summoned to the tower.

To grow my tiny business, I'd lock up the shop in Ballarat on a Friday night, throw the keys to my freshly minted 'manager' – a slightly inflated title for another kid who liked selling the stuff we sold – and drive my van all night up the Hume Highway, or wherever, in order to be on site for events just like this BMX race event. I was taking my business to where the customers were: hundreds of eager young BMX fans keen to blow their parents' money.

On what ultimately became a noteworthy day in 1984, my plans for incremental income generation were placed on temporary pause as I reluctantly responded to the PA call.

The tower was nothing special. In fact, to describe it as a tower would be to insult proper towers! It was just a ladder leading up to a small tin shed about the size of a portable toilet, with only just enough room for one bloke to stand in the breeze with a microphone in one hand and a bit of flapping paper in the other as he called the action while a bunch of sweaty brats furiously pedalled around the BMX track.

I peered up the ladder. A plus-sized gent glared back through thick glasses, his moon-round face and fierce eyes locked on me. 'Are you the guy with *that* Holden panel van parked over there?' he barked gesturing to the unmistakable brightly sign-written Holden 'Neilmobile'.

'Yep,' I grunted.

The look on his face said it all. 'You can't park there, and you haven't paid a site fee to sell your stuff,' he grumbled. 'You need to pay your site fee and move that thing – right now.'

Later I learned this man always tended to be economical and caustic with his words when suffering those whom he perceived to be fools. And I was most certainly the fool.

But in that instant, a momentous link in the bizarre chain of my life fell into place. Serendipity, good management, sheer luck – I really have no logical explanation.

'Are you the kid who has been calling the Mr Motocross Series and the motor racing on the ABC?' he asked.

Indeed I was. I'd been commentating Mr Motocross and motorcycle racing, drags and circuit racing in the previous few years on the ABC, as well as on SBS and Channel 0 (later Network Ten).

'Well, my name's Mike Raymond and I work for Channel Seven,' he went on. 'We've just won the rights to the Australian Touring Car Championship for next year. Here's my number.'

Thirty-seven years later, I can still recite Mike's home phone number without even blinking. I'd rattle it off on these pages now, but I don't think his wife Carol would appreciate the random calls.

I didn't move the van or pay the site fee. Better still, I flogged a huge pile of stickers and lots of Rat BMX clothing, grabbed a fistful of grubby cash and fled home to Ballarat. I rang Mike the next week.

*

That meeting with Mike Raymond, who by the mid-1980s was the prime mover and shaker of Seven's annual Bathurst 1000 TV telecast, in addition to its lead commentator, was my big break, but it was not my first commentary or television gig.

In the late 1970s I'd been forced to stop motocross racing because of injury, but I still had the crazy dream of becoming a racing car driver. I remember stopping at the Maurie Quincey Honda dealership in Alexandra Road, Moonee Ponds in Melbourne around that time with Dad to take a look at a Formula 2 open-wheeler driven by Paul Feltham that was for sale. I don't remember the exact price tag, but the 'sticker shock' I felt when I learned the cost of that car was depressing. My jaw hit the floor, and I remember thinking how absolutely unobtainable that amount of money would ever be.

Right then, the cold reality of real life was hammered home to me. Owning a helmet or being enthusiastic would not lead to me becoming a racing driver. I simply didn't have the money, the connections or the engineering skill to get a driving opportunity at any level. And I didn't even have the first clue how to go about getting them.

I stopped dirt bike racing in 1977, but my decision to make a comeback for the 1978 Australian Motocross titles was what landed me my first job as a broadcaster. However, that was far from my intent.

My bike of choice for my comeback was a 390cc Husqvarna, a pretty cool thing, burgundy in colour, with heaps of power and torque, connected to a six-speed gearbox. It was a wild, nasty, untamed toy that tried to spit you off across every bump and around every corner.

I was practising at a track in Newtown, near Ballarat, in preparation for the Australian titles. We didn't call it 'testing' back then. The Husqvarna had a steel rod mounted to the frame just under and behind the foot peg, running rearwards to the backing plate on the rear brake. While turning at high speed with my right leg out and my foot down, my foot flicked backwards and jammed beneath the rod. I smashed all the metatarsals, the bones connecting my ankle joint out to my toes. Essentially, my foot broke in half.

I was hospitalised, and the surgeons put a metal pin in my foot to help everything heal. So there I was, a very long-haired lout of a motocross rider with nothing to do except

Riding at Newtown motocross track back in 1976. *Crompton collection*

grow more hair while bumbling around on crutches. But that was about to change.

My father had a friend in Melbourne by the name of Bill Clough. Bill was the secretary of the Auto Cycle Union of Victoria (ACUV) and chief electrician of the Victoria Hotel (the Vic) in the CBD in Melbourne. Bill was one of those special people who cross your path and change your life. I don't know how Dad and Bill became friends, but I'm glad they did.

Passionate about motorcycle racing, Bill was one of those special people who give their heart and soul to the sport, ensuring it continues. Without volunteers like Bill, motorsport would simply not exist. We should all be deeply thankful for the flag marshals and scrutineers, as well as all the unpaid workers and administrators who give their bone marrow to make it all happen, and have so done forever.

I was still on my crutches and hobbling around when I discussed the last motocross event at the Vic with Dad and Bill. I was moaning that the circuit's commentators, Ken Dobson and Harry Lowe, were off the pace. They were fine callers in the technical sense, as well as lovely fellows, hard workers who had an undoubted love for motorcycle racing. But I felt they waffled too much about old riders and bikes – BSA Bantams, Triumphs and Nortons and other crappy old oil-leaking Pommy bikes that no one cared about anymore.

Youngsters like me saw all this banter as irrelevant prehistoric chat. I thought they should have enthusiastically been sharing info about the cool new bikes from Japan, and for that matter enthusing about the incredible riders who straddled them in the all-important show.

ON THE AIR

'Well, why don't you do it then?' offered Bill, and in an instant my broadcasting career was born.

I wasn't ready for this response; my unprompted review of the incumbents was merely morning tea chat. But having offered my unsolicited criticism, now I had to back it up.

'Um, maybe, yes, I guess so,' I said tentatively.

After Dad, Bill was the guy who really launched me into the life I now lead, and I am forever in debt to him for what he did for me. When I did look him up in his latter years to offer him my heartfelt thanks, it was too late: he had passed away.

And so it happened. I went along to provide 'expert' motocross rider comments as the guest commentator while still on crutches with my busted foot for an event at Broadford, just north of Melbourne, in 1978 and 1979. As it turned out, it was a combined bikes and car buggies event, co-promoted by the ACUV and the Light Car Club of Australia (LCCA) and televised on Channel 0. For me there would be no gentle introduction to commentary at a regular event where the only people who would hear my waffle would be those having their eardrums assaulted by a scratchy PA system at the track. I was going straight onto live network television as a spotty-faced, long-haired teenager with no formal education, training or skills – other than that I could work out one bike or rider from another.

I had zero idea about anything to do with television or commentary, but I did know the difference between an RM125 Suzuki and a YZ125 Yamaha – how many gears they had, how much grunt, whether they had a special single-ring Wiseco piston, a DG alloy head or special Koni shocks, Renthal alloy handlebars or whatever the gadget of the day was. As a bonus, I could pick the riders without having to look down at a piece of paper. I'd raced against most of these bandits, so it was second nature.

Phil Gibbs was the host of that Broadford coverage, a Melbourne sports broadcaster who did lots of VFA football for Channel 0 in the 1970s. Phil was a real TV pro with a beautiful voice. He was a regular on Melbourne radio and TV, and had joined Channel 0 as Director of Sports in 1964. He'd compered the first live coverage of the Melbourne Cup, and in the 1980s he would foster the talents of Rex Hunt, Bruce McAvaney and Eddie McGuire in the commentary box. All three would become big-time Aussie rules football commentators and personalities on TV and radio.

My commentary debut seemed to go well. Quite by accident – literally – I was in the deep end of the pool, and I presume my peers most likely thought, 'This kid needs a serious haircut, but he seems to know what he's talking about.' Somehow things progressed from there and the phone started to ring. Various motorcycle clubs asked for my services in gigs that landed me $20 and $50 – solid money for a teenager in the late 1970s! I remember sitting at the pub in Ballarat with some of my schoolmates, and they were staggered that I'd earned $100 in one week calling motocross races.

The LCCA was a big deal at the time. It was heavily involved in car racing, as the operator and promoter of the Sandown circuit, in the south-east of Melbourne, a track I'd been to with Dad many times before. The LCCA had a strong membership base and was quite a big organisation. It was all walnut walls, blue blazers and chat about old cars in the bar over a sherry.

Interviewing motocross star Stephen Gall in the early 1980s.
Crompton collection

None of that made any sense to me, but I did a few of the motocross events at Broadford. Then came the question that gave me the next boost to where I wanted to be. The general manager of the LCCA, a guy named Ian McKnight, came to me with a question: 'Do you know anything about car racing?'

Ah, yes, indeed I did! That opened the door to me joining the ABC's television coverage team for the LCCA's events at Sandown. Whether it was touring cars, sports sedans or open-wheeler racing, I didn't care – I would be there in the paddock, with my notepad in hand, asking drivers and teams about their cars, their chances of winning, the colour of their underwear – I wanted to know it all. I was respectful, eager to learn, and hungry to acquire information.

Truth be told, though, I was also petrified of going on air with the established voices of motorsport of the day: Paul Harrington, Adrian Ryan, Drew Morphett, Tim Lane and sometimes the legendary Howard Marsden.

Occasionally someone sends me an old clip or a link from YouTube of some of my commentary or hosting work from that early period, and I cringe. It's totally embarrassing. But working for the ABC brought me closer to car racing. If I wasn't commentating races, I'd sit alongside the likes of Will Hagon and John Smailes and assist them in the commentary box, feeding them notes with information to add to their calls of the races, and keeping a track of the race via a lap chart, jotting down the running order of the cars (or bikes) as they crossed the start/finish line every lap.

I learned a lot about broadcasting from Will and John. Will delivered (and still delivers) motor racing storytelling with such a rich tone and a beautiful vocabulary. I thoroughly enjoyed listening to Will and his colleague Evan Green in those early days and lifted a lot of valuable nuggets from their repertoire. Will always seemed to find the right word to paint and explain the scene.

John also provided a valuable insight and learning for good broadcasting. It's a simple asset that I still apply to this very day. He always researched the topic in detail and took a lot of notes in face-to-face conversation. To this day I still carry a pocket notebook and pen and, while I don't always stand by someone playing cub reporter taking notes, I will walk away from a conversation with a David Reynolds or a Chaz Mostert and jot the key points from our conversation. I never breach confidentiality or key IP, but it's important for our viewers to feel as though we provide an electronic pit pass to the backstage, and note-taking helps me do that.

Back in the days of working on the ABC broadcasts I was still running my business in Ballarat. I'd close it on a Friday night and drive interstate overnight, or first thing on a Saturday to Calder or Sandown. Then I'd be back at the front counter of the shop on a Monday morning.

That was my life on repeat, until the day I headed to the Metro West BMX track at Liverpool Speedway in 1984 and met Mike Raymond.

6

GET YOUR BACKSIDE TRACKSIDE!

MIKE WAS THE ESSENCE of an entrepreneur. He and his brother Steve were something of a double act, working as track announcers for a promotional group called Empire Speedways, which ran dirt track racing at the Sydney Showgrounds.

Mike moved on to Liverpool Speedway later in the 1960s, and his one-liners and catchy nicknames, along with his flair for promotion, meant that the speedway in suburban Liverpool in Sydney quickly became known as the 'Place for Pace'. His call to 'get your backside trackside' was a staple of radio and television ads for speedway and other forms of motorsport for many years.

He moved into television and became the voice and face of motorsport on Channel Seven in the late 1970s. Its annual

Bathurst 1000 touring car telecast was world-leading in motorsport broadcasting.

Despite his always generous build and his distaste for exercise, Mike's energy was boundless. He coined nicknames for all of the top touring car drivers in the 1980s, as he'd done for speedway racers in the years before. Those nicknames live on today among race fans across the country. Ask any of them the nickname and they'll know exactly who you're talking about.

The Baby-Faced Assassin? That was Glenn Seton.

No-Baloney Tony? Tony Longhurst.

Tricky Dicky and Peter Perfect? That'd be Dick Johnson and Peter Brock.

I called Mike a few days after our unplanned meeting at the Metro West BMX track and he offered me a consulting job with Channel Seven in Sydney as a commentator for their motorsport coverage in 1985. Previously, the network had only covered the annual Bathurst race every October, plus some events at Amaroo Park in Sydney, while the other races that made up the Australian Touring Car Championship had been televised by the ABC.

For 1985 this was to all change, and both the series of races that made up the ATCC and the Bathurst 1000 were going to be on Channel Seven. Their aim was to put top-tier motorsport in a regular timeslot on one outlet, so it could be more easily found and enjoyed.

For me, Mike's job offer was an opportunity to get closer to my first love, racing. Going to Sydney would put me in the middle of the action. I didn't go with the specific purpose of 'being on TV'; that was simply a by-product. For me it was then, and still is today, motor racing first, TV second.

It was a super simple recipe. I loved car racing, I wanted to race cars and I liked and continue to enjoy talking about car racing. There's nothing too complex about any of that.

For some time, I'd had a customer in my shop in Ballarat who'd wanted to buy the business. I had rejected his advances a few times, but now I decided it was time to take him up on his offer. A deal was quickly done for the stock and goodwill, landing me with what seemed like plenty of cash in my pocket.

Pretty soon I splashed some cash, treating myself to a brand-new, navy blue 3 Series BMW. I told anyone who would listen that I was going to head up to Sydney, semi-retire and cruise along in life and try my hand at getting closer to car racing. Maybe even spend some money to drive one!

That 318i BMW had no power, but it had the most beautiful paint finish and door-closing feel! If BMW had put as much effort into making it go faster as they did in making the doors close nicely, they might have sold some more of them.

As it happened, Mike's job offer was not the only thing that prompted my move to Sydney. My motocross commentary had led to a chance encounter with Vincent Tesoriero, the Mr Motocross series promoter, as well as Ian O'Brien (known as 'Fish', given he was an Olympic gold-medal-winning former swimmer), who was running the outside broadcast outfit, Videopak, which produced the Mr Motocross TV coverage. This opened the door for me to cover racing for SBS, particularly the traditional Easter motorcycle events that were still running at Bathurst from the 1970s into the early 1980s.

So I'd been making many trips to Sydney for motocross and commentary work – and I had met a girl. Cathy worked for SBS Television, where the then Head of Sport was a chap named John Rowley. Today, John's son Rich still does a pile of camerawork for me. He works closely with me in my production business and others in motorsport as a top-line, highly sought-after video cameraman here and overseas.

Things just clicked into place for 1985. The business was sold, I had cash in my pocket, a girlfriend in Sydney, Mike was giving me the chance to be part of Channel Seven's coverage and I also had an opportunity to do some consulting work for a bicycle and accessories company called General Accessories, which later became known as TI Industries.

They were the Malvern Star manufacturer and the Raleigh Bicycles importer in Australia, and I'd been a successful dealer for them in the past. Now they needed some help in the Sydney market, so they got me on board to help troubleshoot their dealer relationships.

Also in this period, my motocross connections got me an amazing experience on Triple M radio in Sydney. One of Vincent's partners in his advertising agency was Hamish Cameron, who went on to become General Manager of Triple M and later General Manager of Chief Entertainment.

'Oh, you're coming to Sydney? Great! We'll use you on Triple M!'

From there sparked a working relationship with Doug Mulray. Being around him was like being strapped to a rocket. He instantly dubbed me 'Neils on Wheels' at a time where there were one million people listening to his and Andrew Denton's show. It was huge, and listening to that show was a part of Sydney culture at the time.

One year they did a Christmas show and I found myself in the Ansett Golden Wing Lounge in Melbourne Airport singing 'Jingle Bells' live on radio. I started singing it very, very quietly, barely above a whisper, with Mulray booming down the line at me to sing it louder, which made the whole lounge stop and turn around! It was bloody embarrassing!

Add all of that up, and my new life in Sydney was immediately busy and it's never slowed down since.

I've always loved the technical elements of motorsport, but the overwhelming appeal for me has always been the allure of the overall show. That was what paid everybody's bills. Being in the presence of Mike Raymond in that era, I got a massive dose of the show business and entertainment aspects of the sport.

You'd be wasting your time talking to Mike about wheel bearing tensions and other technical jargon – he simply could not have cared less. He was all about seeing a daredevil racing driver dance a mud-flicking, 800-horsepower Sprintcar sideways up against the wall at a speedway at over 160 kilometres per hour in a scorching race with three other drivers, and then watching them cross the line together in a grandstand finish. Mike was all about the adrenaline of motorsport, and for that he was unapologetic.

It was in 1985 that the trajectory and growth of motorsport in Australia genuinely changed. Channel Seven had done amazing things for a long period of time at Bathurst since they first telecast the race (then known as the Armstrong 500) in 1963, but other coverage of racing was disconnected. Some events were on the ABC, some were on Channel Nine and some on Channel 0, so there was never uniformity on where to find motorsport 'on the box'.

Mike recognised that if you could position the sport in one place so it could be found regularly by viewers, they'd buy in and the network would profit. And he was right – they did right through to when Channel Seven lost the rights of what had become V8 Supercars to Network Ten in 1997.

Mike was a cheerleader fiercely fighting for motorsport, no matter whether it was with network heavies who didn't share his vision.

The world will never know how much he threw his political weight around for the cause of motorsport. I remember listening to him explode on the phone in the Channel Seven offices in Epping, Sydney, battling against those who didn't support motorsport. Often, he would have to bulldoze through to get what he wanted.

In those days, Channel Seven wasn't really a united network – it was more a brand under which separate stations operated. You had HSV-7 in Melbourne, ATN-7 in Sydney, BTQ-7 in Brisbane, TVW-7 in Perth and ADS-7 in Adelaide, all of them essentially separate entities that got together and called themselves Channel Seven.

It was no easy task in the VFL heartland of Victoria to convince HSV-7 in Melbourne to put motor racing on instead of the football. That was why so many telecasts in the 1980s were aired late on a Sunday night and stretched into the early hours of Monday morning.

Mike had heavy-duty battles back in those days with CAMS – the Confederation of Australian Motor Sport, now known as Motorsport Australia – the governing body of motorsport in this country. He never liked the 'blue blazer brigade', as he called some of those in positions of power at CAMS in those days – they just weren't his type of people.

Mike was trying to drag them and the industry into a more commercial and TV-driven era. For some of them that was just too hard.

Mike was tough and rubbed some people the wrong way; a few never got over it. He was an old-school kind of guy. He was fiercely proud of the connection to American motorsport that he had developed during his years in speedway. He had close relationships with people like Johnny Rutherford, John Cooper and A.J. Foyt, and opened my eyes to that world. Mike was also a big part of the team that gave us RaceCam, the amazing feat of Australian engineering that put TV cameras in race cars, and driver chat in your living room. Motorsport was beamed onto TVs around the nation in a way that no other country had achieved.

I never asked the question, but I guess Mike saw something in me that I perhaps didn't see in myself at the time. He had no trouble giving me a whack if I wasn't doing the job as he needed it to be done, but he was never nasty. In that period, along with journalist Peter McKay and his wife Sharyn, Mike and his lovely wife Carol had a huge influence and provided a lot of solid guidance. Beautiful, intelligent, loving people.

I met Peter at a Dunlop tyre launch event and we've been the greatest of friends ever since. Mike also added him to the Channel Seven motorsport family for a time, and he commentated and reported on the sport on the broadcasts in addition to his 'real' job as a talented and highly respected print journalist. Peter was also a very, very good race car driver.

The blend of our on-air team was all about range. Mike was the leader of the line-up, the 'team captain'. Garry Wilkinson was a silky-smooth TV host. Wilko's a ripping bloke and was perfectly suited to the host role in those Seven broadcasts. He was Ron Burgundy long before Will Ferrell played the movie role, and he knew it, too! He was full of himself in a self-deprecating, tongue in cheek way and saw the humour in what we were doing.

Wilko would get dressed up in all sorts of outfits to record the openers for each touring car telecast. Whether it was riding horses in 'Kelly country' for the Winton round in homage to Ned Kelly, popping up in scuba diving gear from the lake at Lakeside in Queensland, or equipped with a whip and jockey's silks at Sandown, Wilko would do it all. He loved to remind me, with a giant grin, 'Crompton, they'll remember me long after you're forgotten!'

I was 'The Kid', the junior of the team. The others constantly hammered me to be more social, trying to drag me out eating and drinking with a gang after hours at the race events, but I was always about the work: I wanted to stay in my hotel room preparing my notes for the following day's broadcast. (I'm no better now – just ask Mark Skaife!)

Whenever I surrendered and joined the guys for a meal, it was a running gag that Mike even bothered to ask for a menu. All he would ever want was steak and chips 'with nothing else on it', and a Mateus Rosé to wash it all down. Every single time, without fail, that was his standing order. It continued right up to the last meal I had with him.

As much as he and the others got stuck into me about my note-taking and research, Mike knew our broadcast needed elements of real information and detailed background rather than just huff and puff.

The Channel Seven gig was never about the dollars. Mike could have paid me anything and I would have been happy. I readily accepted whatever was offered because all I wanted was to be part of the mission. I reckon that 1985 TV deal earned me maybe $30,000, but if I had bothered to calculate the dollars-to-work-hours ratio, I would have been on peanuts. I ploughed a huge amount of time each week into preparing for upcoming events. Mike understood, and I know from our discussions later in life that he was immensely proud of me. For my part, I was immensely grateful for the chance.

Behind the on-air talent in those days, Noel Brady was a fabulous editor and understood TV production so very well. But I was petrified of him! He didn't accept second best and he let you know about it. You knew exactly where you stood if you underperformed. Today, I'll be on-air in the middle of an intense Bathurst broadcast and suddenly get a text message reading 'Nice one, Crompton' from Noel. It's Brady dipping his gruff hat, having appreciated a two-minute TV story I might have toiled over for a month! Getting a nod from a special peer from those early days still means everything.

Perhaps the most memorable aspect of that era of Channel Seven broadcasting was the red blazers we wore on air. Fans still ask me about them to this very day – especially whether I still have one in the wardrobe at home. The truth is I don't, and I don't know anyone who does! I wish I did.

Those jackets were the uniform of Channel Seven sports presenters from the early 1980s through to 1987. In order to get a red look on air – because the cameras in those days were not exactly fantastic – they were actually more of a crimson colour. They were as ugly as a hatful of backsides, though! They were eventually replaced by navy blue blazers. I reckon my old red jacket is probably out there somewhere in the universe, possibly serving as a dipstick wipe cloth in a workshop!

Mike was totally supportive of me going racing. He saw that there was benefit in having one of his commentators competing. It was handy for Channel Seven to have an insider, one of their own, in a race car.

At his core, Mike was a racer. Playing TV executive was secondary to the fact that what floated Mike's boat was high-quality, high-energy car racing. Had I been wearing his executive shoes today, I would probably not have supported the concept of me racing quite as enthusiastically. But I don't ever recall him saying it was a bad idea – quite the contrary.

Mike finished with Channel Seven at the end of 1995, and we'd get in touch once or twice a year. Whenever you called Mike, the phone never had time to ring. He must always have been sitting by the phone. His immediate 'hello' sounded like a clipped 'yeah-low'. Our last conversation prior to Mike's sad passing in November 2019 occurred courtesy of one of my closest friends, Phil Harrison.

Phil was in the car with Peter McKay and Mike – both rowdy passengers – and they were driving back from visiting Allan Horsley. 'H' was Allan Moffat's Mazda Team Manager, and had co-promoted Supercross events with Phil and also Phil Christensen. He had been unwell and the boys rang to update me, but they also took the chance to slag me off as a collective – as they should have, of course.

I have kept Mike's email notes often sent following Bathurst 1000 telecasts of recent years. 'Good job, kid,' they often read. They are priceless.

As the Executive Producer of the *Shannons Legends of Motorsport* TV series in 2015, I dragged Mike and Wilko back onto the studio floor at Channel Seven in Docklands, in Melbourne, to talk about the old days. I was sitting in the control room, Nathan Prendergast was directing, and a dear friend, Col Southey, a sports department executive from Seven, was sitting behind me.

I was supposed to be managing and producing the segment times and supervising the hosts, Bill Woods and Aaron Noonan, but I became misty-eyed as Mike and Wilko regaled us with stories from the 1980s and early 1990s. I completely dropped the ball and stopped looking at the clock and began watching the show as a fan. Later, it took a lot of Nath's editing to get the show back on track. We loved it, Col loved it and was full of praise; it was a special marker in the journey.

I was honoured to be asked by Mike's family, his wife Carol, son Andy and daughter Lyndal, to speak at Mike's funeral. I finished my contribution to the service with these words: 'Three weeks ago after Bathurst, Mike sent me a personal note and concluded with, "Take a bow, young man". It's you we should all bow to today, a great leader, mentor and friend. Thank you, Mike Raymond, and farewell.'

Mike made a massive contribution to my life. I'm forever grateful that we met, and I loved him.

Reflections

Peter McKay – Australian motoring/motorsport journalist

Where do you start with Crompton? He's a contradiction on many fronts: a bloke whose world is technical and mechanical and yet he possesses a surprising love and curiosity of nature.

The motor sporting world knows Neil (back a bit) as a fine race driver with a pair of Bathurst 1000 podiums and an outright Bathurst 12 Hour to his name. Had he not had the relentless distractions of his media life always lurking, perhaps he could have achieved even more on the racetrack.

But there is no one better in the frantic, pressure-cooker confines of the commentary box, where he multitasks at a frightening level while also painting vivid word pictures of a tumultuous sport that tends to travel at a 300-kilometre-per-hour blur.

In front of a camera, Neil makes it look so effortless, articulating his thoughts in a steady, logical flow. He is a one-take wonder, his polish camouflaging the hours of preparation.

The kid who started his business life with his own bicycle shop in Ballarat at the age of 16 has certainly done good. His decision to take Mike Raymond's advice and relocate to Sydney got his media career rocketing.

Getting his love life firing wasn't so easy. After a date with a comely lass he met in sin city, Crompton reported in the following day.

'How did it go?' he was asked.

'Not so good,' he replied.

'Oh, how come?'

'We got back to her place where she invited me inside for a coffee. I had to tell her that I didn't drink hot beverages.'

The stuff I recall fondly too is his thoughtfulness with my girls. He patiently taught Lauren, then seven, to water ski. Initially dragging her up and down his backyard pool before graduating to his speedboat. Memorably, he took them off to the Royal Easter Show, returning a couple of hundred bucks lighter, wearily waving sample bags and kewpie dolls on sticks. He orchestrated a visit to the zoo too, describing this as his form of stress relief.

He is a great friend, though one we don't see near as much as we'd like. He's the hardest-working bloke I know. And one of the smartest. Our mutual mate Phil Harrison reckons there must be two of him.

With Peter McKay, our team and the Mitsubishi Cordia at the Winton 300, 1985 – my first car race. *Crompton collection*

7

NOT IN THE LUCKY SPERM CLUB

WITH NO WEALTH OR racing lineage, and no real technical idea of how to go racing, the next period of my life in motorsport was all about trying to leverage every possible connection and moment. As my friend Derek Daly, the former Formula 1 and IndyCar driver, put it when we worked together on the IndyCar TV coverage in Australia in 1996 and in America in 1997, I wasn't a member of the 'lucky sperm club'.

In 1985 came another important marker in the history of Australian motorsport: the first Australian Formula 1 Grand Prix was held on the streets of Adelaide, in South Australia.

Mitsubishi, which was based in Adelaide, sponsored that first F1 Grand Prix and part of that deal included a celebrity race, which featured a fleet of Cordia GSR Turbos.

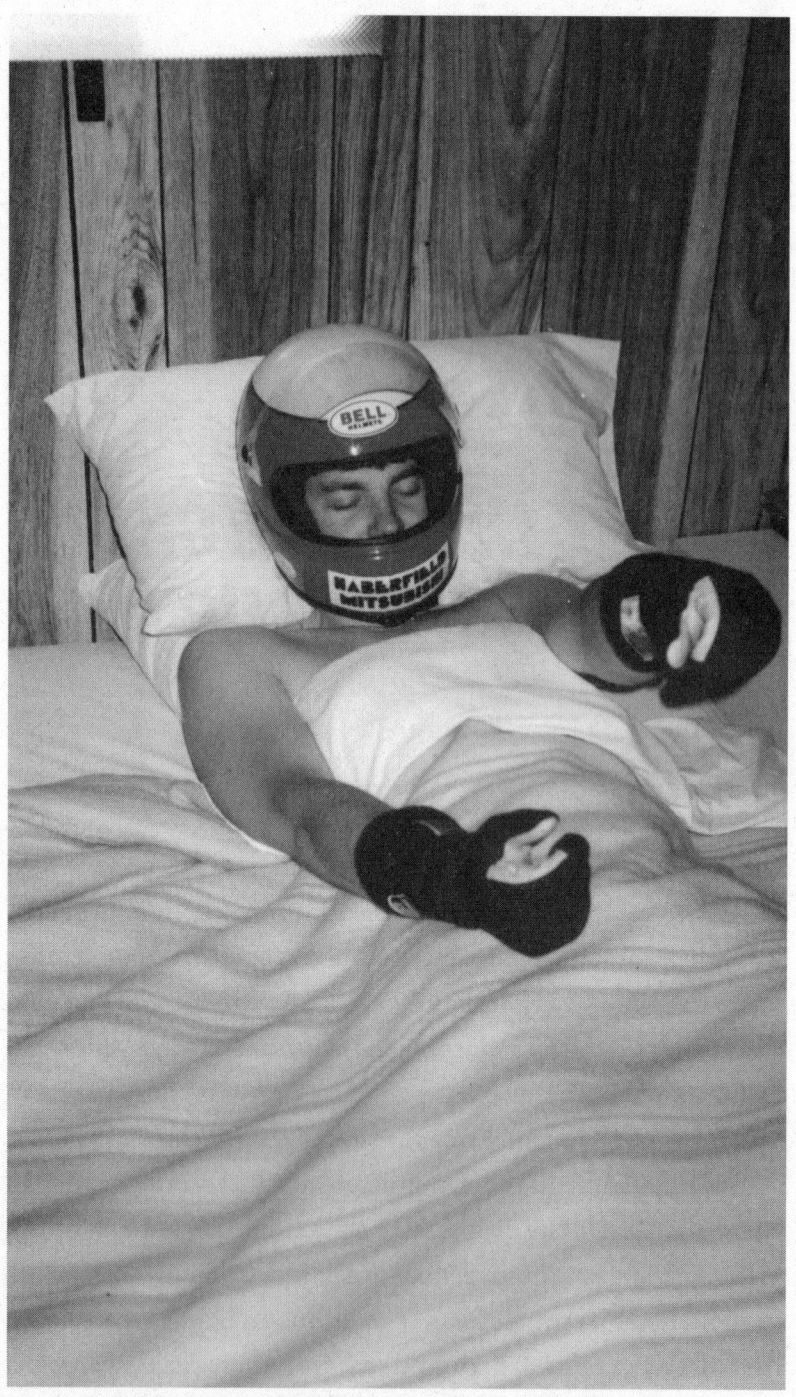

Preparing for my 1985 Winton race car debut – in bed! *Crompton collection*

Manufacturers before and since have used celebrity races as marketing tools for their latest and greatest models. In case the Cordia passed you by – and I imagine there's every chance it did – it was a front-wheel drive, three-door, liftback coupe powered by a turbocharged 1.8-litre engine.

Even glimpsing a photo of this beast these days triggers recollections in me of that car being a case study in understeer. It was also afflicted by massive torque steer under-acceleration (common in powerful front-wheel drive cars when the power and torque of the engine causes the steering to load up as the front wheels spin faster), and it left me with aching forearms for weeks!

The turbo lag was really bad. You'd put your foot on the gas pedal and the engine would 'think about it' first, before the power of the turbo would kick in. You then needed 'turnbuckle' wrists to be able to drive it once it 'lit up'.

A batch of 17 identical cars were prepared for the Grand Prix event, and I somehow put together a deal with Sydney dealer Haberfield Mitsubishi for the use of their car after the Grand Prix was over for the inaugural Winton 300 production car race in early December at Winton, just outside Benalla. Production car racing, as the name suggests, was for vehicles more closely aligned in specification to their road-going counterparts.

The Mitsubishi motorsport manager of the time, John Grant, helped connect me to the Haberfield dealership, who loaned me the car. Racer Phil Ward, a mate of my journalist pal Peter McKay, prepared the car at his Sydney workshop and I laced together funding from anywhere I could dig it up.

I knew the marketing manager from Castrol, John Sawczak, from my motocross days and raised a few thousand dollars from him to go towards to the running costs. I raised a few more bucks here and there from various sources, including Channel Seven, and even scored some additional financial backing ($500) from the enthusiastic promotional manager of the 2WS radio station in Sydney, Craig Denyer. Subsequently, Craig's involvement with the sport has spanned many years, including running the highly popular V8 Utes category, and his son Grant has become rather famous in his own right via his prime-time television career that netted him a Gold Logie in 2018.

McKay qualified our mighty Cordia ninth on the grid and we finished eighth, five laps down on the winning Mitsubishi Starion of Peter Fitzgerald and Barry Jones. We both moaned about lap scoring anomalies afterwards but, regardless of the grizzling, I was racing again!

I did another event in the Cordia in 1986 at Amaroo Park, in Sydney, and I'm told I finished twelfth after an accident; it's funny how your mind can let go of bad memories. A planned return to the Winton 300 in 1986 at the wheel of a Subaru with Jim Zerefos ended up a disaster. The car had a pile of problems after qualifying in 35th position, and we withdrew on race day, meaning I didn't receive an additional signature on my racing licence from the Clerk of the Course. One condition for securing an international racing licence was having competed in a minimum of five national race events within a 12-month period, and our decision to bail on racing the Subaru would come back to haunt me.

An opportunity jumped up late in 1986 to race at a meeting at Amaroo Park in a Mazda RX-7 Sports Sedan owned by a fellow named Mike Griffin. Mike had raced the 13B-powered rotary with plenty of success and was willing to give me a leg-up. I loved Amaroo. It was my 'home base'. Nestled in the Sydney bushland, it was a wild little action track, and also the place I completed a race driving course with racers Allan Grice and John Smith.

The Sports Sedan category was filled with a crazy assortment of cars, and the rules promoted imaginative thinking and engineering. They had high-horsepower engines with giant wings and didn't weigh much. That combination meant they were lightning quick and turned heads.

The Mazda started its life as a Group C touring car that raced at Bathurst. When the local touring car rules changed in 1985 to move away from locally developed vehicles and adopt the international Group A regulations, cars like the Mazda found a second home in the Sports Sedan category.

The car was prepared and run by Ron Krause, and I had my first run in it at a club meeting at Amaroo Park in late 1986, where I scored my first pole position in car racing and won all three races on my way to taking a new class lap record as well.

I had a tremendous race that weekend with young German driver Ludwig Finauer. Nicknamed 'Goofy', he was an engine builder for Frank Gardner's JPS Team BMW touring car squad, and had proven to have quite a bit of talent behind the wheel as well, so Frank entered him in a few races. He and I enjoyed some vigorous racing, and the event attracted a bit of attention.

In 1987, I tried to compete in events in the Mazda where I knew I could attract attention. That meant racing at events with television coverage on Channel Seven where Sports Sedans ran as a support to touring car events at my local tracks in Sydney, Oran Park and Amaroo Park. I conned

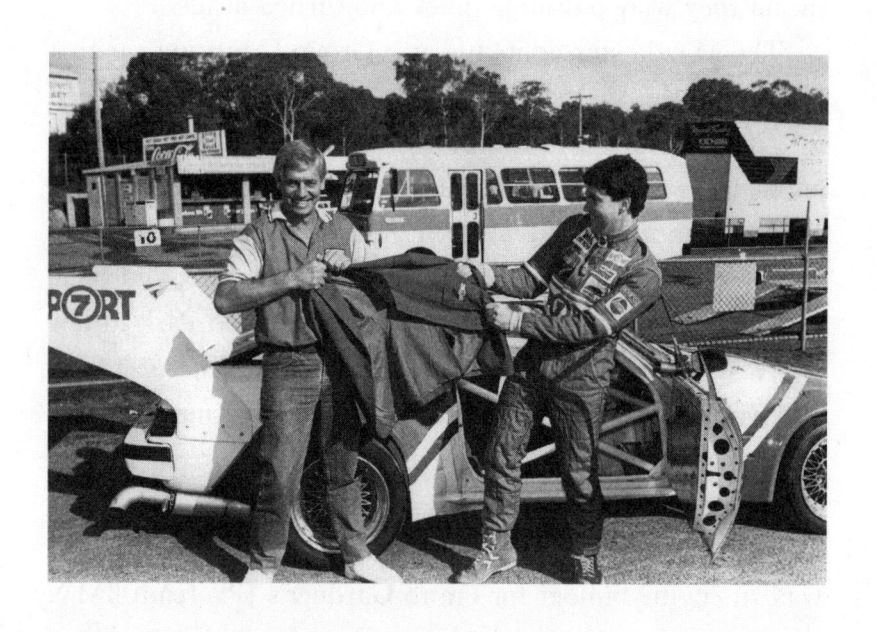

Dick Johnson and me swapping places at Amaroo Park, 1987.
Channel Seven Press

a few more dollars from Castrol and placed some Channel Seven and Triple M signage on it, but the 'Bank of Neil' was still the major financier.

In those days events were less structured. Practice often went for days, and cars from different categories were often mixed. It wasn't uncommon for the stars of touring car racing to be sharing the tarmac with production cars, Sports Sedans and anything else with a roof and an engine.

I found myself on the track at Amaroo Park during one of these all-in practice sessions, and I vividly recall passing Peter Brock in his Mobil Commodore. 'PB' never particularly enjoyed Amaroo, and his heavy, cumbersome V8 Commodore would have been hard work around there at the best of times. My little Mazda, lighter, with wings, decent grunt and bigger tyres, was comfortably quicker than the touring cars and capable of lapping the 1.9-kilometre circuit a few seconds per lap faster, so I was able to sneak past Brock.

Truth be told, it was the equivalent of me hitting balls at him with a size ten tennis racket and him only having a size six with which to hit the returns. But doing stuff like that was still handy given I was trying to get noticed, and it made for some fun pit lane banter and chat afterwards.

If there was one race that did catch some industry attention, though, it was at Amaroo Park in 1987. Held as a support to the AMSCAR touring car event, the race was the end of the Amaroo track championship for Sports Sedans, and Mike Raymond placed a RaceCam in my car.

In a ten-lap race, some of the bigger and more powerful cars fell by the wayside and I found myself in fourth place as we set out for the final lap. With Mike, Wilko and special guest commentator Dick Johnson chiming in (it was DJ's turn to wear the red Channel Seven jacket for the day!), I stuffed my nose down the inside of the third-placed car on the way into the last corner, a fast right-hander that funnelled cars back onto the main straight. There was a slight touch, the front left guard of the Mazda dislodged, but I hung in there and muscled my way past to greet the chequered flag in third place and take the final podium position.

(In a strange side story, my friend Ian O'Brien, who to this day is the senior cameraman on the Supercars TV coverage, then bought the car. 'Mr Fish' had won the gold medal in the 1964 Tokyo Olympic Games in the men's 200-metre breaststroke, to go with his five Commonwealth Games gold medals and nine individual and six relay titles at the Australian Championships. We jacked up some support from Valvoline for the Mazda racing program, and he thought racing might attract some attention for his business. In truth, he just loved car racing – and he still does. Ian is yet another amazing person who made an extraordinary contribution to my life.)

By the end of that Amaroo race, I had completed my fifth weekend of car racing in the Mazda Sports Sedan. The RX-7 had served me very well in those brief appearances, but it wasn't required for my sixth. The next time I went racing, in August 1987, I would be driving a car that, only a few years earlier, was nothing more than a ridiculous daydream.

8

TWO CORNERS AT CALDER

PERFECTING THE BRAKING INTO two key corners of the Calder Park racetrack and one of the biggest automotive divorces in Australian history opened a magical door for me, a nobody from nowhere, to fulfil a dream and drive for Peter Brock's famous racing team.

The 1987 year was huge, both on and off the track, for Australia's most famous racing driver. Brock's season had started in style. On 25 January he and Allan Moffat charged home to lead a Mobil Holden Dealer Team to a 1–2 finish in the Wellington 500 street race, held around the docks and streets of the New Zealand capital.

By the end of February, his race team and business didn't resemble the one that had started the new season as winners.

In addition to his race team, Brock's HDT Special Vehicles business had been a winner, selling hotted-up Holdens to eager customers keen to have a car that came from the same workshops as the team's race-winning Commodores.

Sadly, his insistence on launching his new 'Director' model in late February, without approvals and clearance from Holden, ended up severing what had by then become a fractured relationship with General Motors-Holden. Brock's embrace of the 'Energy Polarizer', a box of magnets and crystals which he fitted to his HDT cars, hadn't endeared him to the Holden heavies, and they'd finally had enough and cut all ties. That stopped the flow of Holden road cars for the HDT Special Vehicles operation to enhance, and stopped the steady stream of parts and engineering know-how for the race team.

A significant number of staff headed for the door, among them his teammates and co-drivers Allan Moffat and John Harvey. Allan and John would tackle that year's inaugural World Touring Car Championship in a brand new, Brock/HDT-built VL Commodore. Brock had to sell the unraced car to Moffat, via a third party, to raise funds to keep his business going in the wake of Holden cutting the cord.

The departure of these two racing legends opened a door, and later in 1987 I walked through it.

The phone rang one day. On the other end of the line was Bev Brock, Peter's partner. 'Peter wants to know if you want to come and have a drive in the car?' she asked.

I thought it was a gee-up. Surely she was pulling my leg?

'No, no, we've had a talk about it,' Bev went on, 'and he'd like you to have a run.'

The test drive was to be at Calder Park, the very place I had watched Brock compete in rallycross as a kid. It was also where he'd carefully handwritten that piece describing a lap of the rallycross track in his Torana for my primary school magazine.

By 1987, the Calder venue was very different. The rallycross roads within the circuit were long gone, and a giant banked oval was taking shape alongside the road course. Its huge mounds of dirt were the basis of what was dubbed the 'Thunderdome', a racing venue for American NASCAR stock cars.

The road course itself had been extended the previous year, from its very simple 1.6-kilometre layout to just under 2.3 kilometres. The old track had a short front straight, a right-hand corner that led onto the back straight, a right, a left and then a right-hander to bring you back onto the main pit straight. It was pretty simple. The extension made the front straight far longer and added a few corners before it brought the cars up over a man-made mountain – which we dubbed 'Mount Jane' after Bob Jane, the long-time owner of Calder – and rejoined the old track on the back straight.

I enthusiastically jumped on a plane to fly to Melbourne. When I got there, I realised there was a giant cast of drivers also keen to take their turn behind the wheel.

I had a very clear view in my head of what I needed to do before I bolted myself into the car and rolled onto the track. From my days as an eager youth, I had closely watched drivers – the way they balanced their car on the limit into a corner, how careful and delicate they were accelerating out of a corner, braking references, how the good guys treated the downshifts, all that stuff. I still do it to this day. I studied what they did in person, in magazines and on television. It was like I was attending a university of motorsport in my mind. I would stare at every frame of what was going on. I had come to see exercising any skill in a race car as something you had to do very precisely, cleanly and smoothly.

I remember that day in that Commodore so well. Brock's 1987 cars were plain white with splashes of red and blue, given his sponsorship from loyal partner Mobil. By today's standards they were very basic cars, with a five-litre V8 engine good enough for about 420 horsepower, but in their day they were 'the business'.

Calder was a simple track on paper: my focus was on being smooth and concentrating on two key corners. You had to have the car wriggling slightly on the wild side limit under brakes at the very end of both straights over the bumpy bitumen. Not locked up and sliding, but not a millimetre too early on the brakes either. There was huge time to gain by smart and brave brake management.

You also needed to be at the absolute threshold of the very heavily loaded left front tyre in both corners at the top and bottom of the track, and needed to be very, very careful with the application of the throttle out of every turn. Stomping your foot was always a temptation, but the stopwatch hated it. I had to feed the accelerator pedal down against the limit of the traction grip and get it flat to the floor as quickly as I could without getting too sideways and having to reset or step off the throttle. These days, there's data to help you read that throttle trace. Back then it came from the seat of your pants and between your ears.

At the start of the day, Brock jumped behind the wheel to set a benchmark time for everyone to aim at. The exact figure is foggy in my mind, but I know that I beat it. The part that isn't foggy is the reaction of one the team mechanics, Tim Collins. 'We've found our man!' he remarked as I climbed out. I got enormous confidence from that test at Calder, and the call came soon after: I was in.

I knew I had done a good job on the test day, but frankly, I was still quite surprised. I was going to drive a Mobil Commodore touring car for Peter Brock's team, and he had personally selected me. This was all a bit surreal.

Some of my peers didn't like it, and from my vantage point today I understand their viewpoint. I'd managed to cut the traditional corners in winning a seat on the team, having served only a very short, non-standard apprenticeship.

But everybody has a different story – there is no 'one size fits all' way of chasing down a ride in the main game. It's always been the law of the jungle, and somehow I had stumbled through the maze, using every available tool: contacts, personal money, media and some earlier two- and four-wheel racing experience.

There was never any discussion about being paid. It never crossed my mind, and it wasn't a factor. I didn't get paid the whole time I was driving for Peter's Mobil team. Putting my hand up for some cash was the last thing on my mind. The team paid for my travel, accommodation and expenses. I was driving for Peter Brock in a Mobil Commodore – that was all that mattered.

*

And that was how the upheaval in Brock's business empire gave me my start as a professional racing driver. Had that

A download with Brock's Mobil team manager Graeme 'Mort' Brown, Sandown, 1987. *AN1 Images/Graeme Neander*

not happened, he wouldn't have lost Moffat and Harvey, and he wouldn't have been looking for drivers to fill the seats of his cars.

If you're involved in motorsport as a driver, this typically means that you're a somewhat self-centred critter. At the time, I reckon I didn't spare a single empathetic thought for Allan or John – both of whom became very close friends of mine later in my life. Peter Brock was looking for new drivers, and I drove the wheels off his Mobil Commodore and got the gig. In retrospect it was quite selfish, but that's all I was thinking about.

There was a lot of conjecture surrounding the Polarizer and the concepts that were attached to it, but I didn't pass judgement on that. Lots of people do life differently to me – so what? I never discussed the Polarizer, Director or any of the turmoil of that period with him in any depth. They were his beliefs and it was his business, so it wasn't for me to pass judgement.

Besides, I was a young guy in my mid-twenties. I'd spent a big chunk of my life to that time dreaming of becoming a race driver. Now I'd got a spot, and so the rest of it was just noise that didn't matter. I was ecstatic that someone was paying for me to go racing, and it just so happened to be my childhood hero.

When Brock realised I could actually drive a race car, that made our relationship even stronger. It felt like it was meant to be – which I acknowledge is a very 'Brock-like' thing to suggest, but I genuinely believe it. Once I was there and driving for his team, it just felt right.

My first chance to race for the Mobil HDT team (Brock was no longer allowed to call it the 'Holden Dealer Team', given his bust-up with Holden) came in the Pepsi 250 endurance race at Oran Park in late August 1987.

In those days, not every touring car race was part of the championship, as is the case with today's Supercars Championship. The Australian Touring Car Championship was decided by a series of sprint races, before a handful of longer endurance races – with two or sometimes three drivers per car – rounded out the year, which culminated in the annual Bathurst 1000.

The Pepsi 250 was very much a standalone race, with no championship points on the line. Peter had brought Tasmanian David Parsons back into the team to share the brand new #05 Commodore with him, while I was entered in the #6 car, alongside the previous year's Australian Formula 2 champion, Jon Crooke.

Our #6 car looked like Brock's brand new #05, given it was painted the same, but beneath the body panels it had actually started its life as the previous model VK: it had been given a facelift to the 1987 livery and VL model bodywork. It was the same car that Peter and Allan Moffat had used at the start of the year to win the Wellington 500 in New Zealand, before Brock's big bust-up with Holden.

Driving the Commodore at Oran Park was a bit of a culture shock. The Mazda Sports Sedan I had been driving was nicer to drive, had bigger tyres and more aerodynamic grip. I don't remember being nervous at all, but learning to drive the Commodore was quite hard, as it slipped around a lot. Oran Park was packed with corners, and over the course of a lap the car was hardly ever driven in a straight line. Compared to Calder, it was infinitely more complex. If Calder had two key points to master, Oran Park had ten.

The challenge of turning out a consistently fast lap there was far more complex than at Calder on test day, and I didn't yet have the depth of understanding I required to get the most out of the car.

Starting from ninth on the grid, Crooke took the first stint in the race. He heavily locked a front right brake on the very first lap, and headed for the pits just to make sure things were okay. That meant we were well behind the field to begin with.

In a classic rookie story, Brock's team manager, Graeme 'Mort' Brown, asked Jon what the problem might be. Jon leaned out the driver's window and shouted that the 'glovebox was on fire' – in reality it was the lingering tyre smoke hanging in the cabin from the bonfire Jon had lit when he locked up his brakes and skidded into turn three. Mort was rather to the point in his firm response and sent Jon on his way.

I jumped in at the halfway mark and slipped and slid my way around on slick tyres on a wet track to eventually cross the line in ninth place – a solid result in a difficult race. It wasn't a world-beating performance, but it wasn't bad.

The next race on the calendar was the Sandown 500 in Melbourne, and there Crooke and I had an ever better run. The traditional warm-up race to Bathurst was another one affected by rain, with constant showers making the track slippery. This time I was given the duties of both starting and finishing the race. From 11th place on the grid, our first pit stop turned into a long one, costing us plenty of time.

The plan was for me to make my first pit stop a lap or two before Brock, so the team could examine the tyres on my car and then make an informed decision on Brock's tyres when he came in. But Brock radioed the crew to inform them he was low on fuel and was coming straight into the pits, so our car was pushed ahead of the pit bay while the #05 Holden was attended to, and the crew then changed the tyres and refuelled car #6.

The time we lost could well have been the difference between a podium finish and our eventual fourth place.

I vividly remember the late stages of that race. Brock's brother Phil – nicknamed 'Splitpin' because of his beanpole build and height – had returned to Melbourne to help Peter run the team in the wake of the Holden break-up, and he was leaning over the pit wall shaking his hand at me, cheering me on like a madman as I pursued the third-placed Skyline of Kiwis Kent Baigent and Graeme Bowkett.

After two races for the Mobil HDT Racing team, my confidence was soaring. The next event on the calendar was the big one, the Bathurst 1000. But I wouldn't be behind the wheel of my beloved new race car.

9

BATHURST 1987

AS IT TURNED OUT, my chances of making my Bathurst 1000 debut in October 1987 were torpedoed a whole ten months earlier, when Jim Zerefos and I decided to withdraw his uncompetitive Subaru production car from the Winton 300 in December 1986. There was no logical way I could have known it at the time, but not competing in that Winton race meant I hadn't received a crucial signature from the Clerk of Course on my provisional racing licence.

The 1987 Bathurst 1000 race was to be a round of the inaugural World Touring Car Championship, and so was subject to higher licensing requirements than in previous years. Despite the racing I'd done during 1987, it started to look like I wouldn't have enough signatures on my racing licence to qualify me for an International C licence, which I needed if I was to compete in that year's race.

When Bev Brock invited me to join the team for the endurance races, it included all the events on the calendar: the Oran Park 250, the Sandown 500, the Bathurst 1000, and then the World Touring Car Championship rounds following it at Calder Park a week later, plus a 500-kilometre race in Wellington, New Zealand. But like a dog that only hears its name amid all the other white noise from its master, all I heard was 'Bathurst'!

When I realised I had a licensing problem, I went on a mad mission to try to do more racing prior to Bathurst in order to get more signatures and convince the powers that be to give me the required licence. I raced the Mazda Sports Sedan again at Winton after the Sandown 500, but I just didn't have enough races against my name, and not enough time to get more done.

Brock's team announced just after the Sandown 500 that, as I'd been unable to procure an international licence, it had engaged Wollongong-based privateer Peter McLeod to share its second car at Bathurst with Jon Crooke. Even so, I was determined to find a way to get more signatures on my licence and argue my case. I even flew to Perth in late September to drive a Commodore owned by Brock's old fishing mate John Farrell in a race at Wanneroo Raceway – a five-lap handicap race against a bunch of street cars.

It was a long way to go for minimal time behind the wheel, and it wasn't enough. It was ten years since I'd first sat in the fork of that tree on top of Mount Panorama, dreaming of being on the other side of the fence in the race, but I wasn't going to be permitted to drive one of Peter Brock's Commodores in the Great Race. The fairytale was temporarily paused.

Brock personally argued to the Confederation of Australian Motor Sport (CAMS) that he wanted me in the team for that race. But not even a good word from the 'King of the Mountain' could make a difference.

I was white-hot filthy about the decision not to let me race. I remember screaming down the phone at Tim Schenken from CAMS, the former Formula 1 driver who today is the Race Director of the Supercars Championship. I count Tim as a good friend these days, but back then I was furious with him. 'What do you mean I can't race at Bathurst?' I bellowed down the phone line, growing increasingly agitated. I screamed, moaned, groaned and cursed.

In the end I threw down the telephone, ending the call. I was livid that I was being denied my chance to compete in the biggest race of the season.

At the time, Tim, CAMS and the Federation Internationale de l'Automobile (FIA), the governing body of world motorsport, based in France, were immovable. It was a World Championship event, and so all drivers needed the relevant International C licence or the required endorsements to qualify for one, and I didn't qualify. I was one signature short. End of story. And the licence rules were designed for a reason: to ensure all drivers were experienced enough to take part.

These days, one of my involvements in Australian motorsport is as a category administrator running the Toyota GAZOO Racing 86 Series. And so I know very well that you simply must have rules or you'll have chaos. You can't make subjective exceptions. As a race administrator, I know all too well now that you'll have anarchy if you make your decisions based on hunches or friendships.

The history books show that the car I would have been driving – the #10 Mobil HDT Racing Holden Commodore VL – crossed the line third in the 1987 James Hardie 1000 at Bathurst. McLeod started the race, and Brock and Parsons joined him as co-drivers after the #05 car's engine expired in a cloud of smoke in the race's early stages. (In those days drivers could switch between any of their team's cars during a race.)

Brock skated his way around in wet conditions late in the race on grooved slick tyres, crossed the line third and was elevated to his record ninth and final Bathurst 1000 win when the first two finishers – a pair of Ford Sierras entered and run by Swiss team owner Ruedi Eggenberger – were excluded from the results because of illegal bodywork modifications.

It was an amazing result, considering the sort of year Brock had endured on and off the track. The only problem was that I wasn't part of it. The notion that, had I been allowed to compete, I could have won Bathurst on debut has been suggested, but I'm not one of those people who thinks that way. It's nonsense.

I broke out the Channel Seven red jacket and patrolled the pit lane during that race instead of slipping behind the wheel. Yep, it sucked by comparison.

I had every reason to mope because I wasn't behind the wheel of one of Brock's Commodores, but I wasn't interested in playing the 'misery card'. Yes, I was disappointed, but I don't remember being in a rage once I got to Bathurst. I was still grateful to be there. In fact, I probably did a better job of the TV gig than I'd done previously because of my recent driving experience.

I gleaned a valuable life insight from that experience. Those initial emotional reactions that flare up come from somewhere deep inside you, so you've got to try to find a way to mentally steer yourself to the other side – otherwise there won't be an 'other side' and the scrapheap beckons. Brock's positive persona rubbed off on me in this regard. He and Bev counselled me, a lot. If I went into a dark cloud because of negative stuff in those days, they'd bring me back with a better, positive perspective.

I did drive a Commodore that weekend at Bathurst, though it was a Group E production car in one of the support categories. It got me another licence signature to secure my international racing licence, and that opened the door for me to rejoin the Mobil HDT team for the next round of the World Touring Car Championship, a week later at Calder Park.

Peter McLeod and I drove the not-yet-Bathurst-winning #10 Commodore (the final verdict that the Sierras were excluded from the top two finishing positions came a little later) on the unique 'link' track, where the regular road course was combined with the new 'Thunderdome' oval to create a totally weird circuit layout.

That meant I did get to drive the #10 Bathurst-winning Mobil Commodore. The only problem was that it was one week after Bathurst. We finished 11th after a puncture delayed our run. Then I was joined by Kiwi David Oxton for the next WTCC round in Wellington, where we ran well until the rear suspension failed.

10

THE KING OF BANKSTOWN

ALTHOUGH HE'S BEEN GONE for fifteen years, Peter Brock floats into my thoughts occasionally. There's heaps of special moments and crazy odd yarns that still make me grin.

Brock and Alan Gow made the decision to sell off the fleet of Commodores and swap to BMW M3s for the 1988 season, and I enthusiastically went along for the ride, driving a third car in selected rounds of the Australian Touring Car Championship and forming part of the driver line-up for the longer endurance races. Reigning Australian Touring Car Champion Jim Richards came as part of the BMW package, linking him up with Brock again to rekindle the combination that won Bathurst three times in a row from 1978 to 1980.

Jim had won the ATCC the previous year wearing the distinctive JPS black and gold colours on the M3. However, by the time we strapped into them in 1988 in Mobil colours they were 'old news' and unable to muster anything like the pace to match the rapidly developing turbocharged Ford Sierra RS500s driven by Dick Johnson, John Bowe, Colin Bond and Tony Longhurst. Regardless, some of the proudest moments of my racing career came in the BMWs that season. Jimmy and Peter were benchmark racing talents of the era, and I was fortunate to be smack-bang in the middle of some sensational battles with them as my teammates and peers.

I recall Richo and I having a ripper battle in one of the AMSCAR Series rounds at Amaroo Park. The tight and twisty Amaroo track was perfect for the nimble 300-horsepower BMWs. Peter was on Channel Seven as a guest commentator, and he loved watching our on-track battle so much that he declared the team would bring three cars to the next event just so he could join in the fun!

The races were off the scale when Brock joined us next time out. The three of us kept passing each other at every second corner. It was fantastic for my confidence. I was going toe to toe with the best in the business. Jim was universally regarded as one of the top touring car drivers in the world in that era, which heightened my sense of achievement, at least temporarily.

Life has natural checks and balances, and after the epic Amaroo Park battles we headed to Oran Park, south-west of Sydney, for a round of the ATCC. I was feeling very comfortable in the car, and keen to take on the world. Then came a knockout punch. Jim was insanely quick, and finished a full lap ahead of me on the highly complex Oran Park layout. I'd been utterly and totally belted by the master. Ouch.

This was a very important lesson, one that sent me flaming back to earth at warp speed. At his peak Jim was a master craftsman, able to wring the last drop of performance out of any car on any circuit in any conditions. He really understood the nuances of the M3, and I quickly realised I needed to better understand the job and Jim's techniques.

The message: never get ahead of yourself, and always park your ego. I've never forgotten this deflating but important lesson.

One night in 1988 Peter and I headed out to Bankstown, in Sydney's west, for a 'meet and greet' dealer function for Dulux Autocolor. We chatted to the audience about how the season was tracking, showed some vision of the race cars from recent events, shared info about the car's performance and later answered questions, signed posters and did plenty of handshaking and smiling.

I thoroughly enjoyed this sort of interaction, and still do to this day. Away from the intensity of the track, it's a pretty cool thing to be able to share the religion of motorsport with like-minded enthusiasts.

One of our shiny white, blue and red Mobil BMW M3 race cars was there as a backdrop for guests to admire up close. Just when I thought we were done and ready to head home, Brock got a fiendish look on his face and made a beeline for the BMW. He jumped in and fired up the sweet-sounding four-cylinder, high-revving engine that had made the German-built M3 one of the most popular touring cars in the world at the time.

I thought, 'Wow, this is pretty cool!' Firing up the engine

to give the guests a bit of an unexpected audio thrill was a nice touch, but what he did next dropped everyone's jaws to the ground. Brock tickled the throttle, lit up more than a few revs, dumped the clutch and shot straight down the middle of the room on the lacquered wooden floor, right between the guests sitting in two rows of plastic chairs!

The King of the Mountain had suddenly become the Crazy Burnout King of Bankstown!

The result was that the beautiful shiny floor was completely stuffed, and Dulux had to fix it. I wasn't sure whether to laugh, cry or run away!

These days, even starting a race car in a confined, indoor area, let alone actually putting it into gear, dropping the clutch and arrowing past the elbows of patrons, would see you marched off by the high-vis-vest warriors of the central office of 'you can't do that', and probably charged with a toilet-roll-long list of offences. But back in 1988 it generated a standing ovation!

*

That year's Bathurst 1000 finally saw me make my Great Race debut, 12 months after the lack of signatures on my licence had stopped me in my tracks.

Prior to Bathurst, I competed in a pair of endurance races, the same events I'd contested for the team in 1987. Brock and Richards won the Pepsi 250 at Oran Park, while David Parsons and I came home fourth, delayed at our first pit stop by a refuelling glitch.

The next race, at Sandown, was the 500-kilometre warm-up race for Bathurst. Peter jumped into my car after his regular car had encountered early race dramas, but engine failure meant we were sidelined not long after he took the wheel. I've never seen a bigger hole in the block of an engine than that day!

For Bathurst, the team paired Peter and Jim in one car, leaving me to share with Parsons. If the BMWs were out of breath trying to keep up with the Sierras, Skylines and Commodores on other tracks, they couldn't get within a bull's roar at Bathurst, where the big grunt cars blazed straight past the M3s on the long runs up and down Mount Panorama. Our team needed to execute everything smoothly if we were to have even a vague chance of finishing near the podium, let alone winning the race.

As things panned out, nothing went smoothly that day – but it did bring some weird relief later. A wheel (from another car) was sitting in the middle of the ultra-fast Conrod Straight, and an unsighted Brock catapulted over the top of it at full tilt. It did plenty of damage, including smashing the oil cooler. That meant our Plan B swung into action: to move Jim and Peter into 'my' car to give them the best chance of a good result. However, that plan quickly fell apart when the engine failed with Jim at the wheel. That meant it was time for Plan C. Once Brock original car's damage was repaired, I climbed in, many laps down but at least out on the track.

When I look back on it now, 33 years later, with a little more perspective, the upside was that I rolled out onto the greatest of racetracks for my first lap in a Bathurst 1000 as Peter Brock's teammate in a Brock race car. Not many years earlier, this was beyond my wildest imaginations. I was even wearing Brock's own sweaty helmet to take advantage of the in-car camera system, as his helmet was wired for sound while mine was not.

One major difference between the cars that weekend was the gearbox. My car had a five-speed Getrag gearbox; however, Peter's car featured a six-speed unit, a $30,000 purchase from British BMW gurus Prodrive, in a bid to try and be more competitive. I hadn't driven the six-speed before, and just as I was trying to find my groove in this unfamiliar car with an extra gear, the earpiece in the helmet crackled into life.

'The boys in the box are going to have a chat,' came the word from the Channel Seven audio director, alerting me that I was about to be connected to the commentary feed.

I went along with it, exchanging pleasantries with Mike Raymond and Garry Wilkinson and waffling along for a little while, explaining what gear I was in and speeds I was tracking, but at high speed that's much harder than it sounds.

Then a weird voice chipped into the discussion. 'Hello, Crompton,' it said. 'Are you listening?'

The BMW's high-revving four-cylinder engine made distinguishing the identity of the new speaker difficult. The radios and my earpieces were crap, and whoever was trying to talk also had a heap of background noise in their microphone.

The mystery voice spoke to me again. 'It's Peter,' the person said.

I had no idea who it was. Peter who?

'It's Brocky!' laughed Mike, and then it all made sense.

It was Peter Brock, with a headset and microphone in the Mobil pits, joining in the conversation. He chimed in as I was cresting the rise at Reid Park, approaching the very same place where, to my right, eleven years earlier, I'd caught my first glimpse of racing action at Bathurst in 1977.

My 1988 Mobil BMW M3 race car.

As well as Mike, Garry and 'PB' in my ears, there was also the Sydney Triple M personality Doug Mulray, a huge breakfast radio star who doubled as an occasional Channel Seven motorsport colour commentator. 'I still reckon Crompton thinks apex is a club,' said Mulray cheekily, as I desperately tried to maintain concentration and avoid disaster despite the wails of laughter in the background. There was no serious talk about how the race was evolving, how my car was going or even what the weather was like. All these blokes could do was launch gags and giggle.

When I think back to it now, there was nothing positive about our team's performance to discuss anyway, so they were probably correct to take the entertainment route.

'I don't know what you guys are doing, but I'm sure it's not to my advantage!' I offered up, all the while concentrating on braking for turn two at the top of Mountain Straight. 'I remember the days when this used to be a motor racing telecast, but it's rapidly becoming a comedy show!'

I was the rookie at the wheel, and Brock continued talking me around the mountain, telling me what gear I should be in as well as offering some good-natured, tongue-in-cheek advice. We were so many laps behind that we could get away with it given there was no competitive pressure. The circus seemed to go on for an eternity, before finally the boys ran out of gags and left me in peace.

What the world didn't know at the time was that Mobil was undecided about continuing their sponsorship of the Brock team. And on the strength of the huge amount of television airtime we received from this impromptu lighthearted banter, Mobil decided to re-sign their deal and continue with Peter. While it was a giggle for those watching at home, it actually helped save the major sponsorship deal for the biggest name in the sport.

*

That year's racing season also included a pair of 500-kilometre endurance races at Wellington and Pukekohe, in New Zealand, on back-to-back weekends. I shared the team's second car with Victorian privateer Tony Noske in the race around the docks and streets of Wellington, and we ran well – until the engine's computer died in the latter stages.

The following weekend, the Mobil team elected to run just one car at Pukekohe, which I shared with Brock. Jim Richards had a calendar clash and was required back in Australia for an AUSCAR race at Calder Park.

Brock was often quite animated in a race car, and there was rarely any doubt about his demeanour. You knew very quickly whether he was happy, sad or somewhere in between. And that weekend at Pukekohe we got a very good example of cranky Peter.

In 1988 the cream of the crop from European touring car racing and Australian racing all assembled for the 500-kilometre enduro at Pukekohe. Our big target for that race was the crack German Schnitzer team and their BMW M3. They had a pair of very fast Italian drivers, Roberto Ravaglia and Emanuele Pirro, and had won the race in Wellington the previous weekend. For Pukekohe they had the rapid Belgian Eric van de Poele co-driving with Ravaglia.

Brock and I qualified seventh-fastest, and the race unfolded well for us. Peter was behind the wheel for the opening stint, and at one point came blazing past the pits on the main straight, furiously waving his arms at us. We were puzzled – we couldn't figure out what he was trying to signal. Our pit was located just before the braking area into turn one, so PB's pace was north of 240 kilometres per hour. So we waited for him to come around a few more times and kept trying to decipher the message. His gesticulations became wilder and wilder, but Mort Brown and I had no idea what he was signalling to us.

'Whaddya reckon he's trying to say?' I asked.

'No bloody idea, Cromley,' said Mort. 'Let's ask him some questions and we'll figure it out.'

We pulled out the trusty lap board. These were used in motorsport for years to advise race drivers of important pieces of information during a race. These days radios allow easy communication from pit to driver, but occasionally they fail and a lap board will be brought out and hung over the pit wall.

Perhaps the engine oil pressure was a problem? So we hung out the lap board: 'OIL P?'

Brock waved furiously at us.

'Nope, must not be oil pressure,' I concluded.

'Maybe it's the water temp?' Mort said.

So out goes the lap board again next time he drives by: 'WATER T?'

That was met with more furious waving.

We asked more questions relating to whether the car had a technical problem, but none seemed to be generating a positive response. By now we were starting to run dry on options, and I began to tire of the game.

'Ask him if he wants a Vegemite sandwich,' I offered. Maybe my stupid humour would lighten the mood.

Out went the lap board again: 'VEGEMITE SANDWICH?'

Brock's arm movements went from furious to ballistic.

'Clearly he's not hungry,' I remarked with a grin.

We eventually came home fourth behind the winning Sierra of Andrew Miedecke and Brit Steve Soper. The Schnitzer BMW of Ravaglia and van de Poele was second, and Larry Perkins and Denny Hulme finished third in their Holden Special Vehicles Commodore.

I pulled in after the race and stepped out of the car, and immediately the debrief began. We asked Brock about all the arm waving.

'Don't you dickheads understand?' he replied incredulously, again repeating the arm gestures he had been making. 'I was asking for the 08 compound tyre!' he said. Now we realised he was drawing a zero and then an eight in the air. '08' was the designation of the harder compound Bridgestone tyres. Things began to make more sense, given his lap speed had died away early in the stint. What didn't make sense was how on earth were we supposed to figure out what all that arm waving meant while he was flying past the pits at 240 kilometres per hour!

At the time, Brocky was livid, his big, black eyes deep and dark. Part of him clearly didn't appreciate our dopey humour! Later, though, we laughed our heads off about it.

I have really fond memories of those BMWs. They were a cool little race car. They were fun to drive, and had a lovely engine induction sound. The beauty was that you could drive them flat-out all day. Brock's Mobil team only spent one year racing those cars before deciding to return to fighting for race wins at the front of the field by sourcing a pair of Ford Sierras from England for the 1989 season.

11

MY FRIEND BROCK

BROCK TOOK A BIT of a shine to me back in those early days. I'm not 100 per cent sure why. At a guess, I know I made him laugh. He roared heartily at some of the dumb stuff we both enjoyed. I can hear him now, and picture him shaking his head with amusement or disgust.

I know I got his attention with that first test for the Mobil team at Calder. Then came the racing in various Brock team cars. I enjoyed some very strong outings, some not so strong, but I always gave everything I had, and he liked my commitment to the cause and my racing capabilities. As a bonus, I worked bloody hard to help him commercially at a difficult time in his life, and I know Peter liked me hustling for sponsors on his behalf.

He, and Allan Moffat too, really respected the fact that I deeply understood what they had both achieved. I was obsessed with my sport, and with their special place within this mad caper. I knew the things that mattered to them, their backgrounds, their cars, their stats. My deep respect for their achievements made a significant impact.

Brock loved to take the piss out of me about anything he could come up with, especially any failures – and particularly those that resulted in me missing out on opportunities. In 1982, with one of my oldest buddies, Bob Haro, the American freestyle BMX guru, I met the Oakley founder Jim Jannard at the Superbowl of Motocross at the Coliseum in Los Angeles, when the business was still a minnow. Jim told me they were looking for opportunities in Australia. Somehow, I didn't follow through on that lead. Of course, Oakley became a ubiquitous brand, and Jim would sell it in 2007 for US$2.1 billion. He now owns islands in Fiji!

Brock also loved the story of the time I allowed myself to be talked out of buying $100,000 of Apple stock in 1997, when I was living in the United States. I loved the ethos behind Apple products, and how Steve Jobs embraced engineering quality and style coupled with a straightforward, user-friendly logic, unlike the mind-bending PC interface of the time. So, when Jobs returned to the helm and started fixing the mess Apple was in at the time, I thought it might be a smart play to invest. It's best not to do the math today, but if you do convert $100,000 of 1997 stock into today's dollars, you'll see why Brock loved recounting the yarn. He would roar with laughter at my almighty near misses.

I also loved taking the mickey out of him, too. One story that springs to mind was the time he, Jim Richards and I went out motorbike riding in the bush. Richo was a brilliant enduro bike rider, highly skilled. If Jimmy had aimed his considerable skills at two-wheel endeavours, he could have been every bit as successful as he was on four wheels.

When the three of us were racing the Mobil BMWs, Jim convinced me it was a good idea to buy a brand-new KTM motorcycle, leave it at his place in Melbourne and go riding whenever I was down from Sydney. On this occasion, we had arranged a ride with my racing mate Brad Jones. Both Brad and I were sharing a room at the Parkroyal Hotel on St Kilda Road. The alarm went off at 5 am. It was pitch black outside, and a classic Melbourne winter's day: freezing cold, with the rain already pouring down.

Jones didn't even bother to lift his head and look through the window. After seeking a brief weather report from me, he muttered an ugly obscenity, rolled over and went back to sleep. He doesn't do mornings well – unless there's a dollar in it!

So I trundled to the outer suburb of Ringwood where Richo lived, and we met up with Brock out in the bush north-east of Melbourne. Peter turned up on a Suzuki acquired from his mate Mick Hone. He looked rather like the cartoon character Elmer Fudd, in mustard-coloured bib-and-brace overalls and one of those heavy chequered shirts, complete with gumboots. Jim and I were fully equipped in serious riding gear, with trick boots, waxed cotton jackets and pants, cool gloves and goggles, the whole shebang. Peter looked completely out of place: we weren't sure whether he was up for a ride or off to herd Little Bo-Peep's sheep!

Off we went – and it was so, so cold. It was one of those days where you had to peel your fingers off the handgrips because they simply stopped functioning!

We moved a few kilometres down the road on a fire trail, and then Richo spotted a wheel track, turned at 90 degrees and rode straight up a steep incline. It's a real skill to ride up that sort of angle: you have to manage the power well, not spin the back wheel and yet not bog down and stop. In fact, I once broke my ankle while doing that with Jim on another ride; I've still got the wire in my ankle as a reminder.

Brock took one look at this riding complexity and pulled the metaphorical ripcord.

'Ah, boys, yeah ... I just remembered, I've got a really big meeting today,' he stuttered. 'Why don't you guys press on?'

Not waiting for a response, he turned and hightailed it out of there! He was gone in seconds. Richo and I still giggle about it to this day.

Brock terrified me on plenty of occasions on public roads too. So much that I always insisted on driving whenever we had to go somewhere together. When I was driving and he was in the passenger seat, he'd call me 'Miss Daisy'. I found that a bit peculiar, given this was a reference to a seriously old Jessica Tandy film, *Driving Miss Daisy*. Had he really watched that movie? It was a constant wrangle between us.

'C'mon, Cromley!' he would say. 'Bloody hell! Drive faster!'

Public roads have so many random hazards that you can't control, so I was never keen to explore any of them at a serious pace. But Peter had such a solid belief in his innate skill as a driver that it never bothered him. Maybe, in fact, he had too much trust in his abilities – to the very end.

I remember being in the passenger seat with him in the streets of Port Melbourne, where the speed limit was 60 kilometres per hour. I can promise you we weren't doing

60! My fear was that some bloke was going to wobble out of a driveway in his 18-wheeler and we would fire straight underneath it and turn a Brock Commodore into a convertible.

In the mid to late 1980s, I often visited his Holden Dealer Team workshop in Bertie Street, Port Melbourne. I still drive to that very street to this day, as one of my current key clients, Toyota, has its national head office there. These days, the building that Brock and HDT were in is long gone, though. There's a car park on the site, and a Bunnings nearby. But back in the 1980s it was a hive of activity of all things Brock.

I recall turning up at the workshop and Peter would be out the back with his beloved clay, making a sill panel shape for the next HDT Commodore road car, or Lada Niva, or some other wacky project, and then he'd be whisking you away to go for another drive. He might have some recalibrated dampers for the front suspension of one of his HDT road cars, and he'd turn to me and beam. 'C'mon, Cromley, let's go for a blaze – you'll love it!'

Ultimately, that's all he ever wanted. He really wanted to play in the sand (er, clay) pit and go for a drive. That's it. That was Peter Brock. Stuffing around with cars, driving at the limit and always keen to impress.

*

There's one moment from my time with Brock I really would like to edit.

I went back to drive for the Mobil team in 1992 at Peter Brock's insistence. By then it was a very different setup.

Brock's race team was no longer his. He drove the race car, while the team, Advantage Racing, was owned and run by Advantage International's Steve Frazer. The company was a major player in the sports rights and marketing sector (it later became Octagon), and they managed Peter's sporting affairs at this time.

Sadly, their sponsorship money ran dry partway through the year, and the two-car team was cut back to one after just four rounds of the Australian Touring Car Championship. I was out of a drive yet again.

It was during that brief period of being back alongside Brock that one of my proudest days in racing came, but I handled it very poorly. It was at the second round of that year's ATCC at Sandown in mid-March. I had a ripping intense battle with Brock in the pair of races that constituted that round of the championship, but in those days we were massively outgunned by the turbo Ford Sierras and Nissan GT-Rs, so we weren't dicing for the lead or charging for a podium finish.

Brock and I crossed the line in each race separated by only a small margin: in Race 1 he finished tenth and I was 11th, and in Race 2 he finished fifth and I was right on his hammer in sixth place; I'd spent some time in front of him before he managed to beat me to the line. Nobody would care about those results – we were not a factor in the broader race – but we were driving the wheels off those things, and it was a great nose-to-tail battle.

'You should be very proud, Cromley,' Brock said to me after the race. 'That was an outstanding drive.'

The team's engine builder, long-time respected industry figure Neill 'Part' Burns (nicknamed during his time with the

Sandown 1992: the race where I led Brock and didn't handle his post-race compliment well. *AN1 Images/Dale Rodgers*

Holden Dealer Team in the 1970s and '80s for his lack of hair on top!), had said the same thing.

'Yeah, piss off, Brock, whatever,' was my grinning, off-handed reply.

Normally there was plenty of needle and banter going on between Brock and me. But this wasn't a time for taking the mickey. Australia's most celebrated racer – my childhood racing hero, was paying me a genuine, heartfelt compliment about the quality of my driving that day. I regret my words to this day. It was a bad misread, and a silly, immature response.

There will always be a few moments in life where you wish you could rewrite the script. For me, this was one of those.

12

LION TALES

'LADDIE, DRIVING MY RACE cars will be like pulling on a pair of comfortable old socks.'

These are the haunting words I'll take to my grave.

'You'll be so familiar, you'll be doing so much driving, you'll become at one with the car. And if it goes well, we'd like you to be part of our sportscar program at Le Mans.'

The words came from the mouth of a world motorsport heavyweight, Scotsman Tom Walkinshaw, after I had signed a deal to drive for the official factory Holden Racing Team for the 1989 season. Tom was dangling before me the possibility that I might also join his TWR (Tom Walkinshaw Racing) organisation's Jaguar sportscar team.

This was all fantastic news, especially for a young driver like me. There was only one small problem. Not long after the euphoric honeymoon period, it turned out to be the Holden 'We Don't Go Racing' Team for me.

Holden's history in the sport is unmatched in Australia. They've won everything worth winning, including the Australian Touring Car Championship (now known as the Supercars Championship) on 21 occasions up to the end of 2020. They've also taken a record 34 wins in the Great Race at Bathurst. The first came in 1968, in a V8-powered Monaro driven by Bruce McPhee and Barry Mulholland. The Harry Firth–led Holden Dealer Team made its debut a year later, with Colin Bond and Tony Roberts taking victory and a young rookie named Peter Brock finishing third.

While Ford came and went from the sport at will, Holden always found a way to stay in the game, providing funding, technical support and political clout to many a Monaro, Torana or Commodore driver and team.

The Cromptons weren't particularly loyal to one motor manufacturer or another, but if we had to cast a vote, we would probably have been a Holden family. Back in those days, people bought a new car every year or two, so our driveway was graced by all sorts of Holdens. And so, despite my emotional attachment to Peter Brock, being presented with the opportunity to drive for the Holden Racing Team in 1989 was a big deal. When Walkinshaw and his local head of Holden Special Vehicles, John Crennan, approached me to become part of the relaunched Holden factory team, I leaped at the opportunity.

Crennan was a former Holden executive who had left to join Walkinshaw and head up HSV, Holden's new performance car partnership, which effectively replaced Brock's HDT Special Vehicles operation. John was very enthusiastic about getting me on board. He said he felt that in me they had found the right young guy to emulate the kind of things Peter had done in his development as a Holden driver and personality. TWR was a huge international operation with a massive reputation and the full backing of Holden. What's more, the multiple British Touring Car Champion Win Percy would be my teammate in the two-car operation.

I met with John at the Parkroyal Hotel in Wellington in late 1988, while I was in town racing for Brock's Mobil BMW team. I wasn't being paid to drive for Peter, so when Crennan and the new Holden Racing Team offered me $40,000, it seemed like a no-brainer. I subsequently met with Tom and John at the Travelodge Hotel at Melbourne Airport shortly after, and the deal was agreed.

For me, the allure was enormous. I was actually going to become a professional racing driver – and professional in every sense of the word. How good was that!

Tom was always economical in his words, and he was quite an imposing figure. At that point he was a big international mover and shaker in motorsport, and a bit daunting to me. Earlier that year, his team had won the Le Mans 24 Hour sportscar classic in France for Jaguar, breaking a long drought for the proud British brand in the classic race.

He'd been a champion driver himself, winning the 1984 European Touring Car Championship, and had taken pole position for the 1985 Bathurst 1000 at the wheel of a Jaguar XJ-S, before deciding to pull up stumps on race driving at the end of 1988 so he could focus on his expanding racing empire.

'You'll flourish in our race cars – it will be like pulling on your favourite old pair of socks,' he told me during our meeting at the Travelodge. 'You'll know the cars, team and your place in the team inside out.'

As history shows, none of this ever happened, though the lure of being considered part of Tom's line-up of drivers for the Jaguar sportscar program in Europe was a real hook.

The deal to join Holden came off the back of the great on-track battles I'd had with Jim Richards and Brock in 1988 in the BMWs. It showed John that I was competitive on track against those two legendary drivers, and I could present well for the brand away from the track.

Holden had a history of being driven by bold personalities. They linked the brand through the ambassadorial nature of motorsport and its personalities, particularly Brock, and many more followed in Mark Skaife, Craig Lowndes, Greg Murphy, Russell Ingall and Jamie Whincup. The drivers became involved beyond the race team, extending to close relationships with dealers and customers.

Holden will remain one of the great examples globally of how to leverage motor racing in the correct way. The racing showed the brand's sporting prowess, and allowed it to showcase its product in a way that translated into sales. It's difficult in 2021 to put this into context, given that Holden is no longer operational and we have a very different automotive landscape. But when you added together the Holden brand, its history, its success in racing, the way it engaged its dealers, the sheer volumes of cars it sold and the percentage of space it thus occupied in the community, joining as a driver was a very big deal.

I was magnetically attracted to joining the Holden Racing Team; effectively, I would be following in Brock's footsteps. But it also meant breaking the very deep bond I'd forged with

Top: The new HSV/Holden Racing Team is unveiled, 1989. I'm right of shot, and next to me is Win Percy, then John Crennan.

Above: A press shot of me in Peter Boylan's Ralt RT20 Formula Holden.

Peter. I stewed over leaving his team. I'm that sort of person. I tossed things around and around in my head for a long time, battling to find the best way to explain my decision to Peter: that I was leaving his team.

From a business standpoint, and considering my career progression, my decision to go to Holden was an easy one to make. But on a personal level it was painful and complex. It meant breaking my bond with the guy who had put me on the springboard into the industry. What's more, he was a mate.

I still have niggles of regret about leaving Brock. At that stage of my career I was slow to understand that motor racing was a dog-eat-dog world. It wasn't all smiles, happiness and fluffy ducks. It was 'kill or be killed' – and I learned that the hard way. Leaving Brock was, on a personal level, very difficult for me.

When I awkwardly delivered the news to Peter, he was astonished, and quickly filled with frustration and anger. He didn't abuse me, but he couldn't believe it. Worse was that my destination was the new Holden team that was replacing Brock's HDT outfit. Tom Walkinshaw was the guy, in Peter's eyes, who had pulled apart the HDT and destroyed his road car business, annexing his spot as Holden's favourite figure. I had joined 'the dark side'.

But Peter got over it and our friendship endured. Ironically, in 1994 Brock himself would sign to drive for Tom and the Holden Racing Team. I often reminded him of this in later years! And even in 1989 the truth was that he had the last laugh, because the factory Holden Racing Team barely did any racing at all! I sat on the sidelines for most of the season as Brock whizzed around in his new turbo Mobil Ford Sierra against the rest of the touring car aces. It was beyond painful.

The year began without a hint of what was to come, as Percy and I tested our Commodores at Calder Park and Phillip Island prior to the commencement of the Australian Touring Car Championship. That test at Calder instantly brought into focus the difference in engineering philosophy between the England-based TWR and Australian-based organisations concerning how best to prepare and run a Holden Commodore race car.

The Brits from TWR didn't agree with the way in which acclaimed engineer (and former driver) Ron Harrop's company was putting together the rear ends of the Commodore race cars at the time. They had their own ideas about what would work, and it was their weird setup that collapsed during one test at Calder. There had simply been too much torque stress on the differential housing, and it had pulled the diff hangers clean out of the floor, so that the car looked like a dog with worms as it crawled up the back straight! The Harrop Engineering–designed rear end was in place for the next test session.

If there was a moment that cemented my place in the Holden Racing Team, then it was the next test session, at the fast and flowing Phillip Island Grand Prix Circuit. That track is seriously fast. I was on a high when I went slightly faster than Win, an internationally renowned and highly respected driver, in that Phillip Island test. Later in the day, when Win was in the car, the engine expired, bringing an end to the day's tests, but to me that didn't really matter. I had proven I could do the job.

So I felt pretty happy with my place in the racing universe as I sat with Win eating some fish and chips near the world-famous Penguin Parade on the edge of the island, but my cheery disposition fell apart not long after.

When the Australian Touring Car Championship kicked off at Amaroo Park on the first weekend of March 1989, neither Percy nor I was on the grid. We weren't there for the second round either, a week later at Symmons Plains in Tasmania, or the third round, at Lakeside in Queensland in mid-April. As it turned out, we wouldn't compete in a single round of that year's championship, an all-important hit-out prior to the most important race on the calendar: Bathurst.

At this point, all communication lines went silent. There were no answers on why we were not racing, and seemingly no light at the end of the tunnel. How could I be a Holden Racing Team driver and not be racing? The whole situation seemed to be covered by a shroud of fog. I'd speak with John, with whom I had a very strong relationship at that point, but I couldn't get a straight answer. Then I'd contact Rob McEniry, Holden's then head of marketing, and I couldn't get a straight answer from him either. In a guarded way, each would point to the other, but not quite fully blame them.

The situation seemed ridiculous, so eventually I jumped on a plane to head to the United Kingdom to see the other corner of the triangle: Walkinshaw. The 30-hour-plus flight from Sydney to England seemed like a long way to go, but I simply had to get to the bottom of what was (or more importantly, wasn't) going on.

TWR's base was in Kidlington, a large village in Oxfordshire. When I arrived, I plonked myself in the waiting area downstairs. And there I sat and waited. And waited. For almost an entire day.

Eventually, Tom emerged from his office. Instantly I could tell from his tone and body language he didn't want to engage in a detailed discussion.

'Oh, I didn't realise you were there,' he said, as he briskly came trotting downstairs with bags in hand. 'I'm sorry, I can't talk now – I'm going to Melbourne.'

It was total bullshit. He knew exactly why I was there, and he simply bolted. I'd flown around the world to see Tom and he barely gave me two minutes of his time. And to make matters worse, he was heading to the country from which I had just flown!

I was livid. Within the space of six months, I had experienced just how harsh motorsport could be.

*

I fell back into the commentary box with Channel Seven, joining Mike Raymond and the broadcasting team for the remaining rounds of that year's championship. This, of course, was a privilege, but a long way from where I expected to be.

I was devastated by the Holden disaster. Truth be told, I don't reckon I ever fully recovered from it. It was the first real confidence-smashing experience of my young racing career, and woke me up to the cold reality of just how tough professional motor racing is. It's tougher than most people could ever contemplate.

Tom was one of those guys who had a firm handshake and looked you straight in the eye. He was a specialist at making you do the talking in any conversation. He didn't do the wrong thing by me, but he didn't explain it either. One thing I will say about Tom, who sadly died of cancer in December 2010, is he never let me down financially. Even when HRT wasn't racing in 1989, he still paid me. I deeply respected him for that.

In a perverse way, though, that made the whole situation worse. When you go racing, you're not doing it for the money. If you strip away all the bullshit in racing, the money is a lovely by-product, a bonus, but it's not the reason you do it. You do it because you love it.

To this day, I don't know why the Holden Racing Team was benched for most of the 1989 season. It must have been about money, or a lack of it between the partners, Holden, TWR and HSV. Perhaps Holden didn't cough up as much as Tom wanted them to. Perhaps there was insufficient sponsorship to cover the racing program. Or perhaps he felt the cars just wouldn't be competitive against the Ford Sierras and Nissan Skylines. Maybe it was a combination of those elements.

After my touring car career stalled during 1989, I jumped into the new open-wheeler Formula Holden series, a category for cars that looked vaguely like Formula 1 machines but were powered by highly modified Holden V6 Commodore road car engines. John Crennan, to his eternal credit, always felt concern about what had happened with HRT, and he went out of his way, using HSV business, to help me get onto the grid.

I decided that the best way forward for me was to try to find a way to keep racing in these new Formula Holden open-wheelers. John Bowe introduced me to a businessman and former driver named Peter Boylan, who was also excited about the new class, which was based on European Formula 3000 chassis cars. It was to become the new premier open-wheeler series from that year onwards, and drivers would compete for the Australian Drivers' Championship and the coveted Gold Star that was awarded to the series champion.

Boylan needed a driver for his Ralt RT20 race car, but he needed help to partially fund it. I didn't have any cash, but I had a relationship with the paint manufacturer Dulux. And they had lots of paint. We all joined forces in a multi-tiered arrangement that saw Dulux provide paint to HSV, as their factories were neighbours in the Melbourne suburb of Clayton. What John and HSV would have spent in cash on paint for HSV production with Dulux was then repatriated at a discount to Peter Boylan for his Formula Holden project. The end result: a multi-coloured, Dulux-backed race car.

I enjoyed tremendous support from Peter in 1989 and 1990. His patronage was a very important and special element of my career. Without it I would never have been able to race open wheelers. People like Peter put their heart, soul and bank balance on the line to help young drivers and I am thankful I was one of them.

It was a big step on John's part. He could have said, 'Bad luck, mate, go away,' but to his credit he helped keep my racing flame alive. All parties profited from the deal: Peter had a sponsor by proxy, John had cheaper paint and I had a race car to drive.

The Holden Racing Team finally did go racing in September 1989 after a deal was salvaged to get the factory-backed operation back onto the track. Larry Perkins had been contracted to run HSV's racing program in 1988, while its road car business was being established, and he was called up to assist again in 1989. A deal was salvaged for his Perkins Engineering squad to prepare and run two cars under the HRT banner for the Sandown 500, the Bathurst 1000 and the Australian Grand Prix touring car support races in Adelaide.

In the lead-up to Sandown, we headed out to Calder for a test session, and I found a very different 'LP' to the man I'd dealt with in the recent past. When I drove with Brock's team in 1987 and '88, he had been quite complimentary about my driving, a great confidant who was forthcoming with tips and insights. But at this Calder test I found myself driving one of his cars, and his approach was cold and direct. He emphatically drilled into all the drivers that there was no need for any of us to be driving too hard.

'Line and length, line and length,' he said, sounding more like a cricket coach than a racing team manager. 'That's all I want to see, not lap times.'

The test didn't last very long. My overwhelming recollection of that day was barrelling down the main straight at Calder at around 260 kilometres per hour, and arriving at the end of the straight with the brake pedal on the floor! With no front brakes and only rear brakes, I had visions of bouncing off a fence.

There was a fence way down the run-off road at the end of the front straight at Calder, with a gate that allowed safety vehicles and facility security access. Thankfully, it was open. I shot through the thistles and rocks that surrounded the outer perimeter of the facility, sailed through the gate at the end of the dirt road at warp speed, and ended up out towards the Sydenham railway station. I came to a rest having miraculously not hit anything.

As it turned out, the material on the brake pads was very thin. They were old pads, with barely any material left on the backing plates. I was angry at Larry, and he was angry at me. It was one of those awkward moments that happen in competitive environments.

The Neil Crompton who performed well in the test earlier in the year at Phillip Island had totally vanished. The Neil who drove the Perkins-run car was a different bloke. I reckon I could have put my grandmother in the car and she'd have done a better job. I'd lost all my confidence, having missed an entire season. I didn't enjoy driving the car; the Calder test was a shocker. The cars weren't quick, but I was hopelessly slow. It all sucked.

Steve Harrington and I finished sixth at the Sandown 500, Percy and I finished seventh at Bathurst, and I finished ninth in both races in Adelaide. They were all worthless results.

*

Motor racing drivers are creatures who depend on confidence, even arrogance. At HRT in 1989, it was the opposite: my confidence was shot.

A year in racing is like a dog year. If you miss one year in the sport, it's like you've been gone for seven real years. As the end of 1989 approached, I was adamant I had to get out of the Holden Racing Team. Then I fell for the three-card trick: Tom apologised, Rob apologised and John apologised. They all said things would be much better in 1990, and as a show of good faith they doubled my salary from $40,000 to $80,000.

Along came 1990, and the Holden Racing Team went racing – sort of. I only drove a handful of times, and once again the promise to run in every ATCC event evaporated. I filled in for Win Percy in very sad circumstances for a round of the touring car championship at Mallala, in South

Australia, after his son had been tragically killed back in England. Otherwise, the only races I competed in were the Sandown 500 and the Bathurst 1000, where Brad Jones and I finished fifth, with Percy and Allan Grice winning the race.

So it was little surprise to many that I completely spat the dummy at the end of 1990. My frustrations exploded. I went berserk to motoring journalist Nick Senior (who later went on to become the Managing Director of Subaru Australia). He ran a story in one of the Sydney newspapers headlined 'Bitter Crompton and Holden split'.

'The combined management of the outlet has done more than enough to ruin my touring car career,' I said in my very public vent. 'I don't need any more of their dithering. I'm bitter towards them for wasting my time – I was promised 23 races. I've done 5. Since the association began, I have rejected good offers to get back to regular touring car racing on the promise and reassurance I was very much part of the future.

'The management of the post-Brock Holden racing era is a very bad joke. I don't think they've done any favours for Aussie Holden racing fans, their dealer network or their sponsors – and still the rot continues.

'I think it was professionally reckless to offer me a job with the TWR Holden Racing Team in late 1988 when they clearly did not have a mandate to do so.'

Candour like this would never be recommended by a PR handbook for aspiring drivers, but I'd had enough.

But then, in a demonstration that my IQ is the equivalent of my shoe size, I let it all happen again in 1991. Tom, Rob and John came back a third time, apologised yet again and invited me back to drive the second car alongside Brad Jones in the Sandown and Bathurst endurance races, which

The HRT crew during my time driving its ride car after I retired from V8 Supercars. This was at Eastern Creek in December 2005.

I willingly accepted. What a silly boy. Looking back, I was just so committed to making it work, when it was clearly never going to. It was like trying to continue in a failed relationship, and refusing to accept the cold, hard facts.

The HRT chapter of my career should have been filled with fantastic experiences. Instead, it nosed me over and into the rocks. In the first instance, the failure was squarely on them. Subsequently, it was on me.

To be a top-line driver like Mark Skaife, Marcos Ambrose, Jamie Whincup, Scott McLaughlin or Shane van Gisbergen, you have to be able to squeeze every last millisecond per lap out of the car and yourself. You need to know the machine inside and out, and have supreme confidence in your capabilities and those of the people surrounding you. I was short on every aspect of this.

John Bowe, the two-time Australian Drivers Champion, two-time Bathurst 1000 winner and teammate of Dick Johnson for 11 years, said to me very early on in my career that I would come to learn the art of driving touring cars in time. He said you needed to be a whisker away from a giant shunt all the time, with the car dancing on the absolute limit. That's the small window where real performance lies in any racing car, and it is right at the ragged edge.

If I'm being deeply self-critical, my personality simply did not cope with the level of deflation I endured during the Holden Racing Team chapter of my career. And I think that's something that goes back to our individual wiring. The superstars have that last, robust, impossible-to-penetrate reservoir of confidence. A key attribute to sporting and racing success is to be able to block out the negative, quickly rebuild, repair and refocus, and come back bigger and better than ever.

That's not something I understood until I was much older. I either didn't have it to start with, or it got broken out of me. I'm not sure which, but that's the difference between being a champion or not.

*

I did manage to write a somewhat stupid piece of Bathurst 1000 history during my time with the Holden Racing Team: I became the first and, as far as I am aware, only driver in the history of the race to use a helicopter to refuel mid-race.

The 1991 race started badly for Brad Jones and me. Our race wasn't even a minute old when he radioed through to tell the team he'd hit the wall at the top of the mountain and was coming into the pits for the crew to check the car over.

Worse was to come later, when I got behind the wheel and found myself on the tail of Allan Grice in our sister HRT Commodore. He had a big slide coming out of the final corner onto Pit Straight, and such was his lack of acceleration that I tagged him from behind, causing a small amount of damage to both cars.

Even worse was to come later in the day, when I jumped into the car for another stint and forgot to switch the auxiliary fuel pump off. It wasn't labelled and I simply overlooked switching it back after the stop. By comparison with today's failsafe methods, which are all carefully conveyed over the radio from the crew to the driver, too much was left to fate back then, and frankly I stuffed it up.

The car eventually coughed when coming out of the Cutting, and I rolled off into the gap in the fence. So there I was, aboard a Commodore that was out of juice.

That was when I had an idea. Hovering above me was ATN-7's chopper, the red Bell JetRanger, with long-serving and skilled pilot Frank Van Rees at the controls. I indicated I wanted to hitch a ride, and Frank landed and then took me back to the pit area. I collected a jerry can of fuel, and Frank flew me back up to the top of the mountain, where I tipped the fuel into the stricken Commodore, fired it back into life and restarted the race. By this time I was under the very strict instruction from Race Control that I was to immediately take the car back into the pits and retire from the race.

'Show me the rule that says you can't use a helicopter to refuel mid race,' I later jokingly said to CAMS Race Director Tim Schenken. But Tim took a dim view of my inventive approach to try and stay in the Great Race.

*

That 1991 Bathurst race was my last start with the Holden Racing Team, and when my tenure ended I sat with John Crennan at Darling Harbour, in Sydney, for a quiet lunch. We continued to be dignified, respectful colleagues.

The HRT operation evolved, eventually turned itself into a powerhouse of the sport, and I ended up becoming involved with it again after I retired from full-time Supercars racing at the end of 2002. Rather than race driving, I was the high-speed chauffeur driver, giving guests rides in the team's dedicated ride car.

Their 'PR2' ride car (PR standing for Passenger Ride, while 2 indicated the number of passengers it could take) was in fact a former race car, the very same ex-HRT Commodore that Craig Lowndes had rolled multiple times down the road at Calder in a highly publicised shunt in 1999. Repaired, it had a seat added in the back and was given identical livery to the race cars of the time in the mid-2000s. Using it meant the team could save its real race cars the strain of thousands of additional kilometres around the country each year, when sponsors, guests and the media enjoyed 'hot laps' at the various tracks.

Mark Skaife – who had acquired the Holden Racing Team from Holden in 2003, in the wake of Tom Walkinshaw Racing's collapse overseas – would arrive on a Monday morning after a race meeting, sprinkle some star dust, take the highest-profile guests for a lap, and be gone by 10 am, leaving me to pound around all day with a scruffy set of tyres!

Occasionally, we ran a new set of Bridgestone tyres that were left over from the company's time as control tyre provider to the V8 Supercar category. The crew would wheel out the fresh tyres, and I'd often take VIP passengers for pretend qualifying laps. It was bloody quick; often I was fast enough to have qualified the car in the front third of the field at the previous weekend's races.

Driving the HRT ride car was a whole pile of fun, and a great way to keep myself connected to the art of race driving.

*

I very nearly made a return to racing in 2007 for the Holden Racing Team, 16 years after my last outing with the team.

By that stage I was well and truly ensconced in my television commentary and analysis role. Channel Seven had the broadcaster rights for the championship again, including the Bathurst 1000, after ten years at Network Ten.

I was sitting at Sandown in Melbourne, preparing some notes for the weekend's broadcast, when my mobile phone rang. It was Rob Starr, an old mate and the longest-serving crew member of the Holden Racing Team. He'd started there in 1991, and by now was Team Manager.

'Can you get down to the garage, Cromley, quick-quick?' he asked.

HRT needed a fill-in driver for Mark Skaife, who had undergone an emergency appendix operation on the eve of the race event and wasn't going to be fit to take his place in the team's #2 Commodore alongside his regular teammate, Todd Kelly.

Given that my business entity had me contracted to Supercars via its television arm (the organisation started producing its own broadcasts for Channel Seven in that season, and continues to do so for the current rights holders, Fox Sports and Channel Seven, to this day), I went to see Wayne Cattach, the CEO of Supercars (then known as AVESCO), and Murray Lomax, the head of the television unit producing the coverage. Would they approve me taking up the opportunity?

They said no, I wasn't permitted to play race driver for the weekend. They were well within their rights, but I was still cranky, especially given the many examples before and after when others in the broadcast team were permitted to put their microphone down for a weekend, or multiple weekends, and step back into a car. As I saw it, it was a chance to put 'one of the team' into the race for the weekend. But when I asked, they said, 'Nah, you've got a job to do.' It pissed me off big-time. HRT ended up flying Tony Longhurst down from Queensland to fill in for Skaife.

As it happens, my link with Walkinshaw still endures, and the bitter disappointment I felt years ago is long gone. Even this year, 2021, I found myself back at the wheel of a Walkinshaw Andretti United Holden Commodore Supercar at a drive day at Sandown. I hadn't been in a Supercar for just over a year.

I was a little nervous for other reasons, but I loved it. I was reunited with my former #1, Rob Starr. It was super cool to have Robbie light up the radio and clear me to start. And so, 32 years later, out of the pit lane I rolled, off went the speed limiter, and into high speed I went for a solid day, turning heaps of laps with eager fans.

13

SKAIFE AND THE KARMA BUS

I DIDN'T HESITATE FOR a nanosecond. 'Sure, mate, absolutely no worries – it's easy flat. No problem!'

On that day I told Mark Skaife a filthy lie, and the karma bus would run me over as payback.

It was 1990 and I was into my second year racing the Peter Boylan–owned Ralt RT20 in the Formula Holden category, while my on again, (mostly) off again HRT touring car career continued to stall.

Mark arrived in the Formula Holden series in 1990, and added real credibility to the category. His Nissan touring car team boss Fred Gibson was one of those guys from that exciting racing era of the 1960s and 1970s when race drivers drove lots of different race cars in lots of categories, often on the same weekend. Fred's mindset was that it would be good for Mark to expand his horizons and chase the Gold Star in a Formula Holden.

After hours, Skaife has always been up for some fun and stupidity, although he was generally a little more earnest and serious in those days. The Winton round of the 1990 Australian Drivers Championship for Formula Holden was held in early April, and Skaife phoned me for some advice about those cars at that track, given I'd raced there the previous season.

'Hey, mate, I'm just interested to know: can you get through the Sweeper at Winton flat out, without lifting the throttle?' he asked.

The devil horns instantly grew out of the top of my head. I couldn't miss this opportunity to try to get one over Skaife. 'Sure, mate, absolutely no worries,' I said. 'It's *easy flat*. No problem!'

There was no way in the world a Formula Holden race car had anything like enough aerodynamic downforce or mechanical grip to get around turn three at Winton without flying straight off the road. I knew that – Skaife didn't.

'Good as gold,' Skaife said – a signature response – and he hung up, happy with the information he'd pinched.

Gibson Motorsport went testing at Winton prior to the next round and, naturally, Skaife put my advice into play. He tried to make turn three flat-out, with the throttle pedal flat to the floor, and succeeded in spearing straight off the circuit at seriously high speed. He bounced into the adjacent paddock, filling the car with grass, rocks and dirt, and maybe the odd insect. Classic! This was an outstanding 'gotcha': gold-plated bullshit.

Skaife's car, a SPA chassis (designed by Northern Irishman Gary Anderson, who designed the first Jordan Grand Prix Formula 1 car), was normally white, but after the impromptu expedition on this day it displayed a lovely layer of 'Winton beige', a stylish film of regional Victorian dust.

Skaife was annoyed, but nowhere near as upset as Fred Gibson. 'Crompton, if you ever tell one of my drivers that sort of shit again ...' he threatened me.

He didn't have to worry about getting even with me, though, because the Karma bus squared up with me in September that year, when Formula Holden supported the Sandown 500 touring car event.

*

Skaifey and I had some ripping races that year, but our epic fight for pole position at Sandown ended poorly for me, leaving me sitting in what was effectively a canoe imitating a former race car! Was the universe repaying me for my Winton 'tip'? Highly likely.

Mark and I traded fastest laps in the hunt for pole position. As there was no dashboard data and live timing in that era, the 'carrot' was the pit board, which suggested either 'P1' or 'P2' each time I passed the pits – although of course the info was one lap old.

In a desperate and dumb move, I decided the best way to get on top of Skaife was to stay hard on the gas for the fast left-hander off the end of the back straight. Yep, flat-out, no lift. It was a 275-kilometre-per-hour approach, and I turned in maybe a millimetre too early. I clipped the kerb on the inside of the corner, a rugged concrete lump, and instantly the car was out of control. It bounced and rotated and launched into the guardrail 100 metres down the road, piercing the fence – backwards, thank God. The deceleration was violent.

I opened my eyes, then checked all my limbs worked and I was in one piece.

It was a bloody miracle.

Bits and pieces of the car were scattered everywhere. Skaife stopped on his way past the scene of what looked like a plane crash. I hitched a ride back to the pits sitting on his sidepod, with the steering wheel in my hand. Brad Jones greeted me in the garage.

I was scheduled to qualify the HRT Commodore next for the Sandown 500, but instead I went and hid in the truck, pale and shaking.

*

The numbers don't lie, and in Mark's case they perfectly capture the amazing career he has carved for himself in Australian motorsport.

Our time together began at Winton Motor Raceway back in 1985, at that Winton 300 where we both drove Mitsubishi Cordia production cars. That adventure laid the foundations for a long-standing friendship and partnership.

Much to our disgust, my television colleague and former fellow racer Mark Larkham and I spent way too much time behind Skaife in those early years. We frequently tease him and ourselves about the lost 'Skaife years'.

Mark Skaife is such a bull. He simply refuses to lose at anything – he's wired to win. Everybody is a competitor, and everything is competitive to him. I've seen it first-hand, up close. Cantankerous, self-assured and highly credentialed, he's also a pain in the arse at times. All teasing aside, we've enjoyed some great times and funny moments together in different chapters of our lives across an extraordinary period in the sport.

In 1990 Mark had a huge crash during practice at the Adelaide Grand Prix in the new Nissan GT-R touring car. He came unstuck at high speed, rolled the two-door coupe and slid down the road on his roof. That really shook him up, and wrote off the car. In fact, it was so badly damaged the team took it to the scrapyard and had it crushed.

A week after the Adelaide Grand Prix, there was another race on the touring car calendar, the Nissan-sponsored 500-kilometre endurance event at the brand-new Eastern Creek Raceway, in Western Sydney, now known as Sydney Motorsport Park. The Nissan team entered its remaining GT-R for Richards and Skaife to co-drive.

'Godzilla', as it was famously known, was still a new toy and had a few teething problems, yet it was clear that the 600-horsepower, four-wheel-drive, turbocharged GT-Rs were incredible, destined to dominate Australian touring car racing. As a result, they were intensely disliked by many Holden and Ford fans.

The word was Skaife was not doing well after his rollover in Adelaide. The Holden Racing Team wasn't competing at that event (hardly a shock!) so I was available for casual steering duties, and received a call from Nissan team boss Fred Gibson. 'Mate, can you be on standby to do the race?' he asked.

'You bet,' I replied. 'I would love to. What's wrong with MS?'

'His neck is no good, he can't walk properly and he's in all sorts of pain and strife.'

'Oh, that's terrible. What time would you like me there?'

I got out to the track and the team asked me to do a few laps in the Friday-afternoon qualifying session as an insurance policy in case Skaife couldn't get into the car. That way, I'd be qualified to drive alongside Richards in the race on Saturday afternoon.

Then Skaifey emerged. He could barely walk – he shuffled with his head on a tilt, his body contorted. He didn't look anything like a driver ready to strap into a race car. But the look on his face said it all: 'This is my car.'

He was smashed up and hurting, but he was going to race that car no matter what – and he did. I was left standing in the pit, all dressed up with nowhere to go. Game over, Crompton.

*

Mark is a very different guy after hours. Away from the track, he's warm, funny and engaging, with a great intellect and giant passion. At his core, he wants motorsport to flourish. He loves it and he's made significant contributions to every aspect of the sport: technical, in governance, sporting, media and community.

A get-together with Mark would come at a cost, though! He has an amazing ability to get other people sideways after a few drinks at such dinners, and just when they're trying to emerge from bed the next morning with a thumping headache, he bounces out on eight cylinders with a grin on his face!

Time has mellowed the fellow I call 'five-time/six-time' (referring to his five championship wins and six Bathurst 1000 wins). He understands how to take the piss out of himself a lot more these days. That most definitely was not on his radar early in his career! If you resisted or teased him back then, not only was he good at running you over with the metaphorical bus but he was also an expert at hooking reverse gear and backing straight over you, making sure you were well and truly finished off, whether it was in an on-track tussle, dealing with the politics of the sport, or just arguing life, politics or business.

I'll always remember his retirement from full-time racing at the end of 2008. I hosted his retirement media conference at Crown in Melbourne. It was a big deal, and Mark was very emotional about it.

He'd sought my counsel in the months before he made the decision, and I remember asking him a simple question. Wrestling with the 'stay or go' decision is incredibly difficult when every fibre of your body is committed to a task or goal. 'Would you rather sit around with your mates drinking beers,' I asked, 'or would you prefer to sort out understeer and oversteer as a race car driver from position 14?'

His answer came almost immediately. 'I'd rather have a beer.'

And there was the answer. It was that simple. And that was where he landed.

Like all of us, he went through periods of withdrawal after finishing up racing, but he's thrown all that effort and energy into his television, track design and automotive consultancy roles since he joined the V8 Supercars broadcast team in 2009. We've enjoyed sharing a commentary box at Supercars events, bringing our passion and experience to the television broadcasts and the viewers at home.

It's funny, though, how there can be periods where we have almost no contact at or between race meetings. That's just how a busy race weekend sometimes plays out, as our roles in between on-track sessions and events take us in different directions. We're often apart at events: he might be sitting on the Fox Sports host desk post-session chatting to Jessica Yates, while I'm in the pit lane or paddock with a notepad in hand, digging up the 'chat' and reaction from drivers or wrangling something in the Toyota 86 paddock. And midweek we're both flying low at a million miles an hour in separate corners of the industry.

But Mark and I have developed a great ability to pick up where we left off, so we can play off each other instantly, no matter whether it's on radio (we hosted a show called 'The Stick Shift' on Triple M for a while), on television or in front of sponsors or corporate guests. We've got the 'light and shade' act pretty well sorted, and can jump between whether we need to be technical in our discussions, humorous or somewhere in between. We definitely have a strong rapport. As I see it, the evidence of that comes when he's not there, as it's always noticeably different.

There are times on air when I have to put my head down and look away from the monitors. Sometimes it's to figure out a certain strategic element within a race; sometimes it's to talk to our team in the production trucks or our 'commentary box engineer', Oscar Fiorinotto, who tracks all the strategy and technical information behind the scenes. When I do any of these things, I feel totally safe leaving the steering wheel of the broadcast to Mark, who always picks things up seamlessly.

Relative to the outside world of motorsport, our Supercars broadcasts punch far above their weight, globally and domestically. If you look at Formula 1 or NASCAR telecasts, they enjoy far greater budgets and resources than we have in Australia, but our amazing engineering and creative teams do a sensational job.

I can always see Skaife's brain freeze whenever I throw a gag, a silly one-liner or something a bit different into the mix that he's not ready for. He always has a strategy for how he wants to explain something on air, but he's never quite ready for a left-field lightning bolt out of the blue. The hardest sessions are the practice session on a Friday when it's quiet and there's nothing happening – they're akin to a midweek training session for AFL or NRL teams.

One time during a practice session I briefly burst into song, and Skaifey just cracked up and couldn't stop. He had tears streaming down face, but he eventually composed himself enough to put his headset back on and continue commentating.

Behind the scenes, Mark has served as a dedicated Supercars board member, he's chaired the Supercars Commission, he's consulted to the governing body, Motorsport Australia (formerly CAMS), and he's worked with expert engineering consultants IEDM on track design and safety. For more than 35 years now he's worked diligently on a daily basis to further the motor racing cause like few others. His work ethic and attention to detail is incredible, and punishing for those who can't keep up.

The serious business and sport of motor racing still compels us both; however, the core passion is pure, just like it was at the very start of our journey. These days, as old mates, we still get to share that giddy excitement and indulge in forensic analysis of the game we love on the telly, instead of in our 'branded onesies'.

Reflections

Mark Skaife — six-time Bathurst 1000 Winner, five-time Australian Touring Car/V8 Supercars Champion

Neil has brilliant levels of competency in everything he does. He also has a mad level of intellect that clearly serves him very well. Whether it be motorsport broadcasting, his love of aviation and flying planes or water skiing, he applies himself 100 per cent to every task in life.

But, most importantly, away from his sporting and work pursuits, he is one of the most loyal, passionate and considerate people I know, especially with his family and loved ones.

People don't recognise how good he was in a car as a race driver. He was very, very good in a race car. He deserves to have more race wins and championships to his name. He got himself heavily involved in the marketing and sponsorship side of things during his times with Wayne Gardner and Glenn Seton's teams and perhaps that added workload deviated him from the core task of driving, but that's not a criticism. Neil always rolled his sleeves up and made those teams better as a collective from his involvement beyond the driver's seat. Not many drivers could, or would, do that.

I think you have to be able to look at yourself in the mirror after your driving career and ask yourself a question: 'Did the people I race against have my respect as a driver?' With Neil Crompton, I can tell you the answer most certainly is yes.

I would argue he's the best motorsport commentator in the world. While talking about race cars comes easily for many, there are countless other elements involved in making television that are time-consuming and hard, but he makes all of those things look easy and that's why I put him up on a pedestal as the broadcasting benchmark.

Neil also has a far better sense of humour than people would imagine. I think he holds back his real character to a certain degree on camera, so not too many people get to see the fun side of an otherwise pretty serious guy. There's a very fun larrikin that lurks in the background behind that serious exterior. He's probably the worst drinker in the world, though. I've had a lot of fun smashing him up on the juice for a long time; he doesn't recover well! Feed him a few beers or Japanese whiskeys and he's no good!

Mark Skaife. *AN1 Images/Graeme Neander*

14

A BITTER PODIUM

FLIPPING THE BIRD TO motor racing fans from a podium is the last thing I thought I'd do in this life, and while I'm metaphorically a fully paid-up member of the hardcore passionate racers' club, sometimes passion can go too far.

The most controversial podium presentation in the history of the Bathurst 1000 came in 1992, and it remains one of the most talked-about moments. Racing fans and casual viewers will remember that as the day Jim Richards gave the seething mob below an unsolicited character reference, as he and his Nissan co-driver Mark Skaife were booed vigorously while being crowned winners of that year's event – the 30th running of the Great Race at Mount Panorama. I had a first-hand view of what unfolded.

'I'm just really stunned for words. I can't believe the reception,' Richo said at the beginning of his short and sharp

A BITTER PODIUM

verbal spray. 'I thought Australian race fans had a lot more to go than this; this is bloody disgraceful. I'll keep racing, but I tell you what, this is going to remain with me for a long time. You're a pack of arseholes.'

I know only too well how bitter the fans below the podium were about the Nissan team that day, because only minutes before Jim's famous, and somewhat uncharacteristic, outburst, I'd shown the mob an extended middle finger when my co-driver, the Swede Anders Olofsson, and I went out onto the podium as third-place getters after a tough day aboard the second of the Nissan team's cars.

Anders was a typical Swede. A cool, calm and experienced racer who had been to Bathurst a few times before, he handled the mob's booing and jeering far better than I did. I was furious. After all, every driver in that race had put their life on the line in horrendous conditions, and here we were copping abuse for it.

Jim and Mark had been awarded victory in the race after a massive rainstorm caught Jim out on slick tyres on the wet track. The factory-supported, Winfield-sponsored red and white Nissan GT-R aquaplaned out of control and crashed into the trackside bank at the Cutting, ripping one of the wheels off. Crawling back to the pits at walking pace, he couldn't avoid slipping off the road and ploughing into a car park of smashed cars at the side of the track.

The race was red-flagged and brought to a stop and, as were and are the rules in motorsport, the race result was defined by the last fully completed lap. That meant victory was awarded, quite rightly, to Jim and Mark. But the fact the win had been credited to a car that was sitting in a crumpled

I've never heard a more hostile crowd than the one at Bathurst in 1992.
AN1 Images/Graeme Neander

A BITTER PODIUM

heap near the kink at the top of Conrod Straight didn't go down well with the fans at Mount Panorama.

It had been an incredibly emotional weekend. It was fair to say that the GT-R was loathed by most of the teams and personnel in the paddock, and by a large percentage of the partisan fanbase, who were keener on a Holden or Ford claiming victory than the Nissan known as 'Godzilla'.

That race was one of the wettest in Bathurst history, and the rain most certainly played to the technical advantage of the GT-Rs. Being four-wheel-drive, they were superior to the rear-wheel-drive Commodores, Sierras and BMWs that were our main opposition in those conditions.

My drive with Peter Brock's Mobil Commodore team had dried up earlier in the year, so the chance to join the factory Nissan team in one of its amazing GT-Rs for Bathurst was indeed a great opportunity, albeit a one-off. The conditions were so bad, though, that I remember at one stage charging down Conrod Straight at more than 280 kilometres per hour with virtually no visibility, the white lines on the edge of the road my only guide as to my position on the track. Having a four-wheel-drive car may have given me a traction advantage but it didn't help me see where I was going through the rain, spray and gloom.

In the wet conditions, you could still hit the same top speed down Conrod Straight as in the dry, but the rain meant you weren't at maximum velocity for quite as long as normal. That didn't make it any safer, by the way.

At one stage I caught the blur of an orange flash of fire out of the corner of my eye: one of the Caltex team Sierras and a black Commodore had collided and caught on fire as I slipped by. It was like one of those dream sequences in a movie where time slows down and you can see everything going on around you as you pick your way through the chaos. It was truly frightening.

As the intensity and difficulty of the racing that day went up and up, so too did my stress. I kept pulling the seatbelts tighter and tighter, bending myself into a U-shape in the race seat. I was doubled up like a half-opened pocketknife.

The day had already had a shocking pall cast over it earlier on, when Denny Hulme, the Kiwi who had won the 1967 Formula 1 World Championship driving a Brabham-Repco for Sir Jack Brabham's famous team, died of a heart attack while at the wheel of the BMW M3 he was sharing with Paul Morris.

Denny's death was a real shock and upset many in the paddock. I loved my chats with Denny, including on that very weekend. He was known as being a bit gruff, but I reckoned he was a legend of a bloke. He'd been there and done that all over the world. His yarns were fabulous. Even as I passed by his stationary car that day, under Safety Car conditions, as the paramedics frantically tried to revive him, I knew Denny was gone. I was devastated.

On the track, the team determined in the latter stages of the race that my #2 car would make its final pit stop a little earlier than the Richards/Skaife #1 car so the team could change the brake pads, inspect their wear (or lack thereof) and make a decision about whether or not to change the brakes of the lead car.

Bringing our #2 car into the pits took us out of a one-two team position, though, and allowed the Shell Ford Sierra of Dick Johnson and John Bowe to climb past us and into second place. I desperately held off making that last pit stop

A BITTER PODIUM

as long as I could. The pitch-black surrounding skies loomed, and I was in constant communication with Fred Gibson on the radio, trying to time my pit stop for brakes and fuel at the right time to make the swap to grooved wet-weather tyres too.

As it turned out, we made the change at exactly the right time, putting me onto the right type of tyre for the conditions earlier than other drivers, but then Richo had his shunt in the massive downpour and that was that.

Before the top three teams walked out to the podium, the chants from the angry mob below were out of control. They were not looking forward to seeing us.

Whatever colours you wear or team you support, a chant of 'you're a bunch of c-bombs' isn't acceptable under any circumstances. It was disgraceful, so I expressed my thoughts via my extended middle finger – and I meant it.

That didn't help the situation, though, and Skaifey prepared to take matters into his own hands, lining his jacket with unopened cans of Tooheys beer from the fridge in the waiting area before he and Jim walked out to greet the angry mob. Full cans had been pelted at Anders and me when we were out there, so Skaifey decided he would arm himself to fight back.

Thankfully, Jim was the voice of reason: he calmed Mark down and recommended he not return serve – and then, without anyone expecting it, promptly gave a verbal barrage of his own!

The sad thing about the whole situation was that I have no doubt most of the people under the podium carrying on like morons would, on any other day of the week, be the very same people we all love chatting with about car racing. We're all members of the same religion – motorsport – but the emotion of events that day clearly overflowed. I understand their passion and emotion, no problem – the industry has been trading on it and encouraging it for years – but I drew the line at being called a 'c-bomb' on the podium that day.

There certainly hadn't been a Bathurst podium before with that same sort of drama, passion and emotion, and there hasn't been once since. But overall, it was a miserable race in miserable conditions, and a great of the sport had passed away in the middle of it all.

Reflections

Mark Larkham – Supercars TV pit reporter, former team owner/driver

I recall standing with Crompo in a quiet corner at the end of the garages in Sandown's pitlane on a cold Melbourne Sunday morning in 2002. We were in a bit of a deep and meaningful (as we do), reflecting on life (as we do). He had proven his pedigree as a successful, professional race driver, and was at an extremely difficult crossroad. The networks were applying pressure and the realisation was right in front of him: 'Am I a Supercars competitor – or a Supercars commentator?'

I can recall he was genuinely torn; such is his love of driving and competing and, at the same time, in my view, the best motorsport commentator on the planet. I say that knowing all who are and all who have come before him. He had banked enough trophies so he made the right call, and the entire motorsport community benefited.

His mix of brain function (which allowed him to drive so well), verbal skill and broad vocabulary, the incredible 'teledext' of synonyms and the split-second thesaurus that revolves in his head – which can be accessed mid-sentence trotting out classic one-liners – all make him a unicorn. Add to all this his deep knowledge of everything motorsport – technically, regulatory, administratively, financially and politically – and you quickly realise he has no peer. Martin Brundle comes close with his deep knowledge of the sport, Leigh Diffey comes close with his beautiful articulation of it. Crompo brings both to the table.

That well-known saying 'Put ya brain in gear before opening your mouth' ... well, I honestly can't recall NC ever being in neutral.

Typically unselfish, hugely generous and with an unquestionable integrity that makes him a role model, he played a significant role in mentoring me in the broadcast space, and still does. Think about that. In 2008 I walked into a big chunk of Neil's space in the telecast, delving into and explaining sporting and technical issues that were often his domain that I know he loves presenting, but he strongly encouraged me to make that my world. Still does. In fact he played a very big role in bringing me back into the telecast for 2021.

I love the bloke, and we should be so lucky he made that decision on that cold Sunday Melbourne morning.

Mark Larkham. *AN1 Images/Dirk Klynsmith*

15

THE ROUGH DIAMOND FROM ALBURY

THROUGHOUT MY TIME IN motorsport, dating back to motocross when I was a kid right through to this very day, there has been one person who has been a constant in my life: Brad Jones. We first crossed paths as teenagers racing motocross (I often remind him that I won the 1975 Victorian Junior Motocross Championship at Wonthaggi, which means he lost!) and we've been in each other's universe ever since.

He was a scrawny brat from Albury with really long hair, while I was a scrawny brat from Ballarat with really long hair. We were both spotty-faced grubs who just wanted to race. Brad's father Phil was heavily involved with the Hume Weir circuit, and the Jones family were all about motorsport.

Brad worked as a spray painter, but he was determined to become a racing driver and made it happen.

We're the same age, though he's much, much, older (well, actually, only four months), and we're the most competitive mates you've ever seen. As old blokes, we'll be blazing along keeping score and getting wheeled around on frames still trying to beat one another to some obscure goal!

We're completely different people – think Oscar and Felix. I'm neat, organised, detailed and punctual. He's none of those things. Although, in fairness, in recent years BJ has been doing serious grown-up things like keeping notes, pitching ideas using documentation and generally behaving like a businessman. I've often wondered: 'Who are you, and what have you done with Brad Jones?'

From racing minibikes as kids to driving cars together at Bathurst and working on media projects, we've done it all.

Brad is a rock-solid character, a rough diamond. Loyal, straightforward and passionate. I really admire what he's achieved, both as a race driver and in business. He's also a funny bugger.

He and his brother Kim started with a grubby emerald-green Ford Falcon XC panel van, and towed their race cars around on a tandem trailer. Pause for long enough and you could almost hear that panel van rusting!

Brad's sponsorship manual back 'in the day' was the Yellow Pages! That was his sales Bible, and he and Kim would call any and every poor bastard who was listed in it. Silent numbers only became an option after the Jones boys had tried to shake down the entire A to Z on multiple occasions!

They worked their way through Formula Ford and production cars, and built up a team, Brad Jones Racing, to the point that they won five AUSCAR titles and a NASCAR championship in superspeedway racing, and secured factory backing from Audi in the 1990s to twice win the national Super Touring title. They have been in Supercars for more than 20 years.

BJR now runs four cars in the Supercars Championship, plus more cars in the feeder Super2 and Super3 Series on occasion. Kim recently retired, and his brother has now well and truly put the B back into BJR. He employs over 50 people and has made a living out of racing cars his entire life. He comes from a humble background, works too hard and survives where even cockroaches perish.

Bradley is a loveable rogue in the old sense, and the sort of guy that I imagine motor racers from the late 1950s, 1960s and early 1970s were. He's great fun to be around and has a heart of gold. He's a hustler, too – and in racing that's a positive rather than a fault. He's dedicated to the industry and to his own business. It's his life – he's the motor racing stayer you cannot kill. Dismiss him at your peril. Plenty of people have tried to.

We've had plenty of squabbles along the way over different things. In our later, grey-haired life we often sit opposite one another at Supercars Commission meetings, me in my role as Chairman (I've also previously been an independent member), and him as a team owner. We've had white-hot war with one another on topics we have differing views about, but then we tidy up later and our friendship endures. Former chairman Steve Horne has told the other members in a meeting, 'Just let 'em go until they wear each other out, and then we'll get on with the agenda ...'

Brad is an important part of the business, given he sits on the Supercars Board and the Supercars Commission. His team runs four of the 24 cars in the current field, and he's 25 hours a day, eight days a week in his approach. He straddles the big corporate teams and the smaller operators. He understands both ends of pit lane.

He takes the business and his business very seriously, but doesn't take himself too seriously all the time. If you stop and look at what we do in motorsport, you'll soon discover a need to find the levity in it all. This is a key point I didn't understand in my younger days, and still I miss it from time to time. Brad can always disarm a situation with a gag, and his humour and approach have rubbed off on me over time. Having a sense of fun like that protects you from the madness and ego-driven politics that permeates the motorsport industry.

I like to tease Brad, especially on air, but I have to put it on the record that as a driver he was very good. He put in some beautiful drives at Bathurst, a race and track which, like me, he absolutely lived for. He finished on the podium six times in the 1000, though he never quite cracked it for a win. Even so, he often saved his best for Bathurst, and he probably would have been able to generate more recognition in his career if he'd just been able to clinch one or two wins in that race along the way. Bathurst is the measure by which many determine whether you have truly made it or not.

Brad and I shared cars on plenty of occasions. One of them was the 1987 Winton 300 production car race, when I co-drove his Perrier-sponsored Mitsubishi Starion. I'll never forget the angry look on his face when he came screaming into the pits, completely unscheduled and against the pre-race plan, to hand over to me for my driving stint. I was standing with Peter Brock, my race suit undone and around my waist, as well as my sunglasses on, just shooting the breeze. Brocky laughed his head off at us, but Brad wanted to kill me for not being ready to take over the wheel from him.

*

When I made the decision to leave Brock's team and join Holden at the end of 1988, it opened the door for Brad to take my seat and drive their second Ford Sierra in 1989. We didn't admit it for many years, but there was a little bit more than met the eye to how the whole situation came about.

I had to advise Brock and team manager Alan Gow that I was leaving, and I brought Brad with me when I made the trip to Coburg, in Melbourne, where the team was based. I left him in the hire car, parked around the corner from the team's headquarters.

'I'm going to go in and deliver the bad news,' I told Brad. 'You wait here.'

I headed in and Brock and Gow greeted me. 'I've got something I need to tell you blokes,' I told them. 'I'm off.'

Brock was astounded. 'How can this be?' he spluttered. 'I'm astonished, I'm astounded,' he said, trying to find the biggest exclamation word he could find.

Having delivered the news, I skulked back to the hire car around the corner, wounded and uncertain.

'How did that go?' asked Brad.

'Not good,' I admitted. 'Brock didn't take it well at all,'

A few minutes passed as BJ and I chatted some more. Then I decided to put my dastardly plan into action and sent Brad in. The ploy was he 'just happened' to be in town, and thought he'd 'drop in' to the Mobil 1 Racing team and say 'hi'.

'Wish me luck!' he said, smiling his devilish grin. And off wandered Brad around the corner.

He bowled upstairs and burst in the door. 'Hey guys!' he exclaimed. 'What's going on? I was in town and thought I'd stop in to see how you were going.'

For Brock and Gow, the solution to their sudden problem was right in front of them – who would have thought it!

'Oh, Brad, you won't bloody believe it,' Brock replied. 'That idiot Crompton has just bloody quit, and we don't have a second driver for next year.'

This was when Jones was able to practise his acting skills, which were truly worthy of an Academy Award. 'Wow, what are you going to do?' he said, shocked.

Brock: 'Well ... how about you? What are you doing next year?'

Gow: 'Do you want to come and drive for us?'

The grubby plan worked perfectly, and Brad walked out as the newest member of the Mobil 1 Brock team. He returned to our hire car grinning like a moron.

*

Everything between Brad and I was a competition. We even created our own scoring system, and we'd allocate points based on anything and everything: how our careers were relative to one another, our individual race results, who had more personal sponsors ... anything and everything was fair game.

When Mark Larkham got pole at Bathurst in 1999, Brad (his co-driver for the weekend) tried to claim double points. Wanker! Worse still, I was with him, leaning on a tree at the top of Mount Panorama watching the Top 10 Shootout when the PA burst into life to announce that Larko had won pole position. Brad bounced up and down in glee and I moaned and groaned. When I stopped driving, we had to make up a new scoring system on a seasonally adjustable basis.

We went to England in late 1994 and, on our travels, visited the race car museum at the Donington circuit that featured a wide range of Formula 1 cars, including the Beatrice-Lola that Alan Jones had raced in the mid-1980s. There was a big sign near all the cars: 'Don't touch!' I turned my back for one second, and when I looked back, Brad wasn't touching one of the cars, he'd leapt the rope and was sitting in it!

'Get out!' I roared, a nervous breakdown about to take over my body.

He simply laughed his face off. 'What are they going to do, arrest us?' he said. Then he insisted I take a photo of him so he could give it to 'Jonesy', Alan Jones.

On the same trip we went to visit the Williams Formula 1 team and meet with Sir Frank Williams himself. I placed my briefcase on the ground briefly before we got into the car to go there. Brad picked it up and put it on my lap, unaware it had mud on the bottom of it that promptly smeared my neatly pressed, fawn business trousers! And that's how I had to look when I walked in the door at Williams Grand Prix Engineering.

While I was apoplectic, Brad just laughed. 'It's not like Frank is going to give you a drive, you idiot! Get over it!'

With Brad Jones and Alan Jones's Beatrice F1 car, Donington Motor Racing Museum, 1994. *Crompton collection*

I was surprised and humbled to be inducted into the Supercars Hall of Fame in 2017, and it was fitting that it was Brad who introduced me on stage.

It was a really special moment, a great honour for me. I wasn't totally comfortable about my qualifications, though – when I look at the group of people in that Hall of Fame, it's a very special list of peers. The honour made me immensely proud.

Brad and I have had some poignant moments, too. At one stage I was in the middle of a day of intense work, and wasn't able to answer his repeated phone calls. When I finally got back to him, I learned that he'd been calling me to tell me his dad Phil had passed away. I felt so incredibly bad that I'd let him down personally when he needed me most. It broke my heart, and I've never forgiven myself for it.

To show how deep our friendship runs, he drove from Albury to Ballarat unannounced to attend my dad's funeral in 2016. I had no idea he was coming. I was incredibly touched. He's been a rock-solid friend through good times and bad.

Through life, you don't have many really close friends. You might have plenty of colleagues, but if you write a list of the people you'd choose to share a dining table with and the number shrinks quickly. Brad is absolutely on my dinner table list – even if the only thing he will eat is steak and chips with tomato sauce, washed down with Fanta!

Reflections

Brad Jones – five-time AUSCAR Champion, two-time Australian Super Touring Champion, Brad Jones Racing Supercars Team owner

Neil is one of those people in my life who I connected with straight away. We were young guys trying to make it in the world of motorsport. Neither of us had any money to spend on racing, so both of us would fight, kick and scream to make it happen. I knew from when we were kids how good a motocross rider he was, and I knew that if he ever got the opportunity, he would do well in car racing. Having Neil as a best mate gave me somebody who absolutely understood the pains and could sympathise with my lows and celebrate the highs.

To come across someone as skilled as Neil was as a driver and as a broadcaster is extremely unusual. You can count on one hand the number of people in the world who have done both to the level he has achieved.

As a broadcaster, he knows what he's talking about and is a master with words. I've always felt he's one of the very best broadcasters in the world. I'm a little one-eyed maybe, but he's the Lewis Hamilton of his particular craft; what he does is at that sort of level of excellence. Until you've tried to work in television and broadcasting, you can't appreciate just how good he is at it. He can fill the role of expert commentator, play-by-play or host. He's done them all. Each of those jobs is so very difficult on its own and he has the skillset to do them all. I learned a lesson when I did some broadcasting work with him some years ago. He's so clever with words and quick-witted that you should never try to level up with him verbally. You've got no chance! When he hit the metaphoric ball at my head, I knew it was better to weave or just let it hit me. Trying to return serve was not an option! Racing together with Neil at Bathurst in the late 1980s and early 1990s is one of the highlights of my career. I've always felt close to him and sharing a car with him was like racing with my brother. We enjoy each other's company immensely and can talk at length about nearly any topic for hours and hours on end. Above everything we've done in motorsport, I'm most proud of the longevity of our friendship in an industry where you tend to have lots of acquaintances but very few real friends.

An emotional moment as my friend Brad Jones inducted me into the Supercars Hall of Fame in 2017. *Mark Horsburgh/EDGE Photographics*

16

THE WOLLONGONG WIZ

HIS TESTICLES WERE THE size of footballs.

It's a crass description, I know, but I can't think of a better way to express his approach to racing. Wayne Gardner, the 1987 500cc World Motorcycle Champion and two-time winner of the Australian Grand Prix at Phillip Island, would easily be the bravest racer I encountered. In all my time in and around the sport, I have never seen a guy with such an overwhelming commitment to taking himself right to the edge of a monumental shunt.

On occasion, this approach got him into lots of trouble, both privately and professionally. Gardner and those top-level motorcycle racing guys from the 1980s and '90s – Wayne Rainey, Kevin Schwantz, Mick Doohan, Eddie Lawson, Daryl Beattie – were all astonishing racers. The racers' racers, in my view.

Wayne was a fitter and turner from Wollongong who climbed out of his trade and became the best in the world at his craft. I was at Phillip Island in 1989 when Wayne won the first Australian 500cc Motorcycle Grand Prix. That race was arguably the most memorable in the history of Australian motorsport, across both two-wheel and four-wheel competition.

His win blew the roof off the joint, creating a hair-raising atmosphere. Thinking about it now, it was surreal to hear that level of passion at a motorcycle race. You could truly hear the crowd roar over the bikes.

The Island was a venue that had been closed for the best part of the previous decade. The famous track had been rebuilt and brought back to life especially for the arrival of the 500cc World Championship, and Gardner put on quite a show.

Those 500cc bikes were phenomenally fast, with noisy two-stroke engines, and were often nasty bits of kit to ride. Gardner rode a fairytale race, passing and re-passing the front pack to lead home Wayne Rainey's Yamaha by just three-tenths of a second. His Phillip Island win on that magical day (and his follow-up win in the same race a year later) cemented him in the hearts and minds of many fans as the guy who popularised international motorcycle racing for the masses in Australia in the late 1980s.

Although motorcycle racing is frequently ignored by the mainstream media in Australia, we have always punched massively above our weight on the world stage, whether in speedway, motocross or road racing. The achievements of riders like my good friend the late Gregg Hansford in the early days, and more recently Mick Doohan, who maintained an incredible grip on the World Championship for many years, have made Aussie motorcycle racers legendary around the globe.

Wayne's arrival on the scene in the 1980s was a case of perfect timing. For one thing, he caught the 'Wide World of Sports' wave on Channel Nine, which often placed him on our TV screens late at night. Calling the action were a couple of the greatest storytellers and characters in motorsport, the late Darrell Eastlake and the late, great Barry Sheene. It was a time when sport was becoming more valuable for big media organisations because live events could be broadcast into Australian homes via satellite.

Gardner wasn't the first Aussie to do well internationally in motorcycling, but he was the first from this part of the world to do well in the full gaze of the media, and therefore the public, and that made him something of a pioneer for the sport. In addition to being the 1987 World Champion, Gardner finished runner-up in the title chase in 1986 and 1988. He retired from bike racing at the end of 1992, and began racing V8 touring cars full-time in 1993, when he inked a deal to join my old team, the Holden Racing Team, as teammate to Tomas Mezera.

At that stage I was driving a Commodore sponsored by GIO insurance and run by Sydney businessman Bob Forbes's small but dedicated team in the suburb of Mona Vale. It was a happy, harmonious team, and we'd managed to add my friend Wally Storey, a highly respected engineer, to the squad earlier that season after he felt it was time for him to move on from HRT. We were very competitive on occasion, and spent the early part of the season with an older, heavier car with a Holden V8 engine rather than the newly permitted Chevrolet-

Top: Aboard the Coke Commodore at Sandown, 1994.
AN1 Images/Graeme Neander

Above: With my long-time engineer and dear friend Wally Storey at Sandown, 1994. *AN1 Images/Graeme Neander*

based powerplant. Ironically, that car was the same chassis in which Wayne had made his Bathurst 1000 debut a year prior, alongside Sydney privateer Graham Moore.

Late in 1993 our team built a brand-new car and I jumped out to the lead at that year's Sandown 500. It was a beautifully built car. I remember that some of the guys on the crew teared up when I hit the front, such was the emotional overload of putting in so much effort to the new car.

*

I'd always enjoyed a solid relationship with Gardner and his manager/media consultant Nick Hartgerink, and in my early Channel Seven days had frequently reported on his racing in the 1980s and early '90s. They gave me great access during that time, and Wayne and I got along well. So you can imagine my displeasure when he rubbed me the wrong way big-time in the first round of the Australian Touring Car Championship at Amaroo Park in late February 1993.

That track had a very slow, tight corner known, appropriately enough, as the Stop-Go Corner. It was a right-hander, and Wayne came charging like a bull trying to get down the inside of me. But his dive was ill judged and he tagged my car, pushing me off the road and into the wall.

Because we'd been friendly in recent years, when we got out of the cars in *parc fermé*, he laughed it off.

I certainly wasn't amused. 'It's anything but funny, mate,' I remember saying to him post-race. 'Wait and watch, pal. There'll be a moment in time when you leave your arse exposed, and I promise you I'll be there.'

That moment came only a few months later, in mid-July, in Round 8 of the championship at Barbagallo Raceway, in Perth. And I didn't miss.

That day was miserable weather-wise, with pouring rain making conditions difficult for racing. Noted 'rain king' Jim Richards had disappeared down the road in the lead, with Tony Longhurst's BMW in pursuit. Gardner and I were racing hard for third place, with his black and white HRT Commodore just in front of my GIO car. What happened next was 100 per cent payback, exactly as I had angrily predicted in February.

The final corner on that track is a 90-degree right-hander that brings you back onto the pit straight. Wayne bombed past me down the inside on the way into the corner, and I responded with a crisscross move. I got my nose back down the inside of the right rear of Wayne's car just past the apex, and turned him into the receiver. I was most certainly the server.

Rough justice, yes, but he had the chance at Amaroo to make his mind up whether or not it was a good idea to pull a low blow move on me, and he hadn't hesitated. Now I did exactly the same to him. I had the choice to lift off the throttle or even tap the brake to make sure I didn't push him off the track. I didn't, and he swiftly disappeared onto the grass on the infield.

Wayne came up after the race and gave me a mouthful of abuse. The language was white-hot, and I suggested to Wayne and his team manager, Neal Lowe, in no uncertain terms precisely where they could shove their point of view.

I finished third in the race and scored second for the round overall, to take my first Australian Touring Car Championship podium finish. As well, I copped a $1000 fine from Peter Wollerman, the CAMS umpire, for the collision. As I saw things, it was a great investment – I would happily have paid more!

Gardner had not got along well with HRT boss John Crennan during the 1993 season, and did a surprise deal with Coca-Cola Chairman and CEO Dean Wills one day at a function in Melbourne, to sponsor his own team for the following year. In an odd twist, given the recent history between us, Wayne bought Bob Forbes Racing and turned it into Wayne Gardner Racing for 1994. Even more bizarre was that he offered me a gig to drive for him!

When Gardner talked to me about me driving for his new team, it was impossible to ignore the dust-up we'd had the previous year. I readily admitted that I'd deliberately dispatched him off the road at Barbagallo. His reaction wasn't what I expected. He said he respected me for standing my ground – as he saw it, it was the sign of a no-nonsense racer and something of a badge of honour. We even had a laugh about it!

I was disappointed that Bob's team had vanished, but he felt selling it to Wayne was the right thing to do, and would take the show to the next level. Bob and his wife, Joyce, were fabulous to work for, and our relationship was excellent. We remain close to this day.

My time with Wayne and the Coca-Cola–backed WGR brought some solid results over the new few years. We finished third on the podium at Bathurst in 1995 driving together, and would ultimately spend four years as teammates, between 1994 and 1997. Along the way, we had plenty of fun, piles of competitive top five and ten results, and achieved great value for our team partners.

THE WOLLONGONG WIZ

I'm proud that we successfully represented a big-time global non-automotive brand in Coca-Cola with a heap of groundbreaking marketing activations. It was a critical growth period in the motorsport business.

*

There's no doubt Wayne underestimated things when he came back to Australia to compete in V8 touring car racing. I think he felt winning in touring cars would be easier than the racing he'd done in the GP circus. But nothing could have been further from the truth. Racing in Australia in touring cars (now Supercars) is tough. The quality and intensity is at a seriously high level.

The magic he could command when riding his Honda 500cc Grand Prix bike at Phillip Island didn't necessarily translate to a touring car. You couldn't just take that skill set and transfer it straight over to car racing and have the masses roaring in approval for you at Bathurst as you stroll off in front of the field.

He started to get irritated with the whole car racing scene, and he didn't suffer fools, which only made it worse. For him, the rhythm of Australian touring car racing was too slow and lacked the risk/reward incentive when compared to GP bike racing. In the touring cars of that era, bravery didn't gain you much time. If you drove those cars with too much bravado, they would slide and you'd be slow – whereas on the bike, the harder and braver you rode, the more lap time you could find.

Wayne's first year in touring cars in Australia with HRT saw him get in a few on-track scraps, and he soon was dubbed

'Captain Chaos' in the press – a nickname that, naturally, didn't go down well with him. Eventually the funds got tight in early 1996 and the team slimmed back to one car for Wayne, though I still co-drove with him in the annual Sandown and Bathurst races in 1996 and '97.

WG had a short temper and no filter, and he was actually proud of that. Often in an industry like motorsport, you'll come across someone – in the media, perhaps, or a sponsor or administrator – who you just don't click with, but you have to grit your teeth and get along with them and make the best of it.

Not Wayne, though. He'd take to them with a metaphorical tomahawk. If he thought you were a dickhead, he'd tell you that you were a dickhead, no matter whether you were the head of a million-dollar corporation sponsoring the team or anyone else down pit lane.

He gave me plenty of insight into how and why he was programmed like this in the early stages of 1995, when the pair of us were subjected to a Cairns-to-Sydney promotional tour and had plenty of hours to fill in between the visits to every Coke outlet, every Hog's Breath Cafe and every bloody Caltex service station along the way. It was the promo trip from hell. While the rest of the industry were enjoying a well-earned break from the 24/7 nature of racing, we were spending our summer break on the road plastering on fake smiles.

The trip involved the Coke race team transporter, a fully painted Holden Commodore promo car, Wayne's Harley-Davidson motorcycle, and too many posters that all needed signing. We took turns rolling down the east coast at the helm of the promo car. Each day was a seesaw of emotion.

One of us would be the good cop, the other the bad cop. On any given day, one of us was a grumpy bastard wishing he was anywhere but on tour, while the other tried to cover up this awkward behaviour.

Along the way, I learned a lot about WG's time in Europe, his ride to the top and his approach to racing. 'When you're lucky enough to do something on a world stage, then you don't have to beg, scrape, creep or crawl commercially,' he told me.

I could understand that. Wayne was a global name. As a global player, Wayne was further up the hierarchy than most and his rationale was he didn't have to grovel. I've seen exactly the same nature prevalent in some very big-name F1 drivers and other international motor racing personalities. I don't agree with the approach, but I understand it.

*

As punishing as that road trip was, there was a big upside to that trip: at a stopover in Port Macquarie, I met a lovely girl named Sarah Mathewson. We became friends, and reconnected years later. Sarah loves telling the story of how we met, because naturally there's a motor racing theme involved. I was trying to find a newsagent in Port Macquarie so I could buy a copy of *Auto Action* magazine.

'He had me at *Auto Action*,' she laughs to this very day.

Sarah and her sister Lisa were sport fishing at 'The Golden Lure' – although I have to say, she remembers this detail, not me! They were standing in the car park where the fish were being weighed when I, a total stranger, lobbed in front of them asking for directions to the local newsagent's. Not only did they tell me where it was, they walked me there to ensure I made it to my destination safely! Sarah remembers that I bought her whole family, including her mum, Joan, ice creams as a thank you. As we were visitors to her fair town, Gardner and I were invited out for dinner with Sarah and her friends at an Italian restaurant later that night.

The night finished late, with a lot of laughs and way too many drinks – so much so that Sarah's enduring memory is of pushing Wayne, with sunglasses on, down the street in the wee hours of the next morning in a shopping trolley!

Sarah and I parted that night as friends and reconnected many years later – so much so that she became my second wife. In 2008 we got married, and we had our daughter, Sienna, soon after.

The trip was beyond punishing, but thanks to the late Peter Trives and Ross Halpin from the sponsorship and marketing team at Coca-Cola Amatil, it turned out that the horror road trip delivered me the most wonderful gift: my beautiful wife and best friend for life! I lost a summer to that trip but ended up gaining a wife!

Reflections

Wayne Gardner – 1987 500cc World Motorcycle Champion

My choice to buy Bob Forbes's little touring car operation in 1993 was a great idea because a key component to the whole thing was having Neil come along with it – not only with a pretty good driving resume with lots of experience, but with a lot of off-track ability to contribute to the marketing and sponsorship side of things. The sort of skills other drivers simply don't possess. He'd be out there looking for extra sponsorship, putting together presentation documents and videos, designing liveries – he was a genius with all of that behind-the-scenes work.

I was so lucky to be able to engage him and make him part of the team. He guided me on the whole process of setting up Wayne Gardner Racing. If we had some disappointments along the way, like all teams, he would be straight back to work Monday morning and banging on doors finding sponsorship and support. His work ethic is the best I have ever seen of anyone. If I was going to employ someone to manage a team and pull it all together, Neil would be the man for sure!

Neil was always a safe pair of hands to share a car with at Bathurst over the years. You knew he would bring it home in one piece. He was a fast driver without being crazy bashing into things. I was a bit more aggressive, and he used to just shake his head at me at times.

I think his contribution to the sport out of the car has been far greater than any driver. He's a genius with the TV work and is a natural talent, always thinking ahead and researching every detail. He's brilliant and professional with lots of experience.

Supercars is all the better for Neil's efforts and contribution. He's brought so much credibility to the sport because of his professionalism. The sport owes him a lot; the Supercars category and company should be celebrating him and his career immensely, he's contributed so much.

Neil's core strength on top of all of his professional skills is that he's an all-round good guy. He backs you up, never lets you down and is reliable as they come.

Cromley's been a great friend to me. He's never done anything wrong by me (well, apart from that day he punted me off the track in Perth!), there's never been a call he didn't answer. Not only was he loyal as a driver and an employee, but he's been a loyal friend, an amazing guy. I value my friendship with him over so many years.

We clowned around together a lot back in the day. We used to call him 'Mr Squeaky' – he was always doing everything so perfectly! A lot of people think Neil is 'Mr Serious' all the time, but geez we used to make one another laugh a lot and get into trouble.

He's a very special guy to me and I'd say was probably my best friend and the most instrumental person in my career during my 'four wheel' car racing period in Australia.

17

LARRIKIN LARRY

'THAT'S NOT WHAT MOTOR racing is all about,' Larry Perkins barked down the phone line a few weeks after Bathurst.

'LP' has a very pure view of what motorsport is. He absolutely hated that in-car banter I'd engaged in at Bathurst in 1988 in the Mobil BMW with Brock on the Channel Seven broadcast. And he was 100 per cent right, in the pure sense of what constituted proper motor racing. What we had done was sideshow alley stuff. That's the way in which Supercars and motor racing globally has tended to skew in recent times, with more emphasis on and tolerance for the entertainment aspect of the sport. But it was the exact opposite of what LP thought was appropriate.

As much as we disagreed on the phone, I respected the fact that LP saw racing in such pure terms. He is the living embodiment of doing things his own way.

Larry worked his way into Formula 1 in the 1970s through sheer skill and speed, his lack of a chequebook the only thing stopping him from him reaching the peak of Grand Prix racing. A gifted and clever engineer whose prowess was matched by his self-taught political skills, Larry came back to Australia after his time in F1, won Bathurst three times with Peter Brock and the Holden Dealer Team, and then set up his own team, scoring three more wins in his Castrol-backed Commodores in the Great Race in 1993, 1995 and 1997.

Despite our little disagreement that day, Larry and I have had a good relationship for many years. For one thing, we share an interest in common sense and a love of planes and flying.

I've had plenty of connection with Larry over the years. His Perkins Engineering business was the engine supplier for my Formula Holden open-wheeler at one stage, and I spent a lot of time with Larry and John Stevenson, who was the Motorsport Manager at Holden for many years, at Larry's shop in Roberna Street, Moorabbin, in Melbourne.

Later, I raced a Perkins-built Commodore when I rejoined Brock in the Mobil team in 1992. Larry had built and run a pair of cars for himself and Peter to drive in 1991, but that business association dissolved and the cars were sold off to Advantage International; there they would run under the Mobil 1 Racing banner. I drove the second car, and LP went back to driving his own Commodore.

LP wasn't a card-carrying member of the Brock fan club by that stage, so he pretty much did everything he could to help me. We swapped car setup notes and he provided lots of input – he wanted nothing more than to see me needle or even beat Brock!

*

In 1993, Larry and I had a classic run-in at Winton. We had some ripping races against one another that year. I was driving the Bob Forbes Racing GIO Commodore, and he was behind the wheel of his Castrol Commodore. Both of us were on Dunlop tyres. I got on top of him at Symmons Plains, in Tasmania, and as soon as we got out of the cars after the race, he crawled under my car to check out the suspension geometry. He wanted to understand how I'd beaten him, so he slid straight under the rear end to check it out!

Racing wheel-to-wheel with Larry was a big deal for me, because I was acutely aware of everything he'd achieved overseas in racing. However, on this particular day at Winton, things got out of control.

We were battling like crazy. I was a bit tardy, with too much mid-corner understeer through the slow corners, and he just kept banging into my back bumper bar. He was losing his patience with me because he felt I was holding him up, while I was rapidly losing mine as he tapped out Morse code on the rear of my car.

This went on for lap after lap, and finally he hooked into me and half-spun me out of the right-hand corner coming onto the old back straight.

That severely pressed my 'hot' button, and after exiting the corner I started moving across on him, with some overlap between us as we continued to accelerate down the road. Ultimately, we both ran out of bitumen as we kept moving further and further to the right, with both of us driving off into the grass on the infield at full speed, locking horns like kids driving dodgem cars at the showgrounds.

Naturally, there was abuse thrown backwards and forwards between us in the aftermath of the race. After getting stuck into one another breathlessly for a few minutes, the naughty schoolboys in us took over.

'This is bullshit,' he said. 'We won't be doing that again, will we?'

I agreed. 'Correct, Larry: you don't run into me, I won't run into you.'

Then we got summoned to see the Stewards in the race control building. We both pleaded insanity and refused to dob the other in. Eventually, they lost their patience with our convenient love-in. 'No penalties, get out!' they said, and threw us out.

Fast-forward from 1993 to recent years, and I was in full flight in the commentary box at Bathurst. As I watched yet another on-track stoush between two drivers, suddenly my mobile phone lit up with a text from Larry. All it said was: 'Remember Winton?'

I couldn't help but smile. Racing drivers have minds like elephants. We never forget a good dust-up.

I have so many fond memories of times I've shared with Larry. The early days at HDT, visiting their workshop in Chetwynd Street, North Melbourne, when he would welcome me in so I could ask dumb technical questions ... the great races we had together in those Commodore/Dunlop years in the mid-1990s ... our war story discussions about his time in Europe, making F1, driving for Bernie Ecclestone and racing at Le Mans ... and many more.

Larry's been an outstanding contributor to Australian motorsport, and I especially love and respect all that he's done to help our mutual friend Allan Moffat in recent years during Allan's health battles. Larry is one of a kind.

18

THE TOILET ON WHEELS

IT'S LIKE DRIVING A 700-horsepower toilet. That's the only way I can describe the feeling of driving a dirt track Sprintcar.

As a racing device, a Sprintcar feels more like you're sitting on it than in it, with your legs dangling and your feet in stirrups. They're totally weird things. These V8-powered methanol munchers don't do anything in a natural way. They don't turn right (because they only need to turn left) and they're made to be driven on the edge, flat-out, sliding the whole time.

Speedway holds a special place in Aussie motorsport history, and there are dirt tracks littered around the country that are busy places every summer. Some of our top Sprintcar drivers have managed to make great careers in the United States on the World of Outlaws trail and the numerous other Sprintcar series that exist there.

The first time I was let loose in one of these mad mud-flinging devices was in 1993, at Parramatta City Raceway. Mike Raymond had been begging me for years to have a run in one, and it was very much a last-minute deal. It was actually forbidden in those days for those with a CAMS circuit racing licence to compete in dirt track speedway racing. So I entered under a pseudonym – Stan D. Wellback (think about it …) – and got stuck in and raced against the speedway regulars.

I had star-studded support. Eddie Irvine was with me that night, a Northern Irishman I'd got to know over the years through mutual friends Malcolm Oastler, Trevor Sheumack and Frank Adamson. Eddie had only recently made his Formula 1 debut with the Jordan F1 team in Japan, and promptly got in a post-race punch-up with Ayrton Senna.

I suggested he also should step in and have a drive. 'No fooking way – you're fooking mad!' he quickly replied in his distinctive Irish accent.

I couldn't doubt his sentiment. Driving that Sprintcar was one of the craziest, best experiences I've ever had in a racing machine.

A night at the speedway starts with what they call 'wheel packing', where all the race cars go out onto the track and drive around slowly to compress the dirt. There are no practice sessions like we have in circuit racing, which help you to get your eye in.

Once it came time to race, it was full-on. When I cracked the throttle open to start the first heat race, the grunt seriously frightened the daylights out of me. After progressing through the heat races, I got through to the A-Main final. I recall my old friend Stephen Gall, of Mr Motocross fame, lapping me as he led away.

It was so cool. I loved the smell of the methanol fuel, the machine's raw and brutal nature, and getting sideways at 160 kilometres per hour. I had a ball, but I completely destroyed a perfectly good helmet and soiled a GIO race suit so badly that we couldn't get the mud stains out! There's a photo floating around of me covered in mud, grinning like an idiot.

The Sprintcar was the most unexpected thrill I've ever had in a race car, and I went back years later and had another crack at Parramatta for a TV story for Channel Ten's motorsport show *RPM*.

I thought long and hard at one stage about putting together a proper budget and racing Sprintcars over the summer. It would be a fantastic way to keep race fit over the break, I told myself. Today, young Supercars star Cam Waters is doing exactly that in the modern era. However, once I did the sums and understood how much extra work it was going to add to my already busy life, I gave myself a mental uppercut and went back to Manly Dam for some more summer water skiing.

Pound for pound, though, Sprintcars are without doubt the most explosive, hair-raising racing machines I've ever driven.

19

A DATE WITH THE DAME

'NEIL AND I HAVE become inseparable,' said Dame Edna Everage in the Australian Grand Prix media conference room after our dalliance. 'It's not a romance yet, but it could be.'

For a brief moment I was the 'toyboy' for Australia's most famous housewife.

Motorsport fans might remember the 1993 Australian Grand Prix in Adelaide for Ayrton Senna scoring his last win for McLaren in Formula 1, and Alain Prost making his last Grand Prix start before retiring as World Champion. However, my memory drifts to my white-knuckled experience that weekend as a passenger alongside Barry Humphries's famous friend Dame Edna Everage in the Celebrity Challenge support race.

That year's race was exclusively for female drivers, with some big names from sport, entertainment, the arts and politics making up the field. Holden provided a fleet of its new German-sourced Calibra models for the celebrities to race around the Adelaide street circuit, and they engaged me to manage the driver training program. I hired a bunch of professional drivers – my good mates Brad Jones, Peter McKay and Tomas Mezera – to help run things in the lead-up.

Dame Edna was a huge drawcard, and Holden's PR manager, Tim Pemberton, made an inspired suggestion that there should also be a 'token bloke' in the field for fun. That ended up being none other than the wonderfully intelligent, articulate and funny Clive James. As a sidebar, Clive just wanted to hang out with us after hours every single night because he had a misplaced notion that we all led the life of playboys. We massively disappointed him in that regard, but still we had a wonderful week together.

The Dame's #1 Calibra looked the part. A huge version of her trademark glasses sat on the roof, and she stood out in a pink race suit with her name on a pink background on the top of the windscreen. Holden's familiar lion logo down the side of the car was pink instead of its trademark red.

At this point, I should probably also clarify something. When Barry is in character as Dame Edna, you must refer to her as Dame Edna. When Barry is Barry, you can say, 'G'day, Barry.'

Humphries was staying at the Hyatt Hotel in the city, and the event organisers wanted me to spend a few days with him to 'teach him how to drive and get him ready for the race'.

'Teach him how to race drive or just drive?' I asked.

I quickly found out that Barry was chauffeured everywhere in limousines and never drove anywhere himself.

I headed off to pick him up from his hotel, and he greeted me with a plan I wasn't expecting. 'Let's not bother about all of this car nonsense, shall we – why don't we go and have a nice picnic,' he declared with a theatrical wave of the hand, his long fringe falling across his forehead.

So instead of taking Barry out to the Adelaide International Raceway to teach him about the nuances of oversteer and understeer, the next thing I know we're driving a Calibra along through the streets of Adelaide to find somewhere nice where we could sit under a tree and have a picnic.

For two days we picnicked under the trees near the Adelaide Zoo! No driver training, just picnics and theatrical stories!

This created one small problem. When Barry – sorry, Dame Edna – got in the driver's seat at the racetrack, it was a tangled mess of missed gears and wrong directions.

Ahead of the race, the CAMS officials reminded me it was my responsibility to sign off on Dame Edna receiving a racing licence. I had to confirm that she possessed the requisite skill to safely participate in a race. Well, I couldn't put my hand on my heart and honestly say Dame Edna was capable of driving in the race. She literally could not drive a car!

The corporate pressure of the situation came into play. Holden had invested a lot of money and effort into the event, and Dame Edna was the biggest drawcard. They had spent hundreds of thousands of dollars on the cars and promotion, so as they saw it, she had to be in the race.

I ended up in meetings with representatives from Holden, the South Australian government and CAMS, and they were all glaring at me to give them the answer I wanted to hear. Ultimately, it was decided the only way Dame Edna Everage could race in the 1993 Celebrity Challenge in Adelaide was if I sat in the passenger seat.

'Argh, this is not good,' I grumbled, stuck in a situation I couldn't extract myself from. I wanted to be racing the GIO Commodore touring car, but our budget didn't stretch to that event, so I could either be Dame Edna's passenger or go and lick an ice cream in the grandstand.

Race day arrived, and Dame Edna and I sat stone cold last on the grid, 25th in a field of 25 cars. For the sake of safety, I'd had another rear-view mirror fitted within the car so I could see more of what was happening out of the back window. There was a high probability, I knew, that it could all end poorly. My mind wandered as we sat on the grid. I had visions of us crashing in the middle of the racetrack, with diamantes flying around everywhere, jewellery, makeup and all sorts of crap flying out of the car – and I'd be responsible for all of it!

The race began, and we had barely got rolling before Dame Edna loosened off the race harness, reached around the back of the seat and pulled out a bunch of her signature gladioli! She started heaving flowers out the window to the nearby marshals, all while we were driving along! 'Hellooooooo, possums!' she shrieked out the window.

Dame Edna's next stunt was even more worrying. She incorrectly spotted the run-off road beyond turn four at Wakefield Street, and instead of turning right to follow the track, she tried to keep going straight ahead! I reached across from the passenger's seat and took the wheel to keep us on the track.

We'd been driving so slowly in the early laps that the race leaders – netballer Michelle Fielke and aerial ski jumper Kirstie Marshall – were already about to lap us. Potentially, one bad move could see me embarrassing a national entertainment treasure, one of Australia's leading vehicle manufacturers and myself in one fell swoop.

I needed to give the Dame a gentle hurry-up. The midweek picnics had not prepared us well.

'Ah, Dame Edna, you're gunna have to pick up the pace,' I said gently, when really screaming would have been more appropriate. There was no response.

Out of the corner of my eye, as we drove back onto the pit straight, I happened to glimpse the great Ayrton Senna and McLaren team boss Ron Dennis in deep conversation near the start/finish line, which was opposite their pit garage.

Dame Edna, probably unaware of their lofty position in motorsport, at that very moment accelerated and attempted to change gear. Instead of going from second gear into third, however, she missed the shift, and slotted the lever back into first gear and put her foot flat on the accelerator pedal. The Calibra shrieked in protest, revving off the clock. It howled and over-revved horribly in front of everybody. I could almost hear the engine valve springs unwind!

And then, with her open-face helmet covered in diamantes and thick make-up, Dame Edna turned to me in desperation, looking straight at me. In a split second she had morphed into Sir Les Patterson. 'HELP ME, HELP ME, HELP ME!' he boomed!

I reached across, whipped the lever out of the first gear position and told him to push the clutch down again so I could get the car back into third gear. Senna and Dennis briefly swung their heads around, searching for the source of the unwinding engine sound. I lowered my helmet visor and prayed for the chequered flag ...

Reflections

Sarah Crompton – life co-driver

A heart-shaped blackboard hangs in our kitchen and it reads: 'Every single day I find a new reason to fall in love with you, Neil, my darling.'

I scribbled this over five years ago thinking I would update that little board every week with a new witty quote to inspire our family, but I haven't touched it since. Unchanged not through laziness, simply because the message is still current and rings true. Our relationship is consistently fair, transparent, respectful and romantic. Neil is the same man in business as he is in his personal life as a father and husband, a man of great integrity. (Well, maybe not so much romance in his business life ...)

I learned early on that whoever Neil worked for, with or was happily committed to as a brand ambassador meant I was pretty much married to them also. It feels that way because he is so considerate of everyone he partners with that they become part of our family.

One special memory I have of my law-abiding citizen of a husband, which makes me just love him even more, is a tale I love to share. We had spent Christmas in Port Macquarie with my family and Neil suggested we check out the Boxing Day bargains at Harvey Norman, as he is always insisting on upgrading my parents' devices or just participating in some festive consumerism.

We were driving past Miedecke Motors car dealership and he would have been recounting a story about Andrew Miedecke's racing career, or maybe telling me about Andrew's new plane. Suddenly, Neil had a look of panic on his face as he slowed down. In an uncertain tone, shaking his head, Neil started: 'Oh no, I had one of your Mum's rum balls this morning.'

A little confused I said, 'Yeah, they're good, aren't they! Why, what's wrong with that?'

'Ah, I may have even had two and the police are up ahead doing RBT!'

I like to recall the Victorian ad from years ago but with a twist: 'If you eat rum balls then drive, you're a bloody idiot.' Of course, my responsible husband was under the limit and blew 0.00%. Surprise, surprise!

My husband surprises me with something almost every day. Good and bad, we tackle it all. What we have is precious.

With my co-driver for life, Sarah, and our daughter, Sienna. Taken in California in November 2018. *Crompton collection*

Top: Behind the wheel in my push and pedal car. My dad made the caravan! (Crompton collection)

Bottom: In one of my dad's many Goggomobils, in Ballarat, 1964. (Crompton collection)

Top: Me on my motocross bike. Although I was on two wheels, I always pictured myself racing cars. (CROMPTON COLLECTION)

Bottom: Meeting my hero Peter Brock at Calder Rallycross in 1972. I'm the kid standing next to Peter. (CROMPTON COLLECTION)

Top: My Ballarat shop, Navajo Action Sports & Cycles, was way ahead of the times. (Crompton collection)

Bottom: My first Bathurst 1000 telecast with Channel Seven, in 1985. Allan Moffat and Mike Raymond are second and third from right; I'm second from left. (Channel Seven Press)

Top: In an up-close pit studio interview mid-race with Peter Brock, Bathurst 1000, 1985. (CROMPTON COLLECTION)

Bottom: I missed out on driving in the Bathurst 1000 in 1987, but a week later I drove the Mobil Commodore at Calder as part of the World Touring Car Championship. (AN1 IMAGES/GRAEME NEANDER)

Top: In the Sandown pits in 1989. I'm in the car, Wally Storey's on my left and Peter Brock is leaning in from my right. (Crompton collection)

Bottom: Among the action in the pits, interviewing Klaus Ludwig at the Bathurst 1000, 1987. (Channel Seven Press)

Top: I had two legends as teammates in the Mobil BMWs in 1988 – Peter Brock and Jim Richards. (Crompton collection)

Bottom: Pit stop for my Commodore during practice for the 1991 Bathurst 1000. (AN1 Images/Graeme Neander)

Top: Racing my Formula Holden at Mallala in 1990. (AN1 Images/Graeme Neander)

Bottom: Sprintcars were like toilets on wheels but very fast! This is me hanging on to one at Parramatta in 1993. (Crompton collection)

Top: On the grid with my former HRT teammate Win Percy at the Bathurst 1000, 1992. (Crompton collection)

Bottom: With Wayne Gardner at the launch of his new Coke Commodore team in 1994. (Press Shot)

Top: I was third at Bathurst in 1992 in this Nissan GT-R. What a weapon of a race car. (AN1 Images/Graeme Neander)

Bottom: 'Hello possums!' Dame Edna at the wheel at the Australian Grand Prix in Adelaide in 1993. I was in the passenger seat. We survived. (AN1 Images/Graeme Neander)

HOLDEN
Mobil

CANADIAN
C·A·R·T
SUPER TOURING CHAMPIONSHIP
BMW
OYOTA

Top Left: Peter Brock was keen for me to be his co-driver for his first 'last' Bathurst 1000 in 1997. (Crompton collection)

Bottom Left: On the podium in Vancouver after a win in 1997. Peter Cunningham is on the left and BMW driver Randy Pobst on the right. (Crompton collection)

Above: This is the in-car 'RaceCam' camera that my Coke Commodore was to carry for the Bathurst 1000 telecast, 1995. (Press Shot)

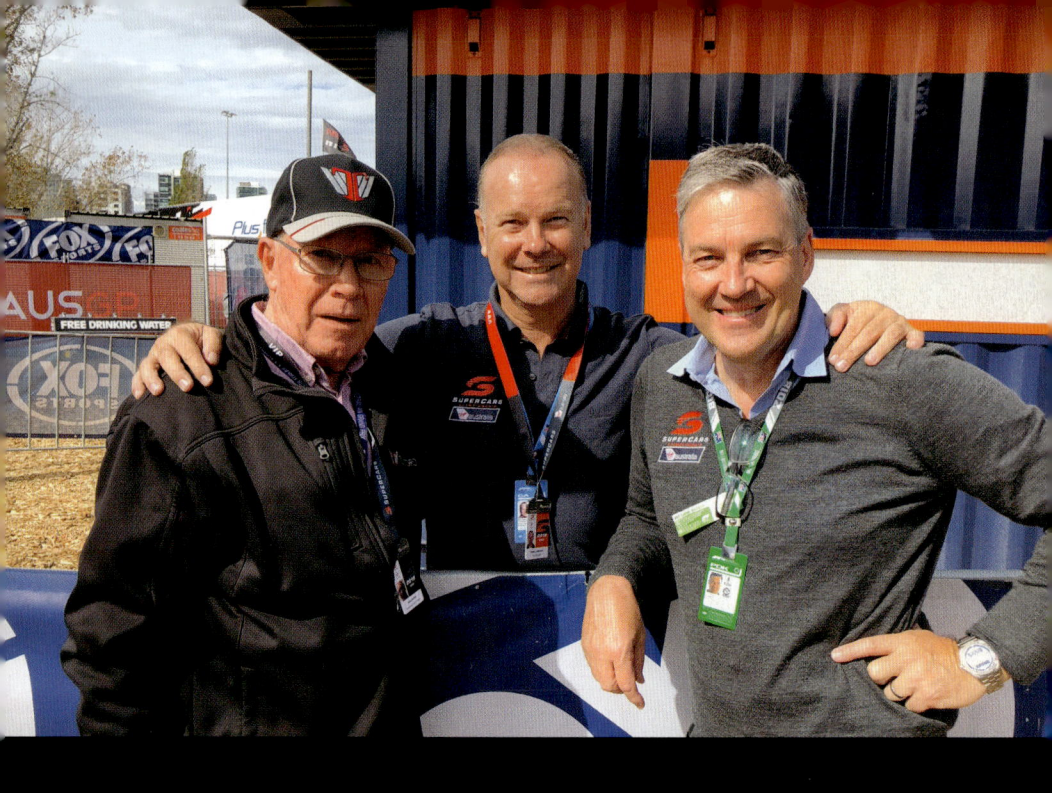

Top: With Allan Moffat and Mark Larkham at Albert Park, 2018. (Crompton collection)

Bottom: The 'Green Eyed Monster'. Craig Lowndes and me with our Gibson Motorsport Falcon, ahead of its debut at Bathurst in 2001. (AN1 Images/Graeme Neander)

Top: The V8 Supercars TV team in Sydney, 2014: (left to right) Greg Murphy, Mark Larkham, Mark Beretta, me, Riana Crehan, Mark Skaife and Aaron Noonan. (AN1 IMAGES)

Bottom: On the set of the *Shannons Legends of Motorsport* TV series with Dick Johnson and John Bowe at the Bowden family's amazing car collection in Queensland. (IAN WARD)

Top: With my wife, Sarah, and great friend Mark Skaife at my 60th birthday. Before the cocktails began! (CROMPTON COLLECTION)

Bottom: My daughters, Emma and Sienna, came to watch me drive one of my old 00 Motorsport Falcons in a demo at the Muscle Car Masters at Sydney Motorsport Park in 2013. (CROMPTON COLLECTION)

Top: I started water skiing when I was six – and I still love it. (CROMPTON COLLECTION)

Bottom: Hélio Castroneves and I were in the Tasman team in the USA back in 1997. In 2021 he became a four-time Indianapolis 500 winner, just the fourth driver in history to do it. He's an amazing guy. (CROMPTON COLLECTION)

At the 2000 Queensland 500, one of my last events driving for Glenn Seton's team.
(AN1 Images/Andrew Hall)

20

THE AMAZING ALLAN MOFFAT

'I LOVE YOU, MAN, I love you,' he said.

Those quietly spoken words moved me to tears. The man I once disliked as a kid was holding me tightly, like a long-lost brother, whispering in my ear.

Once a great gladiator of Australian motorsport, these days dementia has gripped Allan George Moffat, and he often doesn't recognise even those closest to him. On that day, 16 December 2020, at the funeral of his former teammate and fellow racing legend John Harvey, I could see the spark in his eye. He knew exactly who I was.

Moffat spotted me through the crowd of 200-odd people and smiled and waved, so I headed over to greet him. That was when he grabbed me in a fatherly embrace that went for a few minutes. It was a deeply touching moment.

That day, I had spoken at John's funeral and talked about the brilliant performances John and Allan had turned on in 1987, in the inaugural World Touring Car Championship. They won the very first round at Monza, in Italy, in a V8 Commodore, and drove as a two-man crew (when all other cars had three drivers) through the rain and fog of the punishing Spa 24 Hours race in Belgium, finishing in a wonderful fourth place overall against some of the biggest and best funded factory teams the world could muster.

Allan's career is packed with achievements and victories like those. Clearly, his stand-out efforts are his four Bathurst wins – in 1970, 1971, 1973 and 1977 – at the wheel of a range of mighty V8 Falcons, and four Australian Touring Car Championships.

For many years now we've been good friends, yet if you rewind to 1983 at Wanneroo Raceway, near Perth, Allan Moffat simply terrified me. I was a pit lane reporter that weekend for a round of the Australian Touring Car Championship, working for ABC TV alongside Dennis Cometti, who later became an AFL commentary legend.

Moffat? Well, he was just a nightmare! He was often prickly in those days, and just so hard to deal with. He terrified me with his tough, cold, disengaged responses to even the gentlest of questions. I remember him ripping into me that weekend. I was forced to keep him waiting for an interview while there was a big delay from the team inside the outside broadcast van. Allan didn't want to be there, and he hated waiting. He made very sure I knew exactly how he felt.

Soon after, Moffat's Mazda team manager, Allan Horsley, rang me and said that Allan would like to see me. 'He's impressed that you seem to know a bit about his background,' he said.

Indeed I did understand Moffat's background – and what an amazing background it was. I'd studied and marvelled at his local success and his overseas racing trips, from winning the Sebring 12 Hour in a BMW to racing at Daytona and at Le Mans in a Porsche with the American star Bobby Rahal.

In later years Allan loved to say that when I turned up to meet him at his office/workshop in Malvern Road, in Melbourne, I was sporting a short-back-and-sides haircut and wearing school shorts. That wasn't quite accurate, but he loved to tell that story.

His office was tucked away in the back of a workshop that was actually a BP service station out the front. In the office were some lovely old leather-bound chairs, and they would remain my seating of choice on my many subsequent visits.

That first proper meeting with Allan completely transformed our relationship. I realised that the best way to deal with him was to treat him like a businessman. And without question racing was his business. I learned to be business-like and make appointments with him and address him in a professional manner. If you walked into his tent at the track and approached him when he was deep in conversation or debriefing with his team, he'd eat you alive. So I treated him with the respect he deserved, and we've been great mates ever since.

Allan was way ahead of his time. He signed up some of the world's greatest overseas drivers to share his cars with him. Belgian Le Mans legend Jacky Ickx shared victory with Allan at Bathurst in a famous one-two finish at Bathurst in 1977, and he had the likes of Yoshimi Katayama from Japan, Dieter Glemser from Germany and Brit John Fitzpatrick also drive with him at Mount Panorama.

Allan's workshop had a specialised piece of equipment called a 'flat patch'. You could place a race car on it and adjust the corner weights perfectly. No one else in Australia had one of these back then – it was just another example of Moffat's 'big picture' international thinking.

His commercial credentials were even more impressive. Allan's race team sponsors over the years were quite amazing: BP, the Ford Motor Company, Federation Insurance, Brut 33, the ANZ Bank, Pan Am Airlines, Cenovis Vitamins, Camel cigarettes and Coca-Cola. I mean, who could get a bank to give you sponsorship money to go car racing? And then re-up the deal a year later so the team could buy a second car? Allan Moffat did.

He was a self-made man, an expat Canadian who ground out a career through sheer hard work. Allan's a bloke who crafted himself into becoming a professional racing driver. He saw it, fell in love with it and perfected the craft. He understood where and how to find the right equipment and create the right relationships.

The story of his famous Coca-Cola Trans Am Mustang is phenomenal. This American V8 muscle car was gifted to Allan in a special deal, and he brought it to Australia and never looked back, winning more than 100 races in it over a period covering the late 1960s and early 1970s. It made his career.

For Allan to have created such warm relationships with Ford and Kar Kraft in the United States that he was given a brand-new race car free of charge is stunning – the stuff of legends.

In Allan's day, there was no social media and communications specialists were very rare. Today's sophisticated, departmental race teams staffed by 60 or 70 talented specialists were a distant dream. Allan was the butcher, the baker and the candlestick maker of his racing operation. He did it all.

Allan and Peter Brock were the two biggest characters of Australian motorsport through the 1970s and '80s. They were household names. Through that period, Allan was at the peak of his powers, and he relished playing the 'black hat' villain of racing, whereas Peter wore the 'white hat'. Peter had natural Aussie charm, and the backing of Australia's car company – which, let's face it, wasn't really Australian, given it was owned by General Motors from America! He also had the backing of the massive Marlboro brand. Peter was a pin-up boy, whereas Allan was on the opposite side.

Beneath the surface, though, Allan Moffat was no black hat. He was an incredibly intelligent, passionate, outward-thinking, progressive guy.

*

At Bathurst in 1985, I prepared to take part in the Channel Seven broadcast for the first time. Mike Raymond had also brought in Allan as part of the team for the weekend, as he didn't have a drive in that year's race.

Working with Allan Moffat was a big deal for me. Only two years after being terrified of being anywhere near him in my ABC days, now I was standing next to him in a red jacket talking motorsport on TV. I went from being a young fan on one side of the fence to becoming a colleague, and then a warm friend. That's pretty special.

I remember standing on the pit wall that weekend, laughing my guts out. Mike had come up with an idea for the telecast: wouldn't it be great for Allan to drive all the different types of cars in that year's race, and then give his expert opinion in a series of stories screened during the telecast.

One of the cars he drove was the Volvo 240 Turbo of Kiwi Robbie Francevic. Moffat took off out of pit lane, did a lap – and didn't come back into the pits! He just kept going around and around and around. The test drive ended with Robbie storming out on pit straight, waving his fist at Allan to get him to come back into the pits and stop turning laps. Such was the enjoyment Allan took in doing laps around that special track.

*

When we made the *Shannons Legends of Motorsport* TV series in 2014, Allan was the perfect choice as the focus of the debut episode. We filmed it in the garage of the Bowden family's beautiful car collection – the custodians of his famous Coke Mustang – on the Sunshine Coast, and Allan was so good that we decided to film a second episode with him a short time later, at the National Motor Racing Museum in Bathurst.

I've got a lovely photo of him cuddling my wife at that filming day. My beautiful and somewhat crazy wife, Sarah, is very outgoing and personable, and Moffat and his old teammate Colin Bond loved goofing off with her.

I will never forget standing on the stage in the museum in front of the live audience, filming a link for one of the episodes we were shooting that day. We started recording and away I went. I delivered the lines, but halfway through I became aware of some strange sounds in the background. I could hear a very soft voice emanating from the office nearby, which we had set up as a storage and green room in which our special guests could rest and prepare. There were two other voices as well, and clapping ...

The tiny little girl voice was unmistakably my daughter Sienna, aka 'Sis', who was all of five years old at the time. The other two were Moffat and Bond. And the tune was familiar: 'I'm a little teapot, short and stout, here is my handle, here is my spout ...'

Sis had somehow convinced these two legends of Australian motorsport to join her in a rowdy rendition of a favourite nursery rhyme. And off they went, giving their all. Bondy led the lyrics and Moff was on backing vocals and clapping duty. Brilliant! The duo who own one of the most iconic moments in our sport – the magical 1977 Moffat Ford Dealers one-two form finish – singing a nursery rhyme just 300 metres from the famous pit straight where they greeted the chequered flag all those years ago.

It's a Mount Panorama memory I'll never forget. Priceless.

With my good friend Nathan Prendergast, the co-producer of our programs, I caught up with Allan again at the Hilton Hotel in Melbourne in 2015 to film some more interviews. These clips were to be used in the second series. Sadly, just a year after the fun at Bathurst, it was clear the early stages of dementia were beginning to take hold.

With the camera recording, Allan sat in pole position ready to hold court, but it was extremely hard for him to recall any real detail of particular cars, races and people. I had to feed the answers to him. When we stopped the camera we went downstairs to have dinner, and Nathan and I were gobsmacked by the stories that followed. He was completely lucid, right down to the detail of every nut and bolt and spark plug. It was like having a private audience with a librarian walking us through the 1960s and 1970s of Australian racing history.

The story of Allan Moffat is remarkable. I have so much warmth and admiration for him. He's a very special guy, and I'm so proud to call him a friend.

21

A MOUNTAIN WIN

WHEN YOU SAY 'BATHURST' to people, more often than not they think of the Bathurst 1000, the annual touring car race that is the crown jewel of the Supercars Championship calendar every October. But the Mount Panorama circuit has hosted plenty of other varieties of cars and motorcycles racing over the years, including the Australian Grand Prix for both.

The Easter race meetings of the 1960s, '70s and '80s were huge, though the motorcycle events in the 1980s got a little out of control with the unruly behaviour of the troublemakers at the top of the Mountain and came to a grinding halt.

One race that has written its own history is the Bathurst 12 Hour; it started as a race for road-going production cars, but is now held for faster, more exotic GT race cars. I'm proud to say I am on the honour roll as a winner of the race in 1994, in a factory-run Mazda RX-7 with the late Gregg Hansford.

Racing at Bathurst at Easter was revived via the inaugural 12 Hour, staged in 1991, an event put together by promoter Vincent Tesoriero, a guy I had a great history with long before he came up with the idea for that race.

Vincent was a partner in a large North Sydney advertising agency and, via his own business Forcefield Promotions, had come up with the concept of the Mr Motocross series in 1974. That series quickly grew and became a very big deal through the 1970s and into the 1980s, and our paths came together when I began commentating on the Mr Motocross series.

Meeting and working for Vincent also introduced me to my first wife, Sally, in the 1980s. She was his assistant at the ad agency, Harris Robinson Courtenay in North Sydney, and Forcefield Promotions was the business within that ran the Mr Motocross operation. Vincent was very clever and creative, and the motocross series was some of his finest work. Sally's role was to run around and tidy up after him, and she had the task of wrangling me as 'talent', which later in the relationship she noted was hard work!

Phil Harris, Michael Robinson, Bryce Courtenay (yes, the author) and Vincent ran a vibrant business and many of those involved were deeply embedded in the Willoughby Motorcycle Club, which was a very strong club in that period.

Vincent also established his own 'Rat' BMX and MX clothing line, which I sold in my shop in Ballarat and, of course, from my panel van at the Metro West BMX track at Liverpool! That relationship led to Vincent and me bringing out to Australia one of the pioneers of BMX freestyle riding, a

In the number 7 again, this time on the way to victory at the Bathurst 12 Hour in 1994. *AN1 Images/Andrew Hall*

young Californian named Bob Haro, of Haro Bicycles fame, to help promote the brand. Bob remains one of my oldest and dearest friends. Vincent and I convinced the ABC to televise the event, which we staged in Victoria Park in Ballarat on a BMX track I built by hand with other club members. The event was known as the 'Castrol Boss of BMX'.

Fast-forward to 1991 and Vincent created the Bathurst 12 Hour. This provided a platform for me to race again with some old mates in a V6 Commodore. Vincent and I put together the whole program with James Hardie's backing, and I dragged in Peter Brock and Peter McKay to share the driving with me.

The following year, Brock did a deal with Peugeot to run a trio of its little 405 cars. By then I had returned to racing with PB, racing the Mobil Commodore touring cars, so I was part of the nine driver line-up for that weekend's race.

I didn't do the 1993 race, but a chance came up in 1994 for me to join the dominant Mazda factory team, which had won the race outright in both 1992 and 1993 with its rotary-powered RX-7 coupe.

Mazda's racing program was under the control of Allan Horsley – the same Allan Horsley who had been Allan Moffat's Mazda team manager in the 1980s. Nothing happened in motorsport at Mazda that wasn't driven by Allan. I knew him from my ABC era in the early 1980s, and I'd also worked with Allan and his business partners, Phil Christensen and Phil Harrison, commentating the Supercross Masters series, which they had very successfully promoted at tracks around Australia.

Horsley had a promoter's background. He had learned the tricky business of circuit operation at the old Hume Weir circuit, near Albury, before becoming an innovative and groundbreaking promoter at Oran Park, in Sydney.

In fact, he was the first promoter who paid Peter Brock to race in the early days, locking the young gun into an exclusive deal to race at Oran Park. Under the terms of the deal, Brock couldn't race at any other track in New South Wales. Horsley was smart, protecting his investment. He wanted energy, colour and fun in the commentary at those Supercross events. One night at the Melbourne Showgrounds I started waffling about tech specs or some other obscure point and Horsley barked to Phil Harrison, 'Get him off – now!'

So it was great to get the call from Allan to drive one of the green, yellow and silver BP Visco-sponsored RX-7s in the 1994 12 Hour at Bathurst. I was paired for the race with the former international motorcycle racer Gregg Hansford, and we went into the race very well prepared. Gregg was a great guy, a laidback Queenslander who successfully competed on the global stage. In my view he never got the recognition he deserved.

Gregg adapted to cars really well, and Allan Moffat signed him up as a regular member of his Mazda touring car team in the early to mid 1980s. He again drove for Moffat in his Ford Sierras, and won the Bathurst 1000 with Larry Perkins in 1993. Gregg's death at Phillip Island in March 1995, in a two-litre Super Touring crash in a Ford Mondeo, was a terrible shock. I miss him to this day.

The field at the pointy end of the grid for the 1994 Bathurst 12 Hour featured some serious contenders. Gregg and I signed up to drive car #7 while Mark Skaife also joined the squad to share car #1 with Garry Waldon.

The main opposition to our Mazdas were the pair of Porsche 968s run by Melbourne Porsche expert Peter Fitzgerald, who had Jim Richards co-driving his car and my mate Brad Jones spearheading the other. Meanwhile, Alan Jones and John Bowe paired up in a BMW M3.

I did a lot of testing with the Mazdas in the lead-up to the race, and I loved working with Barry Jones, the noted engineer engaged by Horsley to build and develop the cars. Those RX-7s were great cars to drive. The nature of production car racing meant only limited modifications were permitted. The cars ran on grooved 'R-spec' tyres, not the slick racing tyres more commonly seen in racing. Those Mazdas ran along really well, but they were right on the borderline for brakes. You had to nurse them along. Punish them and you'd be in strife.

One of my standout memories from that race was a battle I had with Waldon in the sister car. He's a great mate of Skaifey's, a brilliant driver, with great credentials in production cars, and a fabulous bloke. We got along very well.

I had him covered from the Cutting, all the way across to Skyline at the top of the Mountain. That was my favourite bit of racetrack in the universe bar none, but he had me well and truly covered from Skyline to Forrest's Elbow, the corner that brings cars out onto the world-famous Conrod Straight. Our various strengths and weaknesses meant we were closely matched for lap speed.

I got close enough to challenge him at the bottom of the straight, and the cars rubbed gently side by side on the way into the Chase. A furious Horsley came out onto the pit wall before we finished the lap and shook his fist at us both, then he jumped on the radio and got stuck into us again. The

A MOUNTAIN WIN

sister car had a turbo failure, so Hansford and I remained the sole Mazda chance against the pair of Porsches, and Gregg ultimately brought it home our win.

It didn't occur to me at the time, but Gregg and I had managed to do something the company had hoped to achieve with Allan Moffat in the early 1980s – win a major Bathurst endurance race in a Mazda RX-7.

For sure, winning the Bathurst 12 Hour isn't the same as winning the Bathurst 1000. It's a bit of a 'Diet Coke' win compared to the full-strength October classic, but any major win at Bathurst is special, and I remain proud of the achievement – especially given the people involved, like Gregg, Allan, Garry and Mark.

During that period in my career at Bathurst I was somewhat blessed. I finished on the podium in the 1000 in 1992 with Nissan, won the 1994 12 Hour with Mazda, and scored a third place with Wayne Gardner the following year in the Bathurst 1000 in our Coke Commodore. It was a great feeling to be up there on the podium three times in four years.

The 12 Hour race ground to a halt in 1995. Twelve years later it was revived for production cars at Bathurst, and I couldn't resist the chance to have another crack. In 2007 I finished fifth overall in a Subaru Impreza WRX STi Spec C alongside Chris Alajajian and Grant Denyer, and I went back with my former Ford V8 Supercar teammate and good mate Glenn Seton for further runs in a Mitsubishi Lancer EVO in 2009 and 2010. I really wanted to help deliver a Bathurst win for Glenn, but we had to settle for second place in 2010.

*

Of all my fond memories of that 1994 Bathurst 12 Hour weekend, one stands out – for different reasons.

Hansford and I had hotel rooms next to one another, and on the Saturday night at the hotel I struggled to sleep. But not because of pre-race nerves. All I heard was the endless racket from the room next door.

The main source of the noise coincided with the arrival in town of his girlfriend. And she seemed very pleased to catch up with him. 'Oh, Gregg … oh, Gregg … oh, Gregg!'

Very, very early the next morning, we met to drive to the track together for the big day.

'Morning, Cromley,' he said. 'You all set?'

'Ah, yeah, all good, mate,' I replied. 'I do know one thing for sure,' I added. 'Your bloody name most certainly is Gregg!'

22

SETTING UP SUPERCARS

'SO LET ME GET this straight – you bring the show, you provide the stars, you load up your cars, you drive around Australia, you guys go racing, and the circuit promoter takes all the money from the ticket sales, hospitality and the signage? You lot don't get a dime? Are you nuts?'

Tony Cochrane was a big-time entertainment and event promoter from way back, the man who famously brought Frank Sinatra to Australia. Now it was the mid-1990s, and he was sitting in front of me trying to understand the state of Australian V8 touring car competition. He was gobsmacked.

Tony and his partners brought major acts to this country all the time, but he was simply staggered to learn how things worked at that time in the nation's top category of motorsport. The fact that the performers – in this case, the teams and drivers – paid to play, blew him away. Yes, there was prize money, but nothing about the overall commercial structure looked even close to a sustainable business model for the teams. I could see there was huge potential for touring car racing to be much bigger and better than it was, and Tony was all over it to a level I couldn't even begin to understand.

My initial connection to Tony came via the Gold Coast IndyCar event. He worked for IMG (International Management Group), which ran the Aussie round of the IndyCar Series, and I was belting on his door in the early 1990s trying to find support in my ambition to become an IndyCar driver with Steve Horne in the United States. I got on very well with Tony, and I knew he had a curiosity about the broader workings of V8 touring car racing – or Group A, as the Australian Touring Car Championship was known back then. Tony mused that he thought Group A sounded more like a blood type than a racing category and that the whole thing needed a giant tune-up.

I attended some of the early meetings of the first few iterations of the teams' associations, and they always turned sideways. Everyone got bogged down in the heavy-duty technical politics. Too many of the participants worried about the mind-numbing minor details rather than seeing the big picture. 'His wiper blades are made from lightweight plastic and ours are metal – it's not fair!' – that sort of thing. They were bogged down in irrelevant bullshit, forever fighting about nonsense that did nothing for the fans or the TV coverage. Even worse, it was quite spiteful most of the time.

I felt strongly that someone needed to lead the charge against this self-defeating merry-go-round, and either crash through or crash. It had to be a leader, someone who was passionate about the show, who understood TV, who grasped what the fans wanted and who understood the nuanced thinking of crazy racing folk – or who could at the very least manage them.

I remember Tony turning up in a hire car at Eastern Creek in 1993 in the early stages of his fact-finding of what was going on within the V8 touring car paddock. However, April 1996 remains a major marker in the timeline of Australian motorsport, as that was when I formally connected Tony with my old team boss Bob Forbes, who by that stage was the chairman of TEGA, the teams' association of V8 touring car racing. That moment led to V8 Supercars, and what we now know as Supercars.

After sharing backstage snapshots of the industry via many phone calls, various meetings and several trips to his beautiful house on the Gold Coast, Tony made his move. Initially, many of the key players in Australian touring car racing resisted him. The heavyweights of the sport took a lot of convincing to let Tony Cochrane and IMG steer their future.

At a press conference at Sandown in September 1996, Tony outlined the new arrangement whereby IMG would take over the marketing and promotion of touring car racing. Teams became partners in the business, initially known as AVESCO (Australian Vee Eight Supercars Company, later rebranded as V8 Supercars Australia), and received profits from the business rather than paying to race.

Tony later left IMG and set up SEL (Sports & Entertainment Limited) with his partners, and set out to build the V8 Supercars brand like no one before or since.

It led to racing's version of World Series Cricket from the late 1970s. As with cricket, it was a push to build a bigger, better business, one that would lead to a greater slice of the financial pie for every stakeholder.

It sounds easy all these years later, but along the rough, meandering road there were plenty of political boilovers. In fact, it led to a Bathurst 1000 split, as AVESCO signed a broadcast deal for their TV rights with Network Ten for 1997, but Channel Seven, the former rights holder of the championship and the current rights holder for the annual Bathurst 1000, held firm. The end result was a pair of 1000-kilometre Bathurst races competing for the hearts and minds of fans, a situation that stopped a few years later, by which time it was crystal clear that V8 Supercars had won the war.

Tony was one of those guys who could push all the irrelevant noise to one side and get to the nub of what was really going on, and how to get the sport squarely in the bullseye. He was a very, very good salesman, and it all evolved from there. From a tiny acorn grew an oak tree.

New events popped up on the calendar with government backing and support, including the revival of the Adelaide street circuit. The TV rights figures increased, audience numbers (at the track and onscreen) went through the roof, and the awareness and profitability of the category went to heights never before achieved.

As much as Tony was the highest-profile figure of this revolution, there were plenty of good operators around him. Foremost among them was David White, the Head of Sport for Network Ten. David was the right man in the right place at the right time to push the motor racing franchise. He had the support of the management and the board, and David didn't miss his targets. Sometimes 'TC' and David clashed, even viciously at times – but as a combo, wow, did they smash through some barriers together.

Wayne Cattach also played a key management role at V8 Supercars. Wayne's background included a senior management position at Shell, and then he moved on to run Dick Johnson Racing. He was the perfect foil for Tony as the 'Minister for Common Sense'. Tony had the vision, the sales skill and the flair, but he was also incendiary on occasion. Wayne delivered sage business wisdom and balance to offset Tony, while David drove the TV bus and televised their wild show. It was a match made in motor racing and TV heaven.

The party lasted a long time. In fact, despite different owners and many changes, the show continues strongly to this very day. This is something of which I'm very proud.

There are always threats and challenges to balance against the good news stories, but since 1997 the show has continued to defy gravity. It remains one of the few global motor racing properties that genuinely attracts fans, governments and broadcasters in seriously high volumes.

*

I've often been asked whether I would ever take a senior management position within the Supercars company, and I admit it has crossed my mind on occasion.

In November 2017 I turned down the opportunity to potentially become the CEO of the business. I sat down with outgoing CEO James Warburton in a demountable office at Pukekohe, in New Zealand and I knew what question was coming next. We'd loosely talked about the topic and it was decision time.

'So, do you want to pursue this or not?' he asked.

There were 30 seconds of silence, and then I looked him in the eye. 'No,' I replied.

Juggling the competing interests of governments, broadcasters, sponsors and stakeholders makes it an incredibly complex and difficult task. Tony Cochrane managed to stay ahead of that storm for just on 15 years – a remarkable reign.

A management opportunity in the right circumstances in the future is something I might consider. But the cold reality is that the personalities involved in the Supercars paddock are huge. Typically, many of the key players are unaccustomed to hearing the word 'no' and they will switch political sides in a heartbeat. They can be hard to manage.

However, when it comes to taking on a new challenge or professional opportunity, my mantra has always been 'never say never'.

Reflections

*Tony Cochrane – V8 Supercars Executive Chairman
1997–2012*

Neil helped push me in the direction with my idea of starting AVESCO (the Australian Vee Eight Supercars Company) that today is known as Supercars. He encouraged me, and indeed, set up a meeting to talk to Bob Forbes about Group A touring car racing in 1996 to explain what I would do if I was going to get involved in the category. So, my involvement in V8 Supercars is all completely Neil's fault!

According to some people, he should have never, ever introduced me to the sport because they reckon for the next 20 years it went backwards; you just can't help some dills!

Crompo is an interesting case study in humanity. I really like the guy. He's incredibly intense, very genuine and everything he says is usually well thought out. I grew to observe in the early stages of knowing him that if he said something it was worth hanging off and listening to.

He has an enormous background and experience in Australian motorsport. Neil was more than a capable steerer behind the wheel, a great sounding board for me and an enormous contributor to the industry overall. For me though it's that contribution to the motorsport industry across the board that makes him one of the real influencers of the sport.

He continues to influence to this very day, behind the scenes, in the TV broadcast, the look and feel of the cars, his work on the Commission, his commentary and general observations of the sport. Cromley and Skaifey are interesting book ends, it's a rare double act!

Neil's a serious kind of dude; he's so intense about getting the details right. But he's a ripper to have a beer with, enjoys a joke as much as the next person and has a great sense of humour. No question – he's been and will continue to be a big part of the fabric that is Australian motorsport. One of the good guys!

Tony Cochrane. *AN1 Images/Justin Deeley*

23

THE AMERICAN DREAM

'SO, DO YOU THINK you can get around there flat?'

The words came from the mouth of Kiwi IndyCar team owner Steve Horne, who had me squat, literally, over the famous yard of bricks that form the finish line in my first visit of many to the Indianapolis Motor Speedway.

Crouching down, I looked ahead to the first corner of the famous speedway, home of the Indianapolis 500, the crown jewel of IndyCar racing.

'What do you see?' Steve asked.

All I could see was a nasty-looking concrete wall. The imposing turn one wall looked like it was at right angles to the race track direction.

'Reckon you could get through there flat?' he asked again.

I didn't know what to say and considered my possible responses. On one hand, I could say yes, to prove I was a gutsy race driver. Or I could say no, because I was a thinking man's driver. Either could quickly turn into a big career mistake.

In the end, the truth prevailed. 'Ah, not at first, Mr Horne. Maybe later ...'

I'd hit the jackpot. 'Correct answer,' he replied. 'You build up speed gently at this place or it will bite you.'

I'd passed his first test. Steve was a man of few words and he was something of an imposing figure. Starting the relationship with a poor approach could have been strike three.

The circuit known worldwide as 'The Brickyard', given it was paved with bricks when it was first opened, was imposing, fast and challenging. Speeds reach over 400 kilometres per hour, so it wasn't a place to be messed with. But I was transfixed. I had to find a way to race there.

*

The allure of racing in America in IndyCar first arose during a trip to the Long Beach Grand Prix in California in 1990.

I'd stopped over for the event off the back of a trip from England. My friend Phil Christensen had a mate who was the local marketing manager of Air New Zealand, and that opened a free upgrade for my return flight. Sitting up front was comfy, but the catch was that I had to fly from London to Los Angeles, then to Auckland, and then finally to Sydney.

So I decided to check out the Long Beach race, and from the first minute I saw an IndyCar howl past me, I wanted to be a part of it.

THE AMERICAN DREAM

I'd come from a British Formula 3000 race at Oulton Park, where everything was very polite. There were 1500 people trackside under a dull sky, many of them sitting on tiny folding camp stools with blankets on their laps and pencils in hand to keep track of the lap scoring and results in their programs. Polite applause for the winner was the limit of the post-race celebrations.

When I landed in America and lobbed at Long Beach, the contrast couldn't have been any greater. It was hot, there were 100,000 people jam-packed into the venue, the place was buzzing, seriously fast and loud cars were screaming past me, the Goodyear blimp was floating overhead, the show was being broadcast live on ABC, and people were enjoying their Budweiser beer out of buckets. I quickly fell in love with the IndyCar scene.

My Formula Holden open-wheeler in Australia in 1989 and 1990 had been engineered by Bob Murphy and his brother John. They were both Adelaide boys and had worked in IndyCar in the United States earlier in their careers. Bob connected the dots for me, and that was how I met Steve Horne.

Steve was an English-born expat Kiwi whose father had been the first Ferrari importer in New Zealand. He'd been bitten by the racing bug and built Formula Ford engines while in high school, and had left New Zealand in 1974 to head to England and work on a Formula 5000 team, VDS Racing. As the team grew, Steve headed to America in 1976 to work on their Can Am race program.

In 1982 Steve joined with American team owner Jim Trueman in the Truesports IndyCar team, with the backing of Budweiser. Together they won the 1986 Indianapolis 500 with American Bobby Rahal driving, and also the 1986 and 1987 IndyCar Series championships. Sadly, Trueman died of cancer in 1986, less than two weeks after that special Indy 500 win. Steve and the Trueman family assumed day-to-day operations of the team.

Steve's racing credentials were impeccable. Adrian Newey, who later became arguably the best Formula 1 designer of all time, worked for Steve at Truesports. If ever you can get Steve to open up about it, his story about being summonsed to Italy to meet Enzo Ferrari is epic. The short version is that the 'old man' was in the middle of some serious warfare with Formula 1's governing body, and Adrian, Steve and Bobby were asked to design a Ferrari IndyCar. It happened but the project was stillborn, as Enzo used the prospect of entering Ferrari into another series to get his way in Formula 1.

Steve and I struck up a warm relationship in the early stages, and he heard me out when I made my 'Road to Indy' presentation: my plan to get into the Indy Lights feeder series and, ultimately, IndyCar. Unfortunately, despite endless meetings, sales pitches, sponsor begging and constant trips to and from the United States, I was never able to get something going – but the upside was that Steve became a firm friend and we kept in touch.

He left Truesports in mid-1992 and founded Tasman Motorsports Group soon after, initially running cars in the Indy Lights series and then in IndyCar. Tasman won the Indy Lights championship in 1993 with young American gun Bryan Herta driving, and again in 1994 with Englishman Steve Robertson. Tasman was the Indy Lights powerhouse team, and along the way I also introduced former World 500cc Motorcycle Champion Eddie Lawson to Steve.

Later, Horne added an IndyCar program in partnership with engine supplier Honda. The team had its first win in 1995 on the one-mile oval at New Hampshire with Brazilian driver André Ribeiro, and very nearly won that year's Indianapolis 500 at its first attempt. Canadian driver Scott Goodyear led the race in the closing stages, though was judged to have passed the pace car on a restart too early. He ignored the black flag signifying he needed to take a pit lane penalty, which meant the officials stopped counting his laps. Jacques Villeneuve was ultimately declared the victor.

*

By 1996, IndyCar was a regular racing product on Network Ten, with Bill Woods and I hosting the race telecast. I loved the series. The racing was very close, the cars were cool and I knew many people on the inside.

The icing on the cake that year was the chance to drive one of the team's current-spec Lola-Honda IndyCars in a full-blown test. The team chartered a private corporate aircraft to take the crew to GingerMan Raceway in Michigan, near the shores of Lake Michigan.

One of the team's senior race engineers, Diane Holl, who had come from Benetton and Ferrari in Formula 1, worked with me for the day, as did a bunch of Honda engineers. The teams were not permitted to 'touch' the engines or even start the machines without the Japanese technicians on site. These rules were all part of the elaborate lease agreements for the engines. The teams did not own their engines in that highly competitive era.

Honda Performance Development engineers supervised everything engine-related to look after the precious, very expensive and very high-horsepower V8 twin turbocharged engine, which was mounted on the back of the current-spec Lola chassis that was regularly driven by accomplished Mexican racer Adrián Fernández.

The test had a serious technical angle. Don Halliday, then a senior engineer for Tasman, and formerly of the Brabham Formula 1 team, had invented a device to measure tyre grip and friction on the IndyCar. Don reasoned that 'grip' was, and remains, the most talked-about topic in racing, and he wanted to engineer a logical solution to try and measure it. It also had applications for road and runway use too, given that government agencies could save millions of dollars if they had better knowledge of when to apply salt to icy American roads or runways in midwinter. Understanding grip was the challenge, and I played the role of the 'NASA chimp'. It was a special lifetime experience – an off-the-scale experience, in fact.

GingerMan Raceway was an 11-turn, 3-kilometre track often used as a test circuit by IndyCar teams, though no races were held there. When we arrived the weather was mild but the next day it was downright freezing.

In the lower gears on the ice-cold track, the car was a serious handful. It had a subtle form of traction control to stop the rear wheels from spinning under acceleration, but it was still almost impossible to drive on cold tyres on an icy track. It felt like an 800-horsepower skateboard – it just wanted to fly straight out from underneath me as soon as I loaded the tyre mid-corner.

Top: My IndyCar test in 1996 in a full spec Tasman Lola-Honda is a day I'll remember forever. *James Cassimus*

Above: My 1997 Tasman teammates, Tony Kanaan, left, and Hélio Castroneves, right, both future Indy 500 winners. *Crompton collection*

The team sent me out with strict instructions not to over-rev the engine or touch the rev limiter. I remember seeing the data on the dashboard that the turbo boost was set to 40 inches. I also recall that the steering load felt ridiculously heavy. After I settled in, they dialled it up a notch.

'Okay, now we're going to give you full turbo boost,' the HPD engineer told me.

'Um, okay … how much is that?'

They told me it was another five inches worth – a dial-up to 45 inches of turbo boost, providing another 100 horsepower. That took the engine to an output of about 900 horsepower.

I was very fit at the time – I was 36 years of age, training regularly and racing full-time in touring cars in Australia for Coca-Cola and Wayne Gardner – and yet driving this car made me dizzy in the lower gears. It threw my head back under fierce acceleration, and I had to brace myself against the headrest. It was an insanely powerful device on full boost.

In the corners it generated two and a half times the load of gravity, which effectively meant I weighed 190 kilograms in the turns. But that was nothing compared to the forces on the big ovals where those cars raced. There, at places like the big, fast two-mile Michigan International Speedway and California Speedway in Fontana, drivers were subjected to 4.5 Gs of force. Totally nuts.

The speed literally took my breath away. The engine spun up to 15,000 rpm, the brakes were amazing, and you could slow down for the last corner on that track from 250 kilometres per hour to 115 kilometres per hour in less than 80 metres – the length of four cricket pitches, and less than half the distance required to stop a V8 Supercar travelling at the same speed.

Paul Tracy was there the day before in the Team Penske car, and I managed to get to within one second of his fastest time, which I was happy with given the frigid temperature and my unfamiliarity with the car and track.

The test was one of the most enjoyable experiences I've ever had in a race car. It was magical, although stepping out of that car did bring a slight sense of disappointment. Having a taste of that car was sensational, but it also underscored what I'd missed out on when I was unable to break into IndyCar racing.

*

Not only did Steve Horne give me the chance to drive an IndyCar, but he also gave me the chance to drive an Indy Lights car on the 1.5-mile Las Vegas Motor Speedway. That certainly cured me of any immediate desire to race on ovals!

The team's regular Indy Lights drivers, Tony Kanaan and Hélio Castroneves, were back home in Brazil and unavailable to drive at a TV commercial filming week for Firestone-brand Dayton Tyres, who were sponsors of the Indy Lights series.

Both of those guys have become huge stars in their own right in the years since. Tony won the Indy Lights title for Steve in 1997, then went on to win the IndyCar Series in 2004 and the Indianapolis 500 in 2013. Hélio finished second to Tony during his time with Tasman in Indy Lights in 1997, and is now a legend of the Indianapolis Motor Speedway by virtue of scoring four Indianapolis 500 wins for Team

Penske in 2001, 2002, 2009 and 2021. We're all still close mates to this day and remain in regular contact.

I was given the role of stunt double for the filming and we were there for a full week with directors and various creative tossers everywhere. For me, it was another chance to drive a race car – the TV ad was just a nuisance by-product.

The Indy Lights cars were configured for the ovals and stiff in their springs so as to maximise the effect of the floor as an aero platform. The result was that it was really hard to focus at high speed, so I was literally seeing a blur.

After the early exploratory laps, I asked the Team Manager, Steve 'Boost' Dickson, if he could change the front wing settings to dial out some of the understeer – or the 'push', as the Americans prefer to describe a lack of front-end grip in race cars. Out I went again, and the little V6 Buick was singing away. I was scorching along at 300 kilometres per hour, occasionally bouncing onto the rev-limiter – then suddenly the car snapped wildly sideways in the middle of turn three.

It frightened the living crap out of me! It was hard to catch the slide, and I had a giant 'tank slapper', only just missing the outside fence. Needless to say, I immediately dived straight back into the pit lane to retrieve the understeer we'd dialled out!

After that episode, I focused on being a good boy and helping sell more Dayton tyres, and not playing pretend oval racer!

24
RACING IN AMERICA

I CAN'T IMAGINE TOO many racing drivers have been wandering around the Perth Zoo when they receive a phone call summoning them to a meeting that might bring a sniff of a professional opportunity in the United States. But that's exactly what happened to me in May 1996.

I was in town as the Australian Touring Car Championship was racing at Barbagallo Raceway, just outside Perth. The Coke/Wayne Gardner Racing team had made the decision earlier that season, though, to slim back from two cars to one due to a tight budget and rampant costs. Wayne kept racing, while my car was parked up. I still made the trip west to help handle driving duties and to ferry passengers at a sponsor ride day on the Monday after the race. But race drivers make terrible spectators, so I avoided the track and went to the zoo instead.

That was when the phone rang. It was Steve Horne, Tasman Motorsports Group IndyCar team owner. 'What are you doing?' he enquired.

'Well, I'm in Perth, but not driving this weekend,' I told him. 'I'm standing here looking at a giant elephant turd. Why?'

He asked if I could be in Cleveland the next weekend. 'I've got an idea to discuss,' he said.

So I jumped on a plane to Ohio and went to see him at the Burke Lakefront Airport race circuit. Every year in that era, the airport closed down and was turned into an IndyCar racetrack for the weekend, its ultra-wide runways becoming long, fast straights.

I waited around on the Friday and then the Saturday and started to get nervous that there would be no opportunity to see Steve. But finally I got a ten-minute window of time with him in the team's transporter on the Sunday. I wasn't ready for what he said next.

'We're going to run a Honda Accord in the North American Touring Car Championship next year, and I'd like you to drive the car,' Steve said.

I said yes straightaway, but he shut me down in an instant.

'No, no, you go back home and think it over properly,' he told me. 'Talk to your friends and family, then come back to me and we'll go from there.'

Truth be told, there wasn't much to think about. Steve had offered me a substantial deal to drive for his new program. The dollars were great, and they were American (real money!); he'd also provide accommodation for me and my then wife, Sally, a car, plus some additional return airfares for us to come and go to and from Australia during the year.

Something that really meant a lot to me was that the deal included what Steve called 'sweat equity', a chance to have a minor ownership share of the Tasman touring car team.

So I could hang around in Australia hoping to maybe race the Coke car again, budget permitting, or go to the United States with a solid contract. In my mind I was going to America for good. I locked the deal in with Steve soon after, though we didn't announce the news publicly until a week before Christmas 1996. I was going to be a Tasman driver for the following season.

*

The North American Touring Car Championship (NATCC) had been set up in 1996, based on the success of the British Touring Car Championship. Run for two-litre 'Super Tourers', it was new to the United States, a country where NASCAR stock cars and IndyCar racing were the big dogs in the yard.

Importantly, the NATCC had aligned with IndyCar to be a support event at many of its big races in 1997, giving a great platform for the series even though the style of racing was largely unfamiliar to Americans.

Alan Gow, my former team manager at Peter Brock's Mobil 1 Racing team in 1987 and 1988, left to go to England in the early 1990s and became the tsar of the BTCC, and he became a partner in the NATCC, along with IndyCar team owner and billionaire Gerry Forsythe.

The fields for the 1997 NATCC were small, but the quality at the front end was strong. Our big rivals were the PacWest-run Dodge Stratus cars (PacWest also ran an IndyCar team) of David Donohue and Dominic Dobson, plus another Honda under the Honda American Racing Team banner, driven by American Peter Cunningham. Donohue was American road racing royalty, son of the legendary driver Mark Donohue, who had given Roger Penske his first Indianapolis 500 win in 1972 and was a legend of the sport in North America.

My Honda was sourced from Motor Sport Developments (MSD) in England. A 1996 model, it had been a works factory car raced by Scotsman David Leslie in the British Touring Car Championship. It was a really nice car; however, it was front-wheel drive and somewhat quirky. It took a lot of adjusting to, but we were all set for a racing season that would be one of my best.

The first round was held at Long Beach in April 1997, at the very venue where I'd fallen in love with the concept of racing in America seven years earlier. It was one of my favourite tracks, and our plain white Honda simply smoked the field. I won both races to bounce out of the blocks and into an instant championship lead. I led all the way to the chequered flag in both races, winning the first by 13 seconds and the second by 3.3 seconds.

It was an amazing result, considering we'd had only had a brief test session at a freezing Indianapolis Raceway Park and weren't 100 per cent ready to race. The test was troubled and the car was borderline undriveable. It actually made me think that saying yes to the drive could have been a giant mistake. We'd even flirted with the idea of skipping the first round to be better prepared for the season, but Steve wanted to see where we were in relation to the opposition.

Randy Pobst, one of the BMW drivers, finished second in Race 2 and talked to the press afterwards. 'Neil was an unknown quantity, but we knew Tasman was a quality outfit and I figured Steve Horne wouldn't have taken him on if he weren't any good,' he said. 'I was hoping he'd be a rich-guy Aussie wanker, but he's not. He's quite a driver.'

They didn't know me and I didn't know them, but I got their attention pretty quickly. I felt a mixture of elation and frustration in the aftermath of the Long Beach win. On the one hand I was thrilled to finally get a touring car win on the board, but on the other hand it niggled me to think that the breaks hadn't ever gone my way in Australia.

The second round was at Hutchinson Island in Savannah, Georgia, at an Indy Lights event in May. A third and a second place gave me an 18-point series lead over Donohue's Dodge. But then things got messy in Round 3 in June in Detroit, at the Belle Isle street track. I finished third in the first race behind Donohue and Dobson, but was disqualified in Race 2.

It was the first and only time in my racing career that I was disqualified from a race. I was livid, and Steve was uncharacteristically angry.

I'd crossed the line in second place but there had been two incidents that attracted attention. The first came with Cunningham's Honda. I knew I was faster than him and got a great run out of the fast right/left flowing sequence over the bridge out of turns one and two. I made a dive down the inside into turn three and got wholly alongside. There was side-to-side contact between the cars when he turned into me and his Accord lobbed into the tyre barriers.

To this day, I know the move was 100 per cent fair. The race restarted after his car was removed from the wall, and then Donohue blocked me on the last lap on the main straight. I made a dive under brakes to pass until into turn

11, beyond the fountain, and he tried to block me. I was committed to the move and the Dodge bounced off into the tyre wall and I took second place.

A lengthy Stewards' hearing resulted in me being rubbed out of the results – which also rubbed me out of the series lead.

I thought the disqualification penalty was total nonsense. Cunningham, in my opinion, had brought about his own demise, so I felt aggrieved to be penalised. However, I was most certainly guilty of making a bad move on Donohue. I definitely deserved a penalty for the second incident, but to be excluded from the entire race, rather than perhaps receive a post-race time penalty or financial fine (or both) was ridiculous and extreme.

That left Dobson with 97 points to Donohue's 94. I was now in third place with 91 points.

The next round was in Portland, but we didn't race. Publicly we said we were out of sponsorship, but in fact Steve was white-hot cranky about our treatment in Detroit, and felt he should make a point to the series organisers by sitting out and lowering the car count for the weekend.

The series organiser was Roger Elliot. To illustrate how small the world of motor racing really is and why you should never burn bridges, Roger now handles the US distribution of TV programs my business makes for Motorsport Australia (formerly CAMS), so we're in regular contact these days. We even caught up a few years ago when Roger was in Sydney.

To this day, Steve regrets spitting the dummy. It certainly sent a message to the series organisers, but he knows now that, had we raced and even got a handful of points, we would have had a far greater chance of winning the championship. That stung.

We returned to racing in Round 5 at the Burke Lakefront Airport in Cleveland, the same place where 12 months earlier Steve had offered me the drive. We made the decision to race on the Wednesday of race week, thanks to the backing of McCormick Lines trucking and LCI International, a phone company.

My return to the championship didn't go as well as hoped. A fifth place in Race 1 was unspectacular, and I came home second in Race 2. In Race 1, though, I had been running second when I tried to pass Dobson at the one part of the track Steve had warned me not to try and pass on as it was so dirty. I had track position and was 100 per cent down the inside of his car, but found zero grip and skated off into the tyre barriers.

I hadn't listened to the advice of someone who knew what he was talking about. Steve 1, Neil 0.

Labatt Breweries of Canada and Labatt USA provided additional sponsorship for the next races in Canada, at Toronto and Vancouver. I got caught out by a slipping clutch off the start of Race 1 at the Exhibition Place street course in Toronto and dropped back to sixth, though I came storming back through to finish second. Scoring the fastest lap of Race 1 gave me pole position for Race 2, and I led off the line and never looked back, scoring my third win of the season.

By that stage, having missed a round and lost the points from the Detroit disqualification, I was fourth in the championship, but still only 34 points behind leader Donohue. Anything was possible in the remaining races.

Round 7 took us back to Ohio to the Mid-Ohio Sportscar Course in Lexington, one of my favourite tracks in the United States and our home event, given Columbus was nearby. Again, the clutch slipped at the start of Race 1, again I dropped spots and again I fought back to finish second. A hit from Dobson's Dodge in Race 2 sent me in to a spin but I charged back again and scored third place on the final corner of the race. That hit was pure payback from the Dodge boys, and Dominic drop-kicked me off the road. Needless to say, there was plenty of friction between our two squads. Unlike my situation in Detroit when I was excluded for a similar move, I found it somewhat interesting that Dobson was not.

Round 8, in Vancouver at the end of August, helped keep my narrowing championship chances alive. Victory in both races helped Honda seal the Manufacturers Cup and moved me to third in the points. I had momentum but no time on my side.

In the final round, at Laguna Seca in September, I bookended my year with another pair of wins. Donohue won the championship with 304 points from Cunningham's Honda on 282, and I came third with 280 points. Could I have scored at least 24 points in the round I missed at Portland? Maybe, but we all know that ifs, buts and maybes have no place in racing.

I felt the 1997 North American Touring Car Championship was a great experience and a success. I'd won seven races – more than any other driver that year – and broadened my horizons. I loved living in America, working for Steve and his wife Christine and their team.

To this very day, though, I don't have a single trophy from any of those race wins or podium finishes. The Americans know how to make a cool trophy, and the trophies from that series were worth keeping. At the end of 1997, the NATCC was closed down, and at the end of 1998 Steve decided to sell

Tasman Motorsports Group team to his fellow team owner, Gerry Forsythe, who had also been a partner in the NATCC. Steve sold the whole business, lock, stock and barrel, and provided a full inventory of what was included in the sale. The trophies won by Tasman's IndyCar, Indy Lights and touring car drivers evaporated somewhere along the line in the transaction. I wrote polite letters and made calls to try to get them back, but it came to zero. My requests were simply ignored.

As far as I know, they're probably sitting in a barn somewhere and have never seen the light of day again. It just seems so strange to me that someone with no emotional attachment would want to keep another person's trophies. Weird!

Forsythe renamed the Tasman team as Forsythe Championship Racing, and it continued to run out of the existing race shop in Ohio, with Tony Kanaan as the driver of a McDonald's-backed Reynard-Honda in 1999. Steve stayed on as President until he decided to resign in February 2000.

*

I made a lot of good friends in the IndyCar circus and learned a lot from a master in Steve. In fact, Steve restored my confidence as a driver. He was the best race team operator I ever drove for.

And it wasn't just the racing I loved, but the entire experience. The travel, the shopping, witnessing the size and scope of the opportunities in the United States. The whole thing opened my eyes. Steve and Christine fostered a great

In the pits at Laguna Seca in 1997 in the NATCC. It was the last race of the season – and I won. A great way to end that season. My engineer Phil Harris is standing to the left of shot with his back to camera. *Crompton collection*

family atmosphere among the 80-strong group of people who worked for them. They made each of us feel as though we were an important part of a bigger family. In fact, Steve and Christine remain like family to me.

The Tasman Motorsports Group achieved a lot in a short period of time, and a glimpse of the driver line-up and their achievements gives you an idea why: Bryan Herta, Steve Robertson, Eddie Lawson, André Ribeiro, Adrián Fernández, Tony Kanaan, Hélio Castroneves and Cristiano da Matta.

Steve and I remain very close, and have been since those early days. One of Steve's favourite expressions was 'emotion is the enemy'. He trotted that one out whenever I began to stray outside the boundary lines of the business or on the track. Steve has provided me with great guidance over many years, and we share an interest in flying, too. We've also worked together on the Supercars Commission, Steve as Chairman and me as the Independent Commissioner for six years.

Reflections

Steve Horne – Tasman Motorsports Group IndyCar team co-owner 1992–98, Supercars Commission Chairman 2013–19

Neil is a very honourable guy. If he says he's going to do something, then he does. He's a genuine, heartfelt guy with no surface veneer. What you see with him is what you get.

I first met him in the early 1990s when he came to America with a goal of racing in the USA and I was very proud to give him the opportunity to test drive one of our IndyCars in late 1996, which he did immensely well, and then drive for our team in the North American Touring Car Championship in 1997.

We went to Long Beach for the very first race and Neil went out and cleaned up the whole field and won by a substantial margin. Our 1997 Lola IndyCars were pigs of cars that year and running towards the back of the field, so Neil's success that weekend in the Honda touring car, and Tony Kanaan and Hélio Castroneves running in our Indy Lights cars, gave us a real breath of fresh air.

Withdrawing Neil's car from the Portland NATCC round that year – when I spat the dummy with the series organisers over an on-track penalty that Neil had received – is something I regret to this day. Had we raced in that round, Neil would likely have scored enough points that would have resulted in him winning that championship.

Some may think Neil is very serious and doesn't have a sense of humour, but I beg to differ. I asked him to help out with the marketing side of things of the IndyCar program while he was driving for us and we gave him a desk cubicle among four of the girls in the Tasman office, including my wife, Christine. They all played so many pranks on one another I had to end up separating them and gave him a desk down the other end of the building with the engineers. Swapping my PA Tamy's hairspray can for a can of flyspray was the last straw!

The Tasman team with the IndyCar I tested – team co-owner, my friend and mentor Steve Horne is fourth from left. *James Cassimus*

25

WHEELING AND DEALING

A LIFE IN MOTORSPORT has taught me that wheeling and dealing isn't an option, it's compulsory.

'Wheeling and dealing' is not a negative expression. It is a simple fact that you need to work hard, really hard. You need to get up earlier and go to bed later. You need to hustle, network, connect, communicate, promote, innovate, sell and be extremely pro-active if you want to achieve your goals in racing.

But sometimes the deals sound way too good to be true.

After the North American Touring Car Championship closed down at the end of 1997, I was keen to try to find a way of staying in the United States and continuing to race. Labatt USA had been a sponsor of our Tasman Motorsports

Group Honda, so Steve Horne and I visited their head office in New Jersey for a discussion regarding ongoing backing for me to race sportscars in America in 1998.

When I look back on it now, I see that the whole thing was doomed from early that morning. Somehow, I slept through my alarm and woke to Steve banging on my front door. It was a snowy, cold winter's Ohio day. I sprinted through the shower, got dressed and flew out the door at a great rate of knots.

The short version of that meeting in New Jersey was that Labatt didn't have any additional sponsorship funds available for 1998, but they were still keen to help us. While they didn't have any cash available, they did have an extraordinary amount of beer! They had excess production stock of their Rolling Rock beer sitting in warehouses. Steve and I were blown away when the CEO said they could give us one million cases.

Now, I left school before the end of Year 12, but even someone with my limited mathematical abilities knows that a million cases of beer is a lot of beer, and potentially worth a dime! At least, so I thought ...

The trick was, and please excuse the pun, how to liquidate this offer and turn the grog into racing funds. Steve loved a challenge. 'Okay, we'll go with it,' he told them.

At that point I thought we were flying high. Even if we flogged the beer off cheap – at, say, five dollars a case – we'd have enough budget to rattle the sharp end of any grid at major sportscar events like the Daytona 24 Hour and Sebring 12 Hour. Instantly I recognised I needed to speak with someone who understood the brewing universe. I jumped straight on a plane to Australia and headed to the offices of Carlton & United Breweries in Melbourne to visit an old friend in Ian Kleeman. Ian had done the deal for Rothmans' brand Peter Stuvyesant cigarettes to sponsor Allan Moffat's Mazda RX-7 race cars in the 1980s, and he'd since become CUB's Sales and Marketing Manager.

And that's when I got a serious lesson on the subject of beer licensing. I soon discovered that you can't just unload beer wherever you want. I sadly learned about the very few places we actually could sell the beer. True story – there was one particular country in a far corner of Africa and some dodgy part of the former Soviet Union where the beer wasn't subject to an existing licensing agreement. You couldn't make this up!

Another of our sponsors for the Honda touring car in 1997 was a trucking company called McCormick Lines. The old fella who owned and ran the show was named Larry Hooper. He was a chain-smoking, gravelly voiced old-style American who just loved his motorsport. He backed our car, as well as Tony Kanaan and Hélio Castroneves in their Indy Lights cars. Whenever we discussed the competition, Larry's solution was: 'Why don't you just take him out?' He was a loveable character from a bygone era. I can still picture Larry sucking on a cigarette, and saying, with his raspy voice, 'I'll take care of this for you …'

So Larry ended up wheeling and dealing with all sorts of shady black-market characters on the New York wharfs, trying to turn all that beer into cash. Without a word of a lie, we got squeezed down to 50 cents a case – not a bottle, but a *case* – before we could get rid of it. In the end, we decided that doing business with the New York wharf-based mafia via friends of a trucking intermediary was a little too inventive even for us. Then the CEO of Labatt USA left the company soon after and the whole thing collapsed. Probably a good thing!

As a reminder of just how crazy this motorsport journey of mine has been, I've proudly placed an empty bottle of Rolling Rock on a shelf right in my eyeline in my office. I see it every single day ...

*

Peter Brock's announcement in 1997 that he was retiring from professional motorsport at the end of that season meant there was extra focus on that year's V8 Supercars Bathurst 1000, his last start for the Holden Racing Team.

His farewell tour happened while I was racing the Honda in America, but Peter phoned my home base in Columbus, Ohio, a few times that year to check in. It was always good to catch up on the home gossip. Peter and Bev also sent me a really nice fax after I won at Long Beach, in which he explained that he'd decided to retire from top-line racing at the end of that season. That decision was a big deal, so I was flattered when Peter invited me to come back to Australia and co-drive with him at Bathurst in his 'first' last Great Race start.

I was simultaneously taking calls from another mate, Mark Skaife, because Wayne Gardner's Coke team – my old team in Australia – was talking to him about a drive for Bathurst. Ironically, I was also taking calls from Alan Heaphy at Wayne Gardner Racing, while Mark was juggling similar calls from John Crennan at HRT on behalf of Tom Walkinshaw.

It was funny: Brock, Skaife and I all knew exactly what was unfolding as the team principals were wheeling and dealing on what they likely thought was the 'down-low'. But there's no such thing as 'off the record' in the tangled underbelly of racing, and all three drivers knew exactly what was unfolding!

Brock didn't own or run the Holden Racing Team. He was employed as a race driver, so he didn't have the final say in the decision-making process anyway. The decision by Crennan and Walkinshaw to employ Mark Skaife to drive with Peter, and then take his place in the team for the following year, proved to be the right call. Mark went on to win three championships for HRT (in 2000, 2001 and 2002) and three Bathurst 1000s (in 2001, 2002 and 2005).

I went back to share a Coke car with Wayne at Sandown and Bathurst in 1997, but neither team had the ultimate success in the Great Race. Brock's #05 Commodore, with Skaife on board, was leading when its engine backfired and caused irreparable damage that took it out of the race. Our #7 Coke Holden later took up the front running before it too suffered engine dramas while in the lead.

No matter – we all had fun bench racing on the phone at weird hours for a little old-style 'midnight motors' wheeling and dealing!

26

COOL RACE CARS

I'VE BEEN VERY FORTUNATE to drive some unique and amazing racing cars in various exotic locations around the world. A couple of those special moments have been with the 'King of Pukekohe', four-time Bathurst 1000 winner Greg Murphy.

For starters, we both had the opportunity to drive Formula 1 cars. Well, the cars we drove were once Formula 1 cars, but by the time we slipped into the cockpit that description was something of a creative stretch!

It was 2004, and the Michelin Driving Experience was conducted at Magny-Cours in France, and we were sent on a mission to make a feature story on it for Network Ten's *RPM* TV show. The concept was to 'graduate' progressively: initially we'd drive Porsche GT3 Cup cars, then we'd move to Formula 3 open-wheelers under the guidance of some local instructors who were wannabe national drivers. They had no idea who we were, and vice versa! At that time, Greg was one of the top drivers in V8 Supercars, especially given he had won the Bathurst 1000 the previous year and would back it up with another one five months later.

The local French driving instructors loved a briefing. 'You should change gear here and brakes must come on here, oui?' they stressed to us in 'French-lish'.

That sound in the background was both of us, fast asleep ...

'You must follow us on the track – no passing.'

Uh-huh, sure thing.

Every time Greg and I we went out onto the track, we'd follow them for a lap or two, get bored, and then just bolt straight past them and disappear down the road, having our own private battle!

Unfortunately, the F1 cars we drove were a sad reflection of the real thing. They had been Formula 1 race cars at one stage (mine was an Arrows Grand Prix carbon-fibre tub), but the only part of them that had been in a Grand Prix was probably the bones of the chassis. Mine had some sort of detuned Cosworth engine bolted into the back. I definitely wouldn't say I've tested a legitimate Formula 1 car in the same way I can say I drove a real-deal IndyCar, but we had fun nonetheless, and Magny-Cours was an enjoyable circuit to drive.

*

Back in 1990 I had an amazing experience when I tested a Japanese Formula 3000 car at Phillip Island for the Dome team. It was a Reynard 89D chassis with a Mugen-Honda V8 engine, and the team was in Australia doing some tyre testing ahead of their racing season. Their drivers were the American Ross Cheever and the Swede Thomas Danielsson. (Cheever's older brother Eddie raced in Formula 1 and won the 1998 Indianapolis 500.)

The fast and flowing Phillip Island track was a venue that many international teams of the era, including Nissan's World Sportscar team, used for testing in their off-season. The Nissan guys were there that same day, with Mark Skaife having a drive.

I had several runs. On one the team fitted special Dunlop qualifying tyres, and the grip was just phenomenal. They were only good for one lap, though – just. I went out of the pits and by the time I had reached the Hay Shed corner (with about three-quarters of the lap complete), the front tyres were completely destroyed and there was rubber flailing off them that whacked me on the helmet.

On a more durable tyre, once I was familiar with it, I could go 100 per cent flat-out on the throttle around turn one at Phillip Island in that car, which was near enough to 300 kilometres per hour. The car had so much aerodynamic grip and created so much G-force that it was a real battle to hold your head up.

In that period, Japanese Formula 3000 cars were being raced in the midst of a proper tyre war. They were so fast that they would have been capable of qualifying on the back of the grid for a Formula 1 race of the era. Just incredible.

I also had a run in a Reynard-Judd in the British Formula 3000 Championship later that year, and raced it at Brands Hatch in addition to testing it at Silverstone and Snetterton.

My brief foray into international Formula 3000 took me to England. This is at the famous Brands Hatch circuit in 1990.

This was during the 'awkward' period of me being signed up to HRT but not racing, so I made another withdrawal from the 'Bank of Neil' and had a bunch of expat Aussies over there helping me, including Rick Wyatt, who later worked for the Holden Racing Team and oversaw the build of many of its race-winning cars, Trevor Sheumack, a long-time Michelin tyre distributor in Australia in the years since, and Frank Adamson, who would work for Brock's Mobil 1 team when I drove there a few years later, and would spend many years working for Supercars and, now, Motorsport Australia.

Our whole deal was run on the smell of an oily rag. Soon-to-be F1 but then leading F3000 team operator Eddie Jordan loaned us some gear ratios for our 1989 model Reynard. But in return for that, I had to get out of the car at the Silverstone test so Italian driver Vincenzo Sospiri, who later raced in IndyCars and made a brief F1 appearance, could turn some laps.

That Formula 3000 car was very cool to drive, and the tracks were very different to drive on. Their rhythm was completely different to tracks in Australia. Over there, they were all very smooth, very fast and very flat and flowing, completely different from what we've become used to in Australia, where tracks usually have lots of bumps.

Silverstone was a giant buzz. Driving a serious high-performance race car hard around world famous 'big-balls' corners like Stowe at ridiculously high speed was a special treat.

*

My one-off start at Bathurst in 1992 in one of the Winfield team Nissan GT-Rs gave me a unique insight into the car dubbed 'Godzilla'.

A four-wheel-drive car that pumped out around 600 horsepower from a six-cylinder turbo engine, it was incredibly hard to drive and required a special technique. In modern terms, it was a real pogo stick that bounced everywhere. It jumped and leapt and clearly had a phenomenal traction advantage, but its behaviour, and the way it separated and distributed its drive between the front and rear wheels, was not easy to understand. Mark Skaife and Jim Richards were the masters at it.

My co-driver Anders Olofsson and I found it was hard yards. I tested it at Calder before Bathurst, and I had an ashen look on my face after the opening day of practice at Mount Panorama. I was not on top of the car at all. In fact, I was so far behind it that I felt like I was clinging to the boot lid. I wasn't driving it, it was driving me. I didn't feel confident in the car, and nor did Anders. We were miles away from the speed our sister car had.

Skaifey reckons it was only after he fed me a few beers that night that I went back the next day and went faster in the GT-R. He still roars with laughter about that one.

*

My desire to tackle sportscar racing in America went nowhere in 1998, but I did get a chance to have a test drive of one of those very cool open-top cars in the United States. The same kind that raced in the annual Daytona 24 Hour classic in Florida.

It was a car owned by an American, Jon Field, who had a company called Banana Joe's Sports Bar & Grill. It was sort of like a Hog's Breath Café chain, and he was rolling it out across the United States. The car had a Riley & Scott chassis and a thumping Ford V8 race engine bolted into the back. I drove it all day in testing at Mid-Ohio, and it was cool to drive – awesome, in fact. Jon needed a pay driver to join him, but I couldn't deliver that kind of cash so the opportunity went nowhere.

*

Racing a Ferrari may have seemed like an impossibility when I was a kid, but I managed to tick that box as well in 1998 when I got behind the wheel of a Ferrari F355 Challenge.

John Bowe was the regular driver for the car, which was owned by Ross Palmer (the same guy who backed Dick Johnson in his 'Tru-Blu' and 'Greens-Tuf' days) and it competed in the GT-Production car series that supported the two-litre Super Touring Championship.

John was also racing for Dick Johnson Racing in V8 Supercars, and occasionally the two calendars clashed, so he suggested to Ross and team manager Neal Lowe that I should drive it on those weekends where he couldn't. Yes, that's the same Neal Lowe who I'd verbally tangled with in the aftermath of the Wayne Gardner incident in Perth five years earlier. Small world, huh!

The F355 Challenge model I got to drive was one of a bunch of cars produced especially by Ferrari for its Ferrari Challenge race series overseas. It had a 3.5-litre V8 engine good for about 400 horsepower (more than 200 less than a V8 Supercar of the era), with a six-speed gearbox and a factory-fitted roll cage. A limited number, including Palmer's car, were made in right-hand drive. (A quick check online

Me, F1 Ferrari driver Eddie Irvine and the Ferrari F355, Bathurst, 1998.
AN1 Images/Andrew Hall

shows that anyone with one of these right-hand drive versions these days has got themselves a valuable car. Not many were produced, and not all of them survived their racing lives.)

That Ferrari was a cool little car to drive, though. It didn't have much torque, so I had to keep the engine revs wound up. I drove it at Bathurst in November 1998 in the three-hour GT-Production car race on the Saturday afternoon, the main support race to the V8 Supercar race on the Sunday, in which I was competing in a very fast Falcon alongside Glenn Seton.

My focus was more on the Sunday race, so I didn't stress too much about qualifying the Ferrari, which I was sharing for the weekend with Ross Palmer's son Darren.

There were so many cars in the field, and such a wide disparity of speed between the fastest cars and the slowest, that there was simply no chance to do a fast qualifying lap without getting blocked.

The team was stressed that we weren't starting up the front, but I knew we could find our way forward and compete for the win. Darren started and did a really nice job in the first stint, before I jumped in and drove the wheels off it. We kept moving higher and higher up the field. It came down to a fight between my old mate Jim Richards and me in the closing laps.

Those laps were some of the most enjoyable hand-to-hand combat I ever had at Mount Panorama. Jim was driving the Falken Tyres Porsche 911 RSCS of Peter Fitzgerald. Fitzy was prone to a grizzle and was blowing up deluxe when he saw my progress in the race, suggesting we'd done something dodgy to the Ferrari overnight because we'd been nowhere in qualifying and suddenly we were fighting for the lead.

But the reality was that I'd just never got a clear lap in qualifying. I'd been totally disinterested in riskily weaving the Ferrari between pedestrian-speed production cars, given the 80 kilometre per hour speed differential in some parts of the circuit. But now I threw everything at Jim as the clock ticked down and the three-hour time limit approached. I ducked left and right and kept the pressure on the whole way home.

I could see the tyres on the Porsche were shot. Jim was really battling to hang onto it, though he was proving to be a master at positioning his car where I couldn't take a shot at him. Coming into the last corner at Murray's Corner on the final lap, I tried to brake late and deep down the outside on the left of the road as Jim covered the inside line. But the finish line on the other side of the corner was too close and he pipped for me the win by just 0.288 seconds, the closest finish in an endurance race at Bathurst to that time.

It was an epic race, and fun to battle Jim on that track in such cool cars. I did set the GT-Production lap record in that race too, a mark that I am proud to say still stands today.

*

The Bathurst 24 Hour race was only held twice, in 2002 and 2003, and I had a run in the second of those races in a BMW M3 that had been imported from the American IMSA series by its owner, Maher Algadri of Indonesia.

It was a left-hand-drive V8-powered car and gave me a chance to keep racing at Bathurst, even though I'd retired from racing V8 Supercars at the end of the previous year. The driving crew was John Bowe, Greg Crick and Maher.

Top: Behind the wheel of the Team Australia Champ Car on the Gold Coast in 2005. *AN1 Images/Justin Deeley*

Above: The race of my life – Aussie Racing Cars at Bathurst. *AN1 Images/Dirk Klynsmith*

I loved that BMW, and always had a soft spot for left-hand-drive race cars.

Unfortunately, I got a call in the middle of the night not to bother coming back to the track for my next stint. Maher had tangled up with someone on the track and the car was damaged, so we all got to sleep in!

*

In the mid-2000s I had another chance to drive an IndyCar on the Gold Coast – or a Champ Car, as they were known at the time.

It was a Reynard with a Cosworth V8 engine run for Derrick Walker's Team Australia, and evolved out of a dinner with Derrick earlier in the year in the United States. Will Power was driving for the team at the time, and he'd been my teammate at the Bathurst 24 Hour in 2003 – he drove the team's Porsche 911, which was run alongside the BMW M3 I was driving.

I got a lengthy window of time on the track in the Champ Car on a semi-wet track, and just kept going around and around before they finally kicked me off. It was so much fun. The cars in that era were proper race cars. They looked good and sounded good, and the racing was as good as it gets.

*

By November 2013 I had been out of the saddle of full-time racing for ten years but had done bits and pieces of occasional racing when it fitted into my busy schedule.

Craig Baird arranged for me to drive an incredible McLaren GT3 car at the Highlands Motorsport Park in Cromwell, near Queenstown in New Zealand. It was an opportunity I just couldn't pass up, despite feeling in my heart of hearts that I wasn't properly prepared physically for the task.

Track owner Tony Quinn owned the car, a 3.8-litre, twin-turbo V8 rocket ship, and was good enough to entrust Greg Murphy and me with it for the Highlands 101 GT endurance race. The car was a full-blown, GT3-specification race car of the type that races in the Bathurst 12 Hour.

I found the experience somewhat frustrating. I knew what I wanted to do, but I just couldn't execute it properly. It was a case of being out of the saddle way too long.

Even worse was the fact that the event did a Le Mans start, based on how the famous Le Mans 24 Hour used to be started in France. In the old days, drivers would be lined up on the opposite side of the track to their cars parked in the pits, and they'd sprint across to their cars, clamber in and begin the race.

The modern 'Highlands' variant meant, in my case, that Murphy was sitting in the McLaren ready to start the race, while the other co-drivers and I had to sprint a few hundred metres from pit entry towards the cars. From there each co-driver had to rip a Velcro-affixed tag from the window of our cars, which permitted the driver to fire up the engine and leave the pits to start the race.

My first 25 metres was pretty good, and I blazed past some other co-drivers, but I ran out of puff, limping to the car as Murphy flamed me about how long it was taking me to get there! I had calf and ankle trouble for months afterwards.

Once I got into the car and in the race, though, I had a phenomenal battle with Jason Bright, who was driving an Audi. It went on and on, and I was completely stuffed by the end of my driving stint.

The inside of those GT3 race cars are like a sauna. There's no airflow and there's a carbon-fibre firewall right behind the driver's head that separates the pilot from the mid-mounted engine. We took water packs in the car in order to have some hydration mid-race, but it quickly became a hot water bottle, so it was only when I was driving down the main straight and could put my hand out the tiny window that I could guide some air onto my face.

The McLaren was a very cool car. But you had to understand how the floor worked to be able to drive it correctly. It took me a long while to work out. If you changed the way you managed the throttle, it would change the pitch of the underfloor of the car, which dramatically changed the grip level of the car.

Learning how to manage the aero almost came too late, and for a nanosecond at one stage I thought I was going to have the world's biggest crash. If I hadn't applied some more throttle to straighten the car out, they would have been picking up carbon pieces for an hour!

We were in with a shot to get onto the podium, but I brushed a tyre bundle and it got away from us with an extra pit stop to replace a flat tyre.

*

I jumped into another cool race car in 2015 in the Touring Car Masters class at Sydney Motorsport Park: a 1969 Trans

Am Mustang nicknamed 'Sally' whose regular driver was John Bowe.

JB has been very generous to me over the journey: he connected me with my Formula Holden backer Peter Boylan, the Ross Palmer Ferrari 355 drive, and he also opened the door for me to join the Prancing Horse team and drive their BMW M3 with him at the Bathurst 24 Hour. I had a pile of fun and found myself battling with Bowe (aboard a Torana) and Glenn Seton (in another Mustang). It was like a flashback to the mid to late 1990s!

The Mustang (later driven by Steve Johnson) was a cool old car with piles of power, and it behaved nicely. It felt like we were getting the band back together, with a just a few more grey hairs.

In one of the races, I vividly recall rounding the long left-handed corner called Corporate Hill stuck to Glenn's rear bumper. I smiled quietly to myself: it was history repeating.

As much as I thoroughly enjoyed skidding around in those 2013 and 2015 race outings, deep down I knew it was time to give away the notion of racing. The satisfaction of properly driving a racing car was all about putting in a proper effort. The truth was I wasn't fully focused, fit or wholly dedicated to the task. It was time to stop.

*

I'm often asked to nominate the 'best race' of my career, and that's easy. The best race I ever had was in one of Phil Ward's Aussie Racing Cars, which I drove from time to time after my professional career ended. Phil invited me to race one of his cars at Bathurst in 2006, at the Bathurst International Motor Festival event at Mount Panorama.

The little Yamaha-powered, tube-frame, scaled-down racing cars were great to drive. Once you wound yourself up enough to 'believe' in the capability of the car, it was possible to hang on tight and make it from the exit of the Cutting to Skyline 100 per cent flat on the throttle, but the car was right on the ragged edge when you did that.

An old sparring partner, Paul Morris, and I enthused like kids with our war stories after practice about how hard you could drive the car over the top of the Mountain, and the fact that the boundaries kept shifting — we went on especially about how out of control we could be off Skyline and down the hill! It was truly breathtaking what we got away with.

The racing quality was beyond epic. I don't recall how many races we did or all the dirty details. All I remember is leading one of the races, then being fifth, then third, then seventh — there were cars everywhere. Wardy and his boys, James and Brad, were in the mix with Paul. You could hear other cars but only see them once they were next to you. It was hardcore, seat-of-the-pants, balls-to-the-wall racing on the best track in the world.

I recall leading in one of the races on the second-last lap down into the Chase, then I copped a tap from Paul in the tail. I steered into the slide, tightened the steering lock to the lock stops, picked up the throttle to 100 per cent and spun out of my misery in a cloud of blue smoke, and I still finished just behind the lead pack!

Best races ever? Yep, those Bathurst Aussie Racing Car races with Morris and a bunch of other maniacs win by a mile! Not because they'll ever show in a record book as a grand event with stature, but simply for enjoying the raw excitement of driving at 100 per cent and squeezing everything there was out of those cars, and racing so hard against so many other guys simultaneously.

The late Jason Richards came up to me after one of the races and said, 'Dude, that was epic! You guys are totally mad!'

Driving cars like the McLaren, the Ferrari, Indy and Champ Cars, the BMW M3, the Nissan GT-R, Japanese and British Formula 3000 machines and everything else I have raced over the journey has, without doubt, given me the best seat in the house in motorsport.

Reflections

Mark Webber – nine-time Formula 1 Grand Prix Winner, 2015 World Endurance Champion

I remember sitting in Neil's loungeroom as a young Formula Ford driver, seeking his advice on many elements of motorsport. I was crazily green behind the eyes on the Monday to Friday business of racing in those days and he gave me a crash course on the reality of how the commercial side of the sport worked.

It was an absolute fluke I managed to drop onto the radar of some great guys, including Neil, who were very open with their knowledge, and I soaked it up as much as I could. Good people try and introduce you to more good people and that's what he did for me back in those days.

I had so much respect for him when I was younger, mainly because he had been a single seater driver and I had a lot more respect for guys who had raced 'wings and slicks' cars rather than just touring cars. My natural affinity for that style of racing drew me to him to seek advice when I was younger, and we had a strong relationship from the beginning.

Neil's not a complicated guy. What you see is what you get. It's advertised on the tin with him. He's a total workaholic, so it was hard to ever get him away from work to come to an F1 race overseas, which we finally managed to do at the Belgian Grand Prix in 2012.

Neil has a great way of relating to the audience as a broadcaster. He can narrate so well and build great live theatre around it. He's world-class and I think, to some extent, he's been wasted in Australia because he could have done more abroad. He's world class when it comes to presenting our sport in a way that few can.

I have no doubt you could drop Neil into any motorsport broadcast with any category around the world and he would hold his own, though I reckon his style would suit the Americans for sure. Their culture is right up his alley.

It takes a lot of self-discipline to put in the level of research that Neil does. When you have flat periods when the track isn't giving you much with the race itself, you have to dig into that research and how he orchestrates to be so prepared for those situations is to be admired.

He's a ripping bloke, an absolute cracker.

Mark Webber let me try out his Red Bull F1 car at Spa in 2012.
Motorsport Images/Emily Davenport

27

RACING FOR THE BLUE OVAL

MY FAMILY HAD A lot of different road cars when I was a kid, but a Cortina was the only Ford I recall us having in our driveway. Despite that, the Crompton family was never anti-Ford. In fact, our family friends owned the local dealer in Ballarat, Eclipse Motors.

One of my earliest automotive recollections is visiting the Ford You Yangs test track facility between Melbourne and Geelong as a five-year-old, when Ford decided to run the Falcon-Mobil 70,000-mile Durability Run. The concept was to have a swag of leading race drivers pound around day and night in a bunch of Falcons and prove how reliable the cars were. I have no idea how we came to be there, but it was through Dad and his local dealer connection.

The blue oval has a huge history in motorsport, although I didn't find myself racing one until I returned to Australia midway through 1998 and joined Glenn Seton's Ford Credit–backed team in V8 Supercars. I came close to racing a Ford eight years before that as a stunt-double for Peter Brock's Mobil 1 Racing team.

When I moved to the Holden Racing Team in 1989, Peter and his team moved on to race a pair of Ford Sierras imported from Englishman Andy Rouse that had raced in the previous year's British Touring Car Championship. Brock continued with the turbo Fords in 1990, and at that year's Eastern Creek 500 I ended up at the wheel of his #05 car in practice.

I was on standby to replace Mark Skaife in the Nissan GT-R, though it soon became apparent that Skaife would, no matter how he looked or felt, take his place in his car.

Suddenly Brock's Mobil 1 team manager, Alan Gow, came bursting into the Nissan pits looking for me. 'What are you doing here, Crompton, you idiot?' he asked.

'Well, I might need to jump into the Nissan to do a few laps,' I said. 'Why?'

There was a bit of an emergency, Alan explained. Brock's scheduled co-driver, former open-wheeler star Andrew Miedecke from Port Macquarie, had a massive case of … well, diarrhoea.

'Oh, how terrible for poor Andy,' I said. 'When can I start?'

So here I was, a contracted Holden Racing Team driver, standing in the factory Nissan pit and about to be bundled hurriedly into a Mobil Ford Sierra. What a shocking racing tart I was!

I jumped into the Sierra, grabbed first gear and wobbled off down pit lane onto the track. Instantly I understood why they were so potent. The Sierra touring car featured a two-litre, four-cylinder turbocharged engine. Once the turbo spooled up, it gave plenty of additional punch and made the car take off with a thump in the back!

It was the worst, most horrible racing machine I'd ever driven in my life! It was like the engine was hard-mounted, metal-to-metal, to the cross member. It was a harsh, nasty, vibrating thing to drive.

The way it delivered its power with the turbo is easy to explain. You'd put your foot on the gas pedal and there would be no grunt on offer at all.

Wait ...

Wait ...

Wait ...

Keep waiting ...

And then BANG!

All the 500-plus horsepower arrived at one moment, like there'd been an explosion. The car would lurch sideways with wheelspin and try and spit itself into the nearest trackside fence!

I only did three laps before coming back into the pits, where an official told me I needed to report to Race Control immediately. The Race Director, Tim Schenken, wanted to see me.

I wandered into Race Control and was met by Tim. He was anything but pleased to have seen me on the track in the Sierra. 'Neil, what on earth do you think you're doing?' he exclaimed.

I explained I had just gone out to do some practice laps in the Sierra because Miedecke was unwell.

'But you're not entered in that car! You haven't filled out a single piece of paperwork – and to make matters worse, you're entered in another car! Who are you actually driving for?'

'Well, as a matter of fact, Tim, I drive for the Holden Racing Team,' I pointed out. 'But they're not here this weekend, so I'm supposed to be driving the Nissan, but Mark Skaife's now driving that car so maybe I'm having a drive with PB in the Sierra ...'

He threw me out of his office, clearly unhappy with my fact-based responses! Skaife got into the Nissan, Miedecke got his backside under control and I watched the race at home on TV. There was no fine and no notation on my licence, I just got told off. Naturally, I blamed Gow. Tim and I are great mates these days and he was well within his rights to kick my backside!

*

Racing a Ford next came up on my radar in 1998. My stocks were up after the American racing adventure of 1997. Tasman Motorsports and its boss, Steve Horne, had totally restored my confidence.

I dearly wanted to stay in the United States, but I didn't have the funds or the clout to hang on long enough to be able to leap into sportscar racing. Steve wanted me to stay on at Tasman and maintain a role within the IndyCar team alongside him. That was certainly appealing, but I just wanted to race cars.

I took a call simultaneously from the reigning V8 Supercars Champion, Glenn Seton. He reached out with an offer for me to join his team, and I gladly took him up on the opportunity and moved back to Australia. He ran me in a second Falcon in selected rounds of that year's championship, and I co-drove with him at Sandown and Bathurst.

I had a great relationship with Glenn from my time at Channel Seven and also as a driver. It's a warm friendship that endures to this very day.

He'd left the Nissan factory team at the end of 1988 and established his own team in 1989. He wasn't an overly commercial or managerial guy – his roots were in the workshop. That was something I always admired about Glenn. A second-generation racer – his father, Barry, won Bathurst in 1965 and was a racer and engine builder for years – Glenn said there was a good chance his team would become the official Ford factory team for 1999.

If I made a mistake at that point in time, it was probably being seduced by the allure of working for another factory-backed team. I'd done it with Holden some years earlier and it happened again with Ford, who were coming back into the sport as a major sponsor of Glenn's team.

Glenn Seton Racing was rebranded as Ford Tickford Racing for 1999, but while it appeared from the outside to be a Ford factory team, it really wasn't. The cars were blue with the Ford logo down the side of them, but Ford didn't own or run them.

I came from an era when Ford factory team racing, with stars like Allan Moffat, Fred Gibson and Ian Geoghegan driving, was a big beacon, and the lure of that was special. They had huge support, engineering, money and muscle coming directly from head office. My decision to join Glenn's team proved to be a good one, but it ultimately didn't work out as I had hoped. It was probably a case of bad timing rather than any other influence.

His team had been top runners in the 1990s. They had a supply of very good Bridgestone tyres, he'd won the championship in 1993 and 1997, and his offer was a life raft for me at a time when I felt I was drowning, career-wise. I thought there were sufficient good reasons to sign up to drive for him. Glenn was the reigning champion and his team wanted to sign me up.

This was in an era when V8 Supercar racing became much more corporate. John Crennan and his HSV/HRT operation set a new benchmark for success on and off the track, and there was a huge war between Holden and Ford. At one point around that time the combined spend between the two biggest rivals in the V8 Supercar paddock, taking in both direct and indirect industry support, was estimated at a staggering $40 million.

Every team had support in one way or another. At worst, the smallest teams had supplies of free panels; at best, manufacturers were paying drivers fat contracts and wrestling them away from one another between seasons. In my view, this newly corporate style of motorsport caught Glenn out a bit and eventually overshadowed his manner of operating. He had a smaller race team and a small group of loyal team members in Dandenong, in the south-east of Melbourne, with some factory driven financial support.

Motor racing is full of 'wins that got away' but the Gold Coast V8 Supercar event in 1998 was one that definitely escaped Glenn and I early in our relationship.

In those days, the event on the streets of Surfers Paradise, supporting the IndyCar race, was not a round of the V8

Top: Gold Coast, 1998 – the event I was leading before the car broke and Mark Larkham went by to win. *AN1 Images/Dirk Klynsmith*

Above: On the podium at the Canberra 400 V8 Supercar event in 2000. *AN1 Images/Andrew Hall*

championship, so most teams sent their old cars north and left their Bathurst 1000 cars safely under covers in their workshop, so they couldn't be creased by the concrete walls surrounding the Gold Coast track. Glenn hated the place with a passion, and had damaged one of his Falcons and himself the previous year when the throttle stuck on and he slammed head-first into a tyre wall.

For the 1998 event, I drove one of the team's older cars and he sat out, donning a radio headset to take up race engineering duties instead. It meant I had the chance to drive in front of the same IndyCar community I'd been racing in front of and living within the previous year.

Given the track was made up of regular streets, it had such an uneven surface that you needed to be able to do something we call 'trail braking'. What that meant was keeping a little pressure on the brake pedal as you rolled up to a corner without locking up the inside front wheel. I pushed Glenn to increase the rear spring rate and change the ride heights to better suit the undulations of the streets, and as a result we went from having a car that was a solid top five contender to an absolute jet!

I got held up by Paul Romano in the fast chicane on the back side of the track; if not for that, I'd bet one of my kids' lives I would have been on pole position. Despite lining up fourth on the grid, I knew I had a car capable of winning a race.

These days, Mark Larkham forms a crucial part of our on-air line-up in our TV telecasts of the Supercars Championship. We're great mates, but on that day on the Gold Coast in October 1998 he was just another competitor. I sliced my way past Larko under brakes to take the lead and started pulling away from him.

That was when the racing gods tore up the script. The Watt's link bolt that held the car's rear suspension together broke. I limped back to the pits and was forced to retire from the race. Glenn was seriously cranky about the mechanical failure.

Maybe that car had a 'bad luck halo'. I found out years later that I was driving the same car that weekend that Glenn had in the lead at the 1995 Bathurst 1000, until its engine failed with nine laps to go.

The worst part of that whole Gold Coast scenario was that Larkham went on to win! He'd never won a V8 Supercar race before that day, and promptly went out and won again the following day. I've never heard the end of it ever since, but good luck, Larko. That's racing – these days we get along like brothers. I love the bloke!

*

I stayed with Glenn's team until the end of the 2000 season. We showed plenty of promise and occasionally had strong results. The highlight of the year came when I grabbed a podium result on the Canberra street track, a freezing location for a V8 Supercar round on the Queen's Birthday long weekend in June.

Glenn found himself in a very difficult position politically at around that time. Clearly there were those within Ford who didn't want to be involved with Glenn, and would have preferred to have full control of their own team rather than sponsoring his. I could feel the anxiety, headaches and grief he was dealing with on a day-to-day basis. Neither of us really achieved what we wanted to on the race track.

That Ford Tickford Racing chapter didn't work out as it could have, but Glenn and I remain warm friends to this day. I've also called upon his vast experience and skill as a guest driver in the Toyota GAZOO Racing Australia 86 Series to help coach young competitors.

With Glenn, what you see is what you get. He's a lovely guy, and we'll be close mates to the end.

Adding to the challenges of this period, my marriage to Sally ended. Thankfully, although we made the call to split, Sally and I made intelligent decisions and remained 100 per cent committed to providing the best for our daughter, Emma, as reliable and loving parents. Sally and I each got on with our lives and raised a beautiful daughter. We remain friends to this day.

Reflections

Glenn Seton – Australian Touring Car Champion 1993 and 1997, Supercars Hall of Famer

Neil is very professional in everything he does in life, whether it be as a race driver, as a TV commentator, a businessman or a human being! He's an out and out professional, very detailed, very passionate about motorsport and the industry that he's in.

We've enjoyed a fantastic relationship for many years, and I've witnessed his contribution to Australian motorsport from all angles. In the early years it was from my place as a driver and Neil's as a television commentator. He was the one in the red Channel Seven jacket interviewing me after I won my first Australian Touring Car Championship race at Calder in 1987.

From there he moved further into driving and we were teammates on the track, co-drivers sharing a car in the biggest race of the year at Bathurst, and Neil was an integral part of our team behind the scenes with his knowledge and expertise in marketing, sponsorship and general advice.

He was instrumental in helping establish and grow Ford Tickford Racing in the time he was with me. He did an exceptional job in and out of the car during his time with the team.

Neil has always been very underrated as a driver. He had just come back from the United States when we first drove together in 1998, and his speed, concentration levels and the effort he put in was exceptional. His pace was unbelievable throughout the race at Bathurst that year. People on the outside don't see that stuff, and co-drivers generally get overlooked, but Neil proved he was the real deal that day.

He's wired as a perfectionist. In a way that was perhaps a little detrimental to his driving career, but Neil is so particular and meticulous to everything in life – from combing his hair to putting on his shoes the right way!

I really appreciate our friendship and all of the great things we've been able to do in motorsport together. We're mates for life.

Glenn Seton. *AN1 Images/Andrew Hall*

28

SLIDING DOORS

'SO YOU'RE TELLING ME you're knocking back the opportunity to drive for Dick Johnson?'

It was December 1998, and these words came from Dick Johnson Racing's CEO, Wayne Cattach, a former Shell executive who had joined Johnson's famous Ford team some years earlier to bolster and run the business.

Only a matter of weeks earlier, we had sat, along with Dick, in a hotel room at the Novotel in Melbourne, and they had offered me the chance to drive the team's brand new #18 Shell Helix–sponsored Ford Falcon AU race car in the 1999 V8 Supercars Championship, then known as the Shell Championship Series. I'd be teammates with Dick, the five-time Australian Touring Car Champion, three-time Bathurst 1000 winner and outright Queensland legend.

The 1999 season would turn out to be Dick's farewell

tour, as he made the call that he would step down from V8 Supercars racing at the completion of the year.

I still remember the call I placed to Wayne from my parents' place in Ballarat just before Christmas. He was totally flabbergasted. I was indeed turning down the opportunity to become teammates with Dick Johnson.

I outlined my reasons in a fax (remember them?!) to Wayne, a copy of which I dug out only recently.

'As I noted in my calls, after much consideration, I've decided to decline your invitation and will remain with Glenn Seton Racing (GSR) next season with the possibility of some Sportscar racing in the US too,' I wrote. 'The decision has more to do with comfort, continuity and my performances at GSR, than anything particularly negative about your offer or team. In other circumstances it would be a terrific opportunity, but right now I want to return the faith shown by Glenn and Noel [Watson, Glenn's then business manager] earlier this year as we try to grow our partnership. Thanks again, and best wishes for the 1999 season. (Just don't go too well!)'

My decision had nothing to do with my feelings about Dick or his team. I had known him and his wife, Jill, for a long time. I had a warm relationship with Glenn and the allure of being a factory driver for Ford was also part of my decision. Glenn had given me the chance to return to V8 Supercars the previous year, and loyalty was a big thing for me. I followed my heart.

If I had my time over, I'd have been more ruthless in my racing career, and more cold-blooded in the decisions I made to join or leave teams. If you look at the history books and the results of Glenn's and Dick's teams over the following years, you could argue I made the wrong decision. My potential DJR deal never made it into the public domain at the time. The Kiwi Paul Radisich ended up with the drive alongside Dick, and would spend the next four seasons with the team.

Who knows what it would have looked like had I done the deal to join DJR for 1999? Motor racing is full of sliding doors moments like that one. You can only briefly ponder where you might have ended up had you made a different decision. And that's just life – there's no point daydreaming.

*

At that point, I'd made contact with a bunch of sportscar teams and I was loosely in the running to join the then relatively new Panoz team in the United States, though ultimately I lost out on the drive to Dane Jan Magnussen.

My hunt for American sportscar racing opportunities when the North American touring car project dried up delivered me to Brit Tony Dowe, whom I knew from his time working for Tom Walkinshaw at TWR and spearheading TWR's Jaguar Sportscar program in the United States in the 1990s. By the late '90s he'd ended up at the Panoz team, founded and owned by Dr Don Panoz, an American who had made his fortune in the pharmaceutical industry, and who had a concept to build and race a unique front-engined sportscar.

Tony gave me a chance to get onto the short list, and I flew out to America to visit the team and attend a test with them at Road Atlanta. They had a heap of cars and needed a squadron of drivers, but ultimately I didn't get the chance to drive the team's unique V8-engined beast.

Magnussen had recently raced in Formula 1, and was far more qualified for the gig than I was. I would love to have continued my American racing journey, but what I had done in touring cars didn't hold much sway with the sportscar community over there, so getting an opportunity without a fistful of cash was near on impossible.

29
GIVING BACK

THESE DAYS, JAMES COURTNEY is the oldest full-time driver on the grid of the Supercars Championship. He won the championship in 2010 for Dick Johnson Racing and has always enjoyed a prominent profile in the mainstream media since making the decision to step into V8 Supercars in the mid-2000s after a glittering junior career overseas. However, late in 1998 his career looked very much like it was over before it had really got started.

I had just started driving with Glenn Seton's team, and I was introduced by Kim White to James and his parents, Jim and Deanna. Kim was heavily involved with karting. In fact, he and his son Damien (who later became a V8 Ute champion and competed at a high level in a range of car racing categories) looked after the kart that I used as a training tool, driving it to keep my skills sharp in between car racing events.

GIVING BACK

James had been a two-time karting world champion, and lived overseas since he was a kid, but he was flat-footed and had no leads on making the step up into car racing. No one in his world really knew how to help him reach the next level, and there was a real prospect his racing career was over before it had started.

When James came onto the scene in my world, I was still racing professionally, and I certainly didn't covet the notion of being a driver manager. He and his father asked if I could help, so I reached out to three people I knew well to see if they might assist: Malcolm Oastler (an Aussie who was a gun designer and part-owner of Reynard race cars, and later worked in F1 with British American Racing and Jaguar), Steve Horne and Alan Gow.

Of the three, it was Alan who found the prospect of managing James interesting, and he ultimately took up the option of managing the young driver. He even stumped up the cash to get him into British Formula Ford racing in 1999, and onto British Formula 3 after that. The investment paid off in the years that followed, as James won the British Formula Ford Championship in 2000 and led the British Formula 3 Championship in 2002 before a nasty high-speed testing crash at Monza in a Jaguar Formula 1 car derailed his campaign. Moving his career to Japan, he kept winning in 2003, claiming the Japanese Formula 3 Championship before settling on a future in V8 Supercars.

Had it not been for Alan's cash and foresight, James would probably have been laying carpet in Penrith in the family business. Gow took the risk and plunged his money into James.

I was very tough on James at times back in those early days. Before he went to race Formula Ford in England, I hired a Formula Ford from Brad Jones and went to Calder in Melbourne so I could have a look at James behind the wheel. I laid out the witches' hats on the circuit and growled at him whenever he missed the apexes of corners.

I assessed him from all angles – driving, physical fitness, I looked at it all. And I wrote a comprehensive document for him on what he needed to do to become a professional racing driver. He had a great innate skill for driving fast, but he needed to understand that to get anywhere in the sport, he had to craft himself in every aspect of the business.

We had to apply plenty of tough love to James on occasion. He had impeccable junior credentials and was a likeable young kid, but trying to get him to apply himself and stay focused was a challenge.

I remember one poignant moment with James. We went to see Peter Hill from Globe International, the youth-aimed footwear, apparel and skate/surf business brand. Peter was willing to put some additional funding into James as a forward investment to try to get him into the Formula 1 paddock, or into IndyCar racing in America. It's a model that others have used in their attempts to get to the highest level of international racing, but it would have triggered a lot of debt for James.

James and I met with Peter for a time, then we drove away and sat in a side street for a chat. That was when James completely broke down. With tears pouring out of his eyes, he told me he didn't want to live overseas anymore – he wanted to come back and race in Australia and race in V8 Supercars. He'd missed so much of his life as a teenager living overseas karting, and he didn't want to miss anything else.

I immediately put him in touch with Mark Skaife, and James drove for Skaife's Holden Racing Team in the 2005 endurance races at Sandown and Bathurst. Then he joined Stone Brothers Racing as the NASCAR-bound Marcos Ambrose's replacement for the 2006 season.

James has long since converted his skills into a successful Supercars career, complete with all the normal ups and downs. We see each other at events, and occasionally there's a call in either direction. James is now the elder statesman of the full-time Supercars driver squad.

*

Everyone has somebody, or a number of people, who give them a leg up along the way in the early parts of their career. For me, it was the likes of Mike Raymond, Peter McKay, Mike Griffin, Ron Krause, Wally Storey and Peter Boylan. These people went the extra yard – they didn't get paid, or if they did it was never enough; they just wanted to help in whatever way they could.

His thank you for my help back in the early days today sits on my wrist. Some years ago, out of the blue, as we were sitting in the hotel foyer in Launceston, Tasmania, he presented me with a Breitling watch as thanks for my help over 20 years earlier. It was a touching moment.

Other drivers along the way have asked me about providing driver management services, and I regularly get calls and emails from young hopefuls, but it's not a path I want to pursue. I feel a bit of a duty though as a 'tribal elder' to assist others in fulfilling their motor racing dreams where I can, when I can. I'm happy to pass on advice to young racers,

I worked closely with Neal Bates on the Toyota GAZOO Racing Australia 86 Series. *Crompton collection*

especially about how they might go about their business off the track.

My proudest project as a contributor to the next generation of racers is my involvement in the Toyota GAZOO Racing Australia 86 Series. I've been a Toyota ambassador since 2008, and for years I would wander down to the head office at Caringbah, in the south of Sydney, to discuss all things motorsport with Toyota's long-serving PR and media guru Mike Breen.

I did lots of different things for Toyota over time, but I always wanted to find a way to do something meaningful in motorsport with the biggest automotive player in the Australian market. In 2015 that chance arrived. The Japanese Chief Engineer of the Toyota 86 project, Tada San, declared that the company wanted to race the Toyota 86 in series around the globe, with a vision to hold a World Cup one day to find the champions' champion.

My old friend and former Ford Tickford Racing teammate Neal Bates, a four-time Australian Rally Champion, took on the technical portfolio and my organisation was signed to a long-term contract to administer the series for Toyota.

Since 2016, the 86 Series has been a runaway success, with capacity grids and great racing. New stars are constantly emerging. We found the sweet spot, with the right balance of car and running costs, operating on the main stage at Supercars events, television coverage, and all supported by a significant promotional investment to help unveil the stars of tomorrow with a serious digital and social campaign in support.

To see drivers such as Will Brown, Cameron Hill and Broc Feeney now making their way up the ladder is extremely gratifying.

30

THE KID AND GREEN-EYED MONSTERS

I LEFT GLENN SETON'S team at the end of 2000 with nowhere to go.

Then I took a call from Seton's former business manager Noel Watson and Fred Gibson. They told me, on the quiet, that they were putting together another Ford-supported team for the new season, and they had a big piece of news, although it had to stay secret: Craig Lowndes was jumping from Holden to Ford to drive for it.

Lowndes's move was the biggest story leading into the 2001 season, and one of the biggest news stories in that era of Australian motorsport. And they signed me up to be his teammate.

What I didn't know at the time was that although the team was named Gibson Motorsport, it wasn't completely Fred's project. In the background, the company was owned by Bob Forbes, whom I had driven for back in 1993 before he sold his team to Wayne Gardner.

I noticed something strange when my first pay cheque turned up: it was from a bank in the northern suburbs of Sydney. I didn't understand why I was being paid from a Sydney bank when the race team and Fred were based in Melbourne.

Then Bob Forbes, whom I have great admiration and respect for to this day, called me up. 'Welcome aboard,' he said in his customary quiet way.

I had no idea Bob was the money man behind the 'new' Gibson Motorsport. He had been a great customer of the Gibson team in the early 1990s, and had run a Nissan GT-R built by Fred's team and backed by GIO Insurance as a sponsor. Sadly, their association in 2001 ended in terrible acrimony, and led to the once good friends becoming enemies after a vicious legal dispute.

*

I knew Craig Lowndes, my new teammate, from the time he first arrived on the scene in motorsport. I was in the Coke team with Wayne Gardner in 1994, when a nineteen-year-old Lowndes made his Bathurst 1000 debut, and we both headed overseas to race in 1997 – me in North America and Craig in European Formula 3000, after a stellar season the year prior with the Holden Racing Team that saw him win the Australian Touring Car Championship, the Sandown 500 and the Bathurst 1000.

He made huge headlines around that time, and I found it pretty appealing to drive alongside him and join the team. I've never shirked from being up against a big name or highly talented teammate. I see different drivers in both local and international motorsport who get carried away with who their teammate is or isn't. I always felt that to be the best, you need to go up against the best, and you either progress or you don't.

Being teammates with Craig was great. At that point in his career, he had glided through the system with enormous success. In a race car, he's a freak. And I mean that as the ultimate compliment.

He's the best known living race driver in Australia, racking up seven Bathurst 1000 wins (only Peter Brock has more) and a record 14 podium finishes in the Great Race. He won the Australian Formula Ford Championship in 1993 and three Australian Touring Car/V8 Supercars Championships across 1996, 1998 and 1999.

Lowndes is one of the ultra-rare breed of drivers who has a sixth sense, one more than mere mortals like me. They somehow have some form of accelerometer in their bum that knows what they're going to feel through the seat within their racing car, and can steer and work the pedals in a way to drive faster than seems possible. And when I became teammates with Lowndes, I got to see this in action from close range.

I recall testing up at Winton, in north-eastern Victoria, with Lowndes and the Gibson team on a cold, cloudy, miserable day. The track was patchy wet and he went out of the pits at the start of the day on old tyres, and within just three laps – a warm-up lap, a flying lap and a second flyer – laid down a lap time that was the very best of the day. Even he could not get close to it again over the remainder of the eight-hour session.

'Are you kidding me?' I remember thinking.

I vividly remember going out onto the track after him and arriving at turn ten on my warm-up lap and moving aside as he went barrelling by. What I saw next sums up Lowndes to a tee. I slowed and moved to the left for him, and he arrived down the right side of my car in a blaze. The rear of his car was hopping and bouncing, with the rear brakes partially locked up. He turned the wheel aggressively, smashed over the inside kerb at the apex of the corner and his silver-and-black Falcon launched onto two wheels. Then it dropped back down and he slid all the way to the right-side exit kerb, then rooster-tailed over the edge and just into the dirt like a motocross bike, before setting off down the straight towards the next corner.

I saw all this from the best seat in the house, and instantly dismissed what I had just witnessed. 'Well, he stuffed that lap up,' I thought. 'His time for that one will be no good at all.'

But then I wandered back into the pits and asked my engineer, Ross Holder, to tell me what sort of lap times Lowndes was doing to get an idea of the track conditions. And that was when I saw his time for 'that' lap. Despite looking like he was out of control, he was rocket-ship fast. He has an insane ability to just make a car look wild and weird on the track and still turn out a fast lap time on the stopwatch.

My last Bathurst 1000 start came in 2002 in this 00 Motorsport Falcon with Craig Lowndes. It overheated when a plastic bag blocked the air intakes. *AN1 Images/Graeme Neander*

Another of his great attributes is that he wasn't ultra-fussy about his car. You could change a million things on the setup and he'd still do the same lap time – he could drive around things.

I just couldn't drive that way. In Crompton world I needed a warm-up lap, the first and second flying lap, and probably another two more flying laps, and maybe a trip to the pits to make some setup tweaks to the car, before I could find my rhythm. It's akin to a bowler in cricket needing an over to warm up and get their eye in, before they really start hitting the pitch in the right spot.

The bottom line was really simple: Craig was better than me. He was better in the clinches, and that made all the difference.

As the stars of today's Supercars Championship show, you can't be a driver who chips away quietly and methodically. You have to go out there and wring the car's neck to within a millimetre of its life from the instant you hit the track. You can't leave anything on the table.

*

Lowndes's reign at the top has been extraordinary. To begin with, it was the combination of Craig, the HRT Commodores and Bridgestone tyres that delivered a wave of success. Then he went through the crushing few years when he joined Ford, with very few results to speak of. Off the back of two years with Ford Performance Racing he found his way to Triple Eight Race Engineering in 2005, and he hasn't looked back since. Team owner Roland Dane set up the circumstances he needed to really flourish, and gave him crucial engineering support.

In my period of racing with him, Craig was probably more interested in signing the glovebox of some bloke's Torana XU-1 in the car park at Winton than in sitting down and examining the graph of the shock absorbers in his race car. And I mean that as a compliment to him. If you can get the right structure around a driver and keep it simple, then that can be an advantage. Often that's better than carrying around a head full of conflict and crazy engineering theories.

My deal to join as Craig's teammate at Gibson Motorsport was compromised from the very start. I was due to drive the team's second car in 2001, but it never appeared, and I spent all year (bar the endurance races, when I was co-driving with Craig) commentating for Channel Ten on television. It was a familiar tale. Again, things looked good on paper but didn't pan out.

The team debuted a brand-new car at Bathurst that was quickly dubbed the 'Green Eyed Monster' by the industry. Its silver and black livery and fluoro-green headlights made it a menacing force on the track and one of the most memorable liveries seen in V8 Supercar racing.

But the whole deal just didn't work. Forbes and Gibson split at the end of 2001, and the team was renamed as 00 Motorsport.

I had a new car for 2002. It looked the same as Craig's but they were completely different underneath the panels. His was built from a Ford body shell supplied direct from Ford, while mine was a chassis from On Track Engineering in Queensland, the company engaged to build Falcon V8 Supercar chassis for customers. Nothing we did on the cars ever correlated. What worked on Craig's car didn't adapt to mine, and vice versa.

THE KID AND GREEN-EYED MONSTERS

But I will forever be proud of my drive with Craig in 2002, in my last Bathurst 1000 start.

I was racing at the front in my last stint in a battle with Russell Ingall's Castrol car and Jim Richards in Mark Skaife's HRT Commodore. The car was performing really well, and I was right on Russell's tail and maintaining a margin over Jimmy. Our engineer, Oscar Fiorinotto, had done a beautiful job on the chassis and we were right in the battle. I felt totally in harmony with the car.

I handed it over to Lowndes for the final stint to the chequered flag, and glanced up at the TV monitor after I had got out – only to see our car smouldering. A plastic bag had lodged in the front spoiler. The blockage had choked the supply of fresh air to the engine and the engine cooked itself.

I sat in the front of the truck watching TV, so devastated I literally couldn't speak. I was completely choked up. I don't think we had what it took to win the race on absolute pace, but we were right among the cars that ultimately finished on the podium.

*

I spent a lot of time in 2002 working behind the scenes, convincing Steve Horne to buy 00 Motorsport and come back to motorsport in V8 Supercars. We had very earnest discussions with Geoff Polites, Howard Marsden and Louise Teesdale at Ford (sadly, all three are no longer with us), and Steve and I bailed Howard up on the fence in the pits at Pukekohe late in 2002 in a last-ditch effort to make our case. We had a deal done with Bob Forbes for him to sell the team to Steve, though the deal was subject to Ford's sponsorship continuing.

I knew Steve had the runs on the board in the United States and the managerial skills to turn the team around: it could have been the counterpoint to the then ultra-successful Holden Racing Team on the 'other' side of the manufacturer fence. I was determined to break through all the politics and bullshit that was diverting what should have been a concentrated effort to set up a Ford team that could replicate what was being done by Holden.

It came down to Ford choosing between two parties for its backing for 2003. On the one hand there was Steve and Tasman Motorsports, built from the base of 00 Motorsport. On the other side was English racing business Prodrive, headed by David Richards, who based his bid partly on a proposition to buy Glenn Seton out of his team.

In the end, Ford selected Prodrive, and Ford Performance Racing was born.

Had Steve bought 00 Motorsport and came into V8 Supercars, I reckon I would have continued driving. I was 42 years old in 2002 and might have done another year or even two as a full-time driver for the team, before moving into a management role. But the failed deal between Tasman and Ford was the last straw for me as a professional racing driver. By the end of 2002, I knew my goose was cooked.

I had other opportunities thrown at me, and a myriad of enduro drives, but I was only interested in staying at a front-running, properly funded and properly engineered and managed team with a competitive engine program.

You'd like to think it's as simple as signing up a good driver and putting them into a good car, and everyone lives happily ever after. But it's not. With the technicalities of the sport – all the engineering and setup choices – I think of

THE KID AND GREEN-EYED MONSTERS

it like 1000 ropes hanging from a ceiling. You have to pull the right ones by just the right amount and only in the right sequence in order to succeed. It's that complicated.

Unless every single element in every corner of the business is firing, you will not succeed. That means public relations, commercial, sponsorship, engineering, fabrication, composites, data, vehicle dynamics, electronics, engines, as well as the mental and physical skills of drivers, engineers, owners and management, and all the regular efficiencies of running any normal business.

What I know now, as I look back on my driving career, is that too many times I wasn't quite able to get myself into a position where I could have enough of those things in the correct sequence. I'm not one of those people who says, 'Oh, give me Mark Skaife's HRT car and I would have won the championship for sure.' It's never a single magic bullet that delivers the gold in this business. Motor racing is a giant, complicated, collective team sport.

Look at what Mark did at HRT (three straight championship wins from 2000 to 2002), what Marcos Ambrose did at Stone Brothers Racing (two in a row in 2003 and 2004) and what Jamie Whincup has done at Triple Eight (a record seven championship wins since 2008). Most people would think, 'Yep, the guy with their name on the side of the car deserves the credit for those results.' In truth, a giant apparatus has to be working smoothly for those championships to be won.

Way back in 1985, before I started my racing career, I attended the Allan Grice Race Driving School at Amaroo Park in Sydney. They had little Nissan Pulsar school cars, and Gricey ran it out of his race shop, which was next to the track. He gave a speech to the class members that day, and to this very day it echoes long and loud in my brain.

'You might think that driving the car is the hardest thing in motorsport, or you might think that understanding the engineering will be the hardest thing,' he said. 'You might think that getting the money together is the hardest thing, but you're wrong. Make no mistake: the hardest thing is getting back up off the floor.'

He made this speech to a room full of wannabe racing drivers. I remember thinking, 'Has Gricey gone mad? What the bloody hell is he on about?'

Well, by the end of that 2002 season, I knew exactly what he was talking about.

Reflections

Craig Lowndes — seven-time Bathurst 1000 Winner, three-time Australian Touring Car Champion

Neil and I have always had a fantastic relationship. There's never been any egos between us and I've learned a lot from him both on and off the track.

I might have always seemed comfortable in front of a camera, but when we were teammates, he helped build my confidence in hosting and presenting corporate events where I'd have to get up in front of a live audience of people and talk – a very different task to getting out of a race car and answering questions on TV!

That mentoring continued when I joined him on the TV side of the fence in 2019. I leaned on Neil quite a lot to understand what that environment was going to look like, how to handle it and how to approach it – just as Peter Brock helped me in my early days of driving.

He's got a huge amount of pride in presenting things to a high standard and is very passionate in the way he operates, something that shines through when you sit alongside him as he flies a plane. The time I sat shoulder-to-shoulder with Neil in his little Cessna, flying into a headwind from Brisbane to Townsville – a trip that takes an hour and 20 minutes commercially – is four and a half hours of my life I'll never get back! But watching him manage the controls, the gauges, a map, a stopwatch and passing landmarks must mirror the impressive traffic management that goes on in his brain as he commentates.

At any given moment he's listening to multiple radio channels of drivers, race control and TV producers, plus watching timing screens and TV monitors.

To then be able to articulate the information he's learned – combined with his understanding of what's going on for a driver in the cockpit – into something interesting and insightful, and to break down the complexity of the sport and communicate it in a way that connects with the audience is a rare gift. I consider myself blessed to work with him as a colleague but also to call him one of my closest friends.

My last weekend as a V8 Supercar driver with teammate Craig Lowndes, Sandown, 2002.
Crompton collection

31

IFS, BUTS AND MAYBES

AS GUTTED AS I was at the way my last Bathurst 1000 finished in 2002, nothing will compare to what happened at the end of lap 113 and the start of lap 114 in the 2000 race at Mount Panorama. It makes my stomach churn to this very day.

If there's a 'what could have been' moment in my Bathurst career (and, let's face it, every driver has them), it's certainly the 2000 FAI 1000.

The Bathurst 1000 is so hard to get into a position to win, let alone actually win, and the race has always meant so much to me. So being taken out of contention in the 2000 race still irritates me. That year I was paired with Glenn Seton, in my last start with his Ford Tickford Racing team. All week the weather had been miserable, with deluges of rain the norm in the lead-up to the race, as well as in the early stages of the race itself.

By lap 113, though, the rain had cleared for a time, and our #5 Falcon was in the box seat. Although I wasn't leading the race on the road, I was the effective leader, given that my car was the first in the race order of those that only needed one more pit stop for fuel. Right behind me was Mark Skaife in the HRT Commodore he shared with Craig Lowndes. Next came Garth Tander's Valvoline/Garry Rogers Motorsport Commodore and Paul Radisich's Shell Helix/Dick Johnson Racing Falcon. Tander and Radisich were the two drivers who ended up finishing first and second.

Our car was excellent in that race. It had great pace, and Glenn and I were well and truly in contention. We were one of a small handful of genuine key contenders.

I closed in on a lapped car, a Commodore sponsored by Big Kev cleaning products driven by British Touring Car regular Matt Neal, who was sharing it with its owner, Paul Morris. I reached him at the top of the Mountain, and he started to weave all over the track to stop me from passing. The yellow Commodore was a few laps behind me, so I didn't expect it to be a problem. How wrong I was.

Neal held me up for a couple of laps, which allowed Skaife to get a little closer. To make things even tougher for all of us, it started to spit with rain. I finally managed to get by Neal down the inside at the last corner of the lap at Murray's Corner at the end of lap 113. I was at the extreme left of the track, on the white line, and had to climb the kerb to finally get it done.

I passed him cleanly, with zero contact. There was not a single scratch, not a fragment of paint exchanged – and I say that because later he carried on that he didn't like the way I passed him. Maybe he wanted me to send a politely written invitation asking for his permission to pass? I'm not sure what he was doing, and he wasn't either.

So I set off down Pit Straight. Once I had cleared the hurdle that was the yellow Commodore that cost so much time, my next headache was Skaife, who had reduced the gap and was right back on my bumper.

Under brakes into the next corner, Hell Corner, Neal dived to the inside of my car on the semi-wet track, slid straight past the left-hand side of me, all locked up and out of control, as I was turning down to the inside of the corner. He made strong enough contact that it ripped the bumper and splitter assembly off the front of my Falcon.

It stuffed my car and, because he was following closely, Skaife was also entangled in the mess. Mark's damage wasn't quite as bad as mine, though, and I was forced to limp around the rest of the lap to get back to the pits for repairs.

You could argue that I should have driven down the extreme left-hand side of Pit Straight to block Neal at turn one – why should I have to defend from a bloke who had already been lapped and should not have been racing the effective race leaders?

Driving back around to the pits, I was ropeable. I went off my brain on the car-to-pit radio with probably the biggest explosion I can recall. The language was way too colourful for the pages of this book.

Neal was given a 60-second stop-and-go penalty for causing the incident, but that was of little use to Glenn and I. He'd ruined any chance of success. It was all a great shame.

I've never spoken to Matt Neal about the incident, and I never want to. He's had a wonderfully successful career in

Wayne Gardner and I led the 1997 Bathurst race until the engine of our Coke Commodore blew. *AN1 Images/Dirk Klynsmith*

IFS, BUTS AND MAYBES

Britain over many years, and maybe he was having a bad day or trying to show how tough he was. I'm not sure.

Almost everyone who has raced with some success can tell you why they should have won at Bathurst and then ultimately didn't get the job done. But there's no doubt Glenn and I had a massive opportunity to succeed in 2000. Who knows, though – maybe five laps later something else could have brought us undone.

*

I always seemed to have a 'Bermuda Triangle' period in Bathurst 1000 races. If something went wrong while I was in a good position, it was generally around the lap 100 mark.

Even now, when I'm commentating the race on TV and I see the lap counter click to lap 100, I always glance at the race order and check who's leading and think, 'Geez, this could be another one who falls for a bit of Bathurst evil …'

The 1998 race was my first Bathurst driving with Glenn and the EL Falcon we raced was a fast car. The pair of us were well and truly in harmony with the car. We made a rear suspension damper adjustment at the end of my first stint in the race, and it transformed the car into a real contender for victory. However, a steel-braided power steering hose, which was new and should have been indestructible, somehow fractured and we lost over seven minutes while it was replaced.

The issue arose on lap 98, right in the Bathurst danger zone. We re-joined the race and I drove the wheels off the car in back-to-back stints to set the fastest lap of the race and recover some time, but we ultimately finished up fifth. Still, I reckon it was the best drive I put in at Bathurst, with the most polish. No mistakes, resolute focus, machine-like consistency – I was proud of the output. But because it wasn't a win or a podium finish, no one other than me and maybe Glenn remembers it! Such is life.

The Bathurst Bermuda Triangle struck in plenty of other years as well. Every time that I dared to dream of the ultimate success, the motor racing gods intervened swiftly. The Coke Commodore I was sharing with Wayne Gardner in 1997 blew its engine with Wayne at the helm on lap 90 while in the lead. Craig Lowndes slipped off the road into the tyre wall at Forrest's Elbow on lap 87 in 2001.

The Coke car I drove with Wayne in 1995 was a real understeering pig of a thing that was a struggle to manage under brakes. I speared off the road at the Chase on lap 104 and had to make an unscheduled pit stop on the next lap for a tyre change, just five laps after the car was last in the pit lane. How frustrating. We salvaged third place on the podium out of it.

However, there were other years that were beyond salvageable. I ran out of fuel in the HRT car in 1991 and retired after 100 laps. Gardner slipped on oil and crashed our Coke Commodore at the Cutting in 1994 on lap 100. The Brock Mobil BMW's engine lasted 89 laps in 1988. I made it to lap 112 in the 1997 two-litre Super Touring race in a Peugeot before its engine cried 'enough!'. My co-driver Mark Gibbs crashed our GIO Commodore on a slippery track in 1993 on lap 126.

In fact, when I look back on it, my car completed at least half of the races in every one of the 16 Bathurst 1000s I competed in. I never had a year where I was out of the race in the first stint or missed out on a drive altogether.

IFS, BUTS AND MAYBES

The Bathurst 1000 is the race that matters to me more than any other. I respect every driver and their achievements, and the point of view of many of the modern Supercars drivers who value winning the championship over winning the Bathurst 1000. We rightly celebrate those who win the championship for the high levels of complexity it takes to conquer that mission, but I grew up revering Bathurst. To win it would have fulfilled every conceivable motor racing childhood dream I had.

I led the race, frequently found myself in contention, and drove with some absolute legends, but I never closed the deal and won the thing. I could look at this two ways. I could wander around like a moaning misery guts. Or I could celebrate being in a position of such privilege that I was even able to race up there.

I'm disappointed not to have won the race, but eternally grateful for the chance to have had a shot.

32

THE HOME OF MOTORSPORT

THE FACT THAT I joined Network Ten's motorsport commentary team for 2003 after I finished my full-time V8 Supercar career was no real surprise to the industry. What may come as a surprise to many is that I turned down David White, their Head of Sport, multiple times before he finally convinced me to get on board.

I did have an offer to continue V8 Supercar racing in 2003, from the Sydney privateer Lansvale Racing Team, run by smash repairs shop owners Trevor Ashby and Steve Reed. I thought long and hard about it. They were great blokes and seriously keen motor racing guys – but I did I really want to go back into the slog of helping to build up a smaller team? I decided that I didn't.

David had kept in touch with me about joining Network Ten, whose tagline at the time – 'the Home of Motorsport' – was certainly true, given that they had just added Formula 1 to their existing motorsport portfolio.

Initially I said no. I had no interest in television at that time, but David, to his credit, continued his pursuit and kept refining his offer. He raised the dollar number on more than one occasion, but it wasn't the money that got me to do it in the end. It was being given the opportunity to make meaningful change. I didn't have my heart in it when I started doing it, but I grew into it and got my passion back, and then I started sailing along in the new chapter of my life.

Part of me felt that accepting David's offer was an easy way out – as if I had admitted defeat as a driver. But it turned out to be the polar opposite. I was in my early forties and felt like I was jammed in second gear and unsure of what to do next in life. The opportunity to join the Network Ten team allowed me to change gears, grow and accelerate. It was one of the best things that ever happened to me, so I owe David a lot of gratitude for that.

I insisted that the coverage had to tackle each event like a race team, bringing to light the intricacies of motor racing rather than just the colours, numbers and names. After many years of insight into the inner workings of top teams, I didn't like the way that the TV coverage, here and around the world, generally trivialised the topic with a shallow approach. There's far more to it than just top speeds and crashes.

Our first step in that process was bringing in noted race engineer Ross Holder, a long-time engineer at Gibson Motorsport during the team's successful Nissan and Holden eras. He had also engineered my car in my final season with

00 Motorsport in 2002. After all, if you want to catch the poachers, you need your own gamekeeper! We approached the races and events with substantial written engineering and strategic detail on hand.

I could ask Ross mid-race, 'Why has that team just made that strategic call?' and he'd be across the strategic reasoning, which we could then bring to the viewer in the telecast. It was exactly what we did in the race team.

The Network Ten era lifted Australian motorsport coverage to a new level, and when Ross moved overseas, I brought another former race engineer in from the V8 Supercars paddock, Oscar Fiorinotto. Oscar took it to the next level, introducing customised predictive software and integrating race team engineering and strategy tools into the broadcast unit. He remains in the role to this day.

David White and his colleagues at Network Ten accelerated the franchise of motorsport. He doubled down on Formula 1, IndyCar, World Rallying, MotoGP, V8 Supercars and the weekly magazine program *RPM*, and the network made a huge and successful franchise out of it. I loved the work we were doing, and it was exciting to be more broadly involved in the Formula 1, Indy and *RPM* work as well as the V8 Supercars telecasts.

The old Channel Ten had been a bit of a basket case. Mike Audcent, David's predecessor as Head of Sport, convinced me to do a bit of work for them in 1996 on their IndyCar telecasts. I was initially unwilling, such was the poor position of the network in the landscape of Australian television at the time. 'Do I really want to do this?' I asked myself.

Mike believed I made the complexity of motor racing simple, and when David arrived, he had full network control and put all of its motorsport in the one place on a Sunday afternoon.

*

There was one huge firestorm during my first year with Network Ten in 2003, when I found myself embroiled in a huge blow-up.

At that year's Winton round of the V8 Supercars Championship, I absolutely lashed former racer Colin Bond and the Stewards of the day on-air. Colin, who I count to this day as a great friend, had retired from racing in 1994 and was serving as the Driving Standards Observer for V8 Supercars, a role that provides recommendations on what penalties the officials should issue to competitors.

On track there had been an incident: drivers Greg Murphy and Craig Lowndes had tangled. Craig's Falcon had been sliding through a corner and was destined to slip off the road. Right on his tail, Greg's Kmart Commodore couldn't avoid hitting him and helped Lowndes on his way to the infield. Because of the way the rule book was written, Colin had no option but to ping Murphy for the incident, and the Kiwi was handed a pit lane penalty.

I was enraged after I heard his justification of the penalty in an interview, and I let fly. '110 percent wrong, Colin Bond!' I exclaimed. 'We will buy you a television, maybe a colour one, so you can see the red brake lights come on the preceding car, and I'm telling you, that is 110 percent wrong. That is one of the worst, if not the worst, stewards' decisions I have ever seen. Garth Wigston, Peter Svensson, Keith McKay and Colin Bond, hang your heads in shame.'

I'd only just stopped full-time racing and my blow-up on air overshadowed the racing and our broadcast. I still saw myself as a driver at that time. I blew up pretty much how Murphy did, overflowing with volatility and seething at the penalty.

Simply, when one driver jumps on the brakes in the middle of having his own lose, how the hell can you find fault and penalise the poor soul that is following in his wheels tracks with nowhere to go? This was racing, the rules of the general road did not apply.

I couldn't help but blow my top because it was nonsense.

The way the particular rule in the Operations Manual (the rule book under which V8 Supercars racing is run) was written in the day was 100 per cent rubbish, and I felt it needed to be shot down. It was written in such a way that Colin was obliged to give a penalty whenever one car hit another car from behind, which did not allow for the myriad of unique circumstances that motorsport inevitably throws up.

What that situation taught me, though, was that I should not stick my head too far up above the pulpit. My on-air comments brought me a serious censure from V8 Supercars CEO Wayne Cattach. It got to the point where no one cared about the car racing, and it became commentator versus the judiciary.

Wayne took the opportunity to give me a smashing via email, and told the media that the television commentary had created the situation. That was rubbish. What happened on the track created the controversy, and the rulebook and the way it was interpreted was simply wrong. I was so pissed off about the blistering note from Cattach that I considered walking away from my broadcast role.

Needless to say, I didn't walk away and I've probably been a little more sanguine when it comes to instinctive reactions on air ever since.

These days I have an excellent relationship with both Colin and Wayne and interact with them frequently – it goes to prove the integrity of the relationships is bigger than any blow-ups along the way.

*

In 2006, together with Leigh Diffey, I was given the privileged opportunity to call the Australian Grand Prix on Network Ten with Murray Walker.

Much has been said and written about the legendary Murray since his sad passing in 2021. His contribution to Formula 1, motorsport and broadcasting was gigantic. He was a truly fabulous individual. Intelligent, articulate, passionate and a pleasure to work with. He also taught me a valuable lesson, and a lesson for anyone who cared to pay attention on that weekend in 2006 at Albert Park.

At that time, Murray was a Honda ambassador, and Jenson Button and Rubens Barrichello were both driving Honda-powered cars in the Formula 1 World Championship. At one stage 'Muz' found himself on air live inside the Honda team bunker providing a special update. The point was to provide gems about life behind the scenes in a modern F1 team. However, Murray's access did not enable him to join the driving and engineering group as they had their post-session debrief.

So we crossed to Murray, live, our expert reporter on the spot, and although he was merely standing next to a closed door, in a plain pit garage corridor, he began giving a detailed and passionate dissertation about what might be going on behind the door.

'Jenson is saying this ... Rubens that ... Team Principal Nick Fry told me ... Alastair Gibson, the team's Chief Mechanic, said ...'

Murray did not draw breath for minutes. He sold his story with such passion that the viewers and even his commentary colleagues were transported into the moment. But what he was saying was a total and utter fantasy! It was brilliant. In truth, Murray had zero idea of what was being said or done behind that door, but you would never have known. It was like an episode of *Seinfeld* – a story about nothing – but the way Murray Walker performed his craft, you believed every word and looked forward to the next sentence.

He could have been standing outside the Albert Park public toilets for all we knew, but Murray's incredible gift to inform and entertain made us feel as though we were right there in the middle of the team debrief.

Priceless.

It was a wonderful lesson about how to entertain and inform with nothing more than your imagination and a sharp wit. Murray was a wonderful man, a master of his craft. We stayed in touch for many years, and like the entire motorsport-loving universe, I was deeply saddened by his passing.

*

The Network Ten period reinflated me. We did so many cool things as a unit. I called the British Grand Prix at Silverstone

Top: With Bill Woods on the Channel Ten set in the mid 2000s. The 'Home of Motorsport' was a great home for me. *Channel Ten Press*
Above: David White. *AN1 Images/Justin Deeley*

with Leigh Diffey, while Bill Woods and I went to the German Grand Prix and attended various Formula 1 launches. We visited Williams Grand Prix Engineering and interviewed Sir Frank Williams. I crossed the Pacific frequently to cover IndyCar racing, including the Indy 500, and we produced stories with industry luminaries like Chip Ganassi and Roger Penske.

The V8 Supercars telecasts became the toast of the racing world, and Ten made the best motor racing magazine show in the world, *RPM*. I was given the airtime and the resources to produce hours and hours of material, including in-depth interviews and technical features. It was in this period that we did so much to explain the sport in detail, not just skimming the surface.

I can't think of a single idea that was knocked back. Under David, and with the support of his senior team, Scott Young and Steve Wood, I was given a brush and the entire motorsport world was the canvas.

It was all thanks to the vision and tenacity of David White and the team he built around him.

Reflections

David White – Global President of Media at Lagardere Sports, Network Ten General Manager Sport 1997–2011

I didn't meet Neil properly until 1997 when I invited him to a Ten Sport Christmas lunch. I established very early on that he was not only a good bloke but a very decent human being.

Neil had proven during his time at Seven working with the late Mike Raymond that he was a very accomplished television presenter – some would say a natural – and I was determined for him to be part of our Channel Ten motorsport team. I approached the subject many times with him during the next five years, but his total focus at that time was on his motorsport career.

At the conclusion to the 2002 season, Neil had become fatigued by the pressures of being a professional driver and finally accepted my offer to join the 2003 Ten Motorsport commentary team. However, he did not want to be regarded as a television person. He wanted to be regarded as a racer. That was really important to him. He always wanted to be seen as a driver adding value to the broadcast.

We had a great four years with Neil in the commentary box from 2003 until the end of Channel Ten's V8 Supercars rights deal at the end of 2006. The 2005 Bathurst coverage will always be remembered as the best one ever. The commentary from Neil and the team was entertaining, word perfect and captured the whole story of the race so perfectly.

33

8 SEPTEMBER 2006

'CROMPTON ... IT'S TRUE, HE'S dead.'

I will go to my grave recalling those chilling words.

Friday, 8 September 2006 will forever be Australian motorsport's darkest day. Ask any motor racing fan or car buff where they were and what they were doing on that afternoon when the news came through that Peter Brock had been killed, and they'll likely be able to describe it in extraordinary detail. I know I can.

At that point of our lives, Peter had gone through the convulsions of his on-again, off-again involvement in racing, with several retirements and comebacks, while my life continued to rush in different directions. We didn't see as much of each other as we once had, or would have liked to, but when we did get back together it was always warm, enthusiastic and good fun, with, naturally, plenty of silly chat.

8 SEPTEMBER 2006

We were no longer the 'master and apprentice'. There were no issues with that; we were just old mates now, on slightly different tracks. That's often how life unfolds.

I was bowling along the road with my family in the Sydney traffic that awful Friday in September, totally oblivious to what was going on in Western Australia. The first sign of the nightmare to follow came via a call from Alison Drower, a former colleague who is the wife of rally and stunt driver ace Rick Bates.

At the time, Ali was the Triple M FM radio News Director, and always up for a gag. We had worked together on radio at 'the Ms' in Sydney years earlier, and on Network Ten's *RPM*. Her initial question came from left field, and was not pitched in her usual jovial tone. 'Have you heard the news?' she asked.

I had no idea where this random call was headed. 'What news?' I asked.

'The news that Brocky has been killed in a crash?'

My reaction was: 'Nah, no way – sounds like nonsense to me?' I didn't even know he was having a pedal. Ali was on the car speaker, with the family all listening. I felt a little dumbfounded. 'Say that again, Ali?'

In Western Australia, Peter was competing in a tarmac rally called Targa West, in a low-slung, V8-powered sportscar called a Daytona Coupe. I'd done thousands of hectic kilometres with Brock in all kinds of cars over the years, so it certainly didn't surprise me one bit that he may have had a shunt on the road one day, but I dismissed Ali's suggestion as crossed wires. I assured her that I would check with someone who would know, and would call her back.

If there was anyone who would know what was going on with Brock, it was his long-time friend, PR man and gatekeeper from the glory days of the 1970s and '80s, Tim 'Plastic' Pemberton. The Melbourne-based media manager was the person who suggested Brock call his infamous box of magnets and crystals the 'Polarizer' in the late 1980s. He was still a big part of Peter's world at the time, helping with various projects, including the old 'Humpy Holden' that Brock had just been driving at Goodwood's Historic Revival race event in England the week before he competed in Western Australia.

Tim looked after the Holden Racing Team's press and media liaison work when I drove for them and we did lots of other Holden-related work together.

'Is this stuff I'm hearing about Brock true?' I asked casually, in a somewhat dismissive tone, fully expecting him to tell me Brock had fallen off the road somewhere but was okay.

I'd never before heard the dour tone of Tim's response, and as soon as he uttered the first syllable, there was instantly a sickening knot in my stomach.

'Crompton ... it's true,' he replied. 'He's dead.'

A lengthy stunned silence followed. The hair stands up on my neck to this very day whenever I recall Plastic uttering those words.

Peter Brock was dead.

*

Peter's death really kicked me in the guts. It kicked the whole motorsport industry in the guts too, and the nation –

a nation that only four days earlier had lost another icon, the 'Crocodile Hunter' Steve Irwin. Peter was an industry pillar – the King of the Mountain. The King couldn't possibly be dead.

An entire generation cheered for this bloke. He was part of a golden era and transcended the oddity of driving around and around in circles in a race car to become an icon of popular culture. Whether he was plugging breakfast cereals, oil or tyres, or just turning up on a talk show, he could hold court, big-time. He was truly, as the cliché has it, a household name.

And now he was gone. This was incomprehensible.

Afterwards, I quickly found there was only one way I could deal with the pain and the noise. I shut down and hid. Other than with very close colleagues and organisations, I did no more radio interviews, made no more television appearances, no more chats. Nothing.

It felt like everybody who had ever met him, who ever owned a helmet or watched a bloody car race, was using this as their opportunity to be heard and seen. That wasn't really the case, of course – it was the thunder in my mind – but it was a terrible time.

Peter meant a lot to me. I hero-worshipped him as a racing-obsessed kid, and later in my life he concocted the circumstances to help me become the racing driver I had dared to dream of being. He held a very special place in my head, my heart and my life.

Brock was a complete maniac, but I loved him, and I miss him.

34

FAREWELL, PB

PETER BROCK'S STATE FUNERAL, held 11 days after his accident, was at St Paul's Cathedral in Melbourne's city centre – and it stopped the nation.

Televised live on television around Australia, on every network, it brought households, workplaces and businesses everywhere to a standstill. People paused to watch the broadcast; they gathered in their thousands across the road from the cathedral in Federation Square.

I wasn't originally going to be the one delivering the eulogy at Peter's farewell. It was going to be my mate and one of Peter's best friends, Alan Gow.

Alan was best known to racing fans as the expat Aussie who ran Brock's Mobil team in the post-Holden bust-up era, and helped him navigate the various business and financial potholes he drove into. Alan later moved to England to head up the British Touring Car Championship and prance around in gold-studded blue blazers doing important grown-up things in global motorsport with the international governing body, the FIA, the Fédération Internationale de l'Automobile.

Gow's story is impressive. Alan is a great Aussie motorsport export. Part of the reason I torment him is that when he was together with his mate Brock, they always greeted me with: 'Crompton – you idiot!' This was before, during and after I drove for them.

Gow had been by Brock's side over such a long period of time, but commitments in the United Kingdom meant he couldn't get back to Australia in time for Brock's funeral. So, with the endorsement of Peter's family, he asked me to do it. He's never told me this, but I don't think he wanted to be there, even if he could be. It was all too painful.

I had a larger public reaction to my speech that day than to anything else I've done in my life.

Farewelling my father in 2016 was truly a horrible experience, but farewelling PB was right up there. I was just numb. Tired and red-eyed, I couldn't hold anything resembling a normal conversation. My throat was so tight I could barely utter a word, let alone string together a lucid sentence.

My wife Sarah and I got there too early, and I couldn't bring myself to look at the helmet-adorned casket because it affected me too badly. I was a mess. The more I tried to look down and disengage from what was going on in that cathedral, the harder it was.

Then the moment arrived when I had to step up and speak.

It was not like doing a public speaking gig, where you get a lovely intro followed by a warm 'Please welcome our special guest ...' or something like that. Knowing that I would really struggle, I constructed a strategy in the lead-up to ensure I would do the sort of job Peter would have expected – and deserved.

I knew emotion would be my enemy, so I tried to tackle this mission like any other engagement, to compartmentalise it as a job and channel the thoughts and feelings of others. I tried to kid myself that this would make the task more like a professional engagement than a personal and emotional story.

Ahead of the funeral, I rang everybody I could. All our mates, his mates – guys like John Harvey, Allan Moffat, Larry Perkins, Mark Skaife, Greg Murphy, Brad Jones, Craig Lowndes and many more – for their thoughts and feelings and yarns. I tried to incorporate everybody into the speech, so the words came from 'us' not just 'me'. Despite my long and personal relationship with Peter, I was determined that the thoughts and feelings of the wider industry would be expressed.

As I rolled out the chat, I kept thinking of Peter. I knew he would have wanted me to do a good job, to make him proud, and I was determined to do it properly, invoking the sort of serious concentration and focus that are required when you drive a racing car on the limit. I largely held it together, although there were stumbles and cracks near the last lap when I simply choked.

I stood quietly in the background as Peter was lifted into the hearse, in my foggy thoughts offering a silent, profound thanks for his love, support and friendship. All the boys sent me notes or called afterwards. For once, our frequently dysfunctional motor racing family was united.

Completely smashed, mentally and physically, I ambled back to the Crown Casino to have a quiet drink. I was clutching Sarah, and Mark Skaife and Wayne Gardner came with us in support. The day was a painful blur. I excused myself and went to my room to sleep off the nightmare and the exhaustion.

In the aftermath, I got crook. I was about as sick as I've ever been in my life, with the most debilitating cold or flu or whatever it was. It went on for weeks.

Meanwhile, the phone was constantly ringing, and my email was pinging with messages from newspapers, magazines, radio stations and TV news. Everybody wanted a comment or a tribute. I didn't want a bar of it. It was selfish of me but just I couldn't deal with the pressure.

Bathurst that year brought some closure for so many people, and Mount Panorama was the obvious place for it to occur. But to me it felt like a month-long funeral. That made it really difficult and I'm sure it was that way for many others. I didn't appear at any other events or gatherings. All these years later, I know this aftermath was entirely appropriate, and a meaningful way for so many friends and fans to honour Peter and celebrate his life.

I've since tried to work out why I had such a lingering aversion. Motor racing and larger-than-life characters and machines represented such a powerful fantasy for me when I was a little kid. It was a perfectly neat little picture. As a fan of Peter's from an early age, then a friend, and eventually driving for him, life for me was all wonder, smiles, gags – it was a golden experience. Maybe it was all too good to be true?

I think his death hit me with the brutal reality of the risks in motorsport. That harsh realisation was one I preferred to ignore, and if I'm truthful I still do.

Regularly I receive media requests, usually around September every year as the anniversary of his death nears, from documentary makers and other organisations asking for my 'Brock stories', memories and thoughts. A couple of times in recent years I've participated, including in an episode of *Shannons Legends of Motorsport*, but on the whole I just don't want to participate in any tributes, shows or programs.

I only recently watched the video of the funeral. My good friend Nathan Prendergast, a motorsport television guru, and these days the Head of Supercars Media, edited an amazing clip in memory of Peter for one of our many shows. It incorporated elements of my speech, and we also had the original file vision of the funeral. I sat alone and watched it all in my Sydney office meeting room one quiet Saturday afternoon. It brought me to tears.

My lack of engagement in the aftermath could be misinterpreted as disrespect; however, it was precisely the opposite. I did everything that I could possibly do on the day of his funeral. I said what I really wanted to say. I felt I spoke on that day for myself, for our industry and for all those who worked with and loved Peter.

*

In the days that followed Peter's death, many industry peers shook their heads and wondered why he continued competing in any form of the sport, particularly when he'd won everything there was to win – and especially in the risky discipline that is tarmac rallying. This form of the sport features unprotected trees, rocky embankments and steep drop-offs, all ready and waiting should you make a mistake or have a mechanical failure.

For the road racing community, the contrast of our competitive setting compared to a tarmac rally is huge. For the circuit racers it's all about risk mitigation: sand traps, empty space, sealed runoffs and guardrails, thank you very much!

But why not be like Peter and live forever young? Peter did not like being bound by convention. I certainly don't act or think 'old' now, and he definitely didn't. I just remember thinking at the time of his death, 'What a waste.' I still think of that to this very day.

Brock was the guy who had everything – extraordinary natural skill, a presence, the ability to articulate, good looks. He was a sponsor's dream. In the back end of his life, he should have been enjoying being the revered, respected legend of his sport, passing his judgement on those who came after him, offering his trademark positivity, rolling in and out of a racetrack or studio whenever he felt like it, all the while 'clipping the ticket' for a dollar along the way. His last ten, 15, 20 or whatever years should have been beautiful.

I've had moments where I've been frustrated that he was driving that car so hard in that event in Perth in 2006. But that's terribly unfair to Richard Bendall, who owned the Daytona Coupe, and it's unfair to Mick Hone, his close friend and navigator, who was a fine former Superbike racer himself.

It's also mostly unfair to Peter and his passion for driving fast cars – that was something he wanted to do.

These days I can rationalise it all a lot more, but at the time I found myself constantly asking, 'Why was he doing that?' It's just deeply saddening to think he's not here to enjoy his sunset.

Reflections

Alan Gow – Chief Executive, British Touring Car Championship and President of the FIA Touring Car Commission

Neil is one of the best communicators in motorsport. He can explain, inform and entertain viewers on even the most complex of subjects and make it palatable for them to understand. He plays down his own ability far too much.

As a driver, Neil was extremely underrated. The shame of his career as a driver is that it wasn't the other way around – given he started life as a broadcaster and moved into driving. Initially, people didn't take him seriously enough. To them he was a 'talking head' who wanted to drive cars. But we all know that in fact it was the other way around: he was a racer who used broadcasting as his way to get into race driving.

Peter and Bev Brock loved him, and it was Peter who first suggested giving Neil a test in one of the cars. I was running Brock's Mobil 1 Racing team and I'll admit that most people on the team, myself included, thought, 'Pfffft, we need a proper driver, not a media guy in the second car.' But once he got behind the wheel, you could see he was the real deal.

When Peter died, I was asked if I could say a few words at the funeral, but I absolutely chickened out of that one. I just couldn't do it. Neil stepped up to the plate and did a fantastic job. It was clearly the hardest gig he's ever done. Not many people could have done what he did that day. I'll be forever in his debt for doing that. I can't think of anyone who would have done it better.

Alan Gow. *AN1 Images/Justin Deeley*

35

THE TIGHTROPE OF TV

SINCE I JOINED NETWORK Ten in 2003, my role has changed in the Supercars broadcasts. Initially I sat in the 'expert' chair, providing analysis and comments from my driver's viewpoint as someone who had a firm understanding and experience of what it takes to race at the top level.

That role is distinct from what is described as 'play-by-play', meaning the commentator whose role is to focus on and energetically describe what the viewer is seeing on their screen. The play-by-play commentator talks about what is happening, and the expert talks about why it's happening and what it means.

Locating the sweet spot in motorsport broadcasting is a high-wire act without a safety net. If you go okay, you survive; if not, those in 'executive-land' and the court of public opinion will send you through the trapdoor.

THE TIGHTROPE OF TV

As time has passed, I now find myself straddling the two roles, as both analyst and caller. My aim is to make the broadcast as warm, friendly, energised and informative for as many viewers as I can.

In my view, we're squarely in the entertainment business. When most folks plonk in front of the TV, it's a chance for them to escape their daily reality and be entertained and informed. Motorsport is something of a fantasyland in the eyes of many. It's a colourful, larger-than-life universe of characters, heroes, high-performance machinery and emotion, and it's our job as broadcasters to bring all that to life and deliver a cracking show.

To unpack this in greater detail, it's always my intention to ensure that a viewer with no connection to motorsport can understand and enjoy what is unfolding on track, while at the same time not frustrating regular or even expert viewers by diminishing key detail. And believe me, that's no easy balancing act. You can go too far in either the 'tech' or 'show biz' direction at any given moment, and I constantly stress about trying to ensure the mix is right.

I make mistakes, plenty of them, and I typically kick my own backside harder than anyone else ever could. Perhaps one of the best-known examples came during the Top 10 Shootout at Bathurst in 2006, when I was alleged to have dropped the 'c-bomb' during the coverage while throwing to a commercial break. I didn't say that particularly nasty word, but I agree it sounded like it.

That came in the wake of Brock's death, the funeral and all the emotion that went with it. I was as sick as a dog, and as I went to throw to the commercial break during the Top 10 Shootout, I wanted to say, 'After the break the big guns are coming out,' as there were only the last few cars left to go onto the track to compete for pole position. My voice was struggling, and I spat out a mangled word – 'cuns' instead of 'guns'. It was an honest mistake and, for some, it sounded shocking.

If I had the magic eraser of life, I would erase that one.

*

I much prefer two heads in the commentary box, as three's a crowd when it comes to energy, analysis, considered balance and breathing space. In the current era, Mark Skaife and I actually deliver both play by play and expert comments rather than having separate roles, which is somewhat rare but it works well.

If you look at Sky Sports' Formula 1 coverage, for example, there's a greater distinction between the roles of David Croft and Martin Brundle. Crofty is very much a broadcaster who calls the action, while Martin, as a veteran of 158 Formula 1 Grand Prix starts, can add and expand on that with authority.

About 99.9 per cent of my commentary is ad-libbed, though on occasion I will prepare for a probable outcome. For example, when the Supercars Championship is going right down to the wire and there's only one race to go, I will have at my fingertips a bunch of notes for circumstances that I think might arise. I jot down notes, not a word-for-word script, that will allow me to build up to the outcome and capture the moment of achievement in which a driver takes the championship.

I'll cover off their pathway in the season, leading to that special moment of success – and having already typed it

THE TIGHTROPE OF TV

earlier in the week, it's embedded in my thoughts so I tend not to require a piece of paper in front of me. I'm well prepared to call that special moment with the reverence, energy and positioning it deserves.

Because of the soundbite nature of the world we live in, I also put some thought into the preamble ahead of a race as well. Sometimes I structure how I am going to call the start of a race when the cars burst away from the grid, sometimes I don't. If it's Bathurst, I'll always plan what I would like to say at the start. But once the lights go out and the cars leave the grid, it's all ad-lib from there for the next six or seven hours.

Bathurst seems to fly by. I love it and it's all over way too soon. It's a huge job, before, during and after the Great Race, but in many ways I find it easier than the multi-race formats.

*

There's so much more data and information available now to fans and broadcasters than when I started on television. And there's also far more airtime to fill. Back in the day, we were only on air for a race on a Sunday afternoon, but now we do multiple races in a weekend, plus practice and qualifying sessions and pre- and post-session analysis. So we have to be conscious to avoid repetition. And that's way harder than it sounds. To get around this, you have to dig even deeper in preparation.

I treat broadcasting as serious work: race meetings are not social events for me. I might go out to dinner once with my colleagues, but most nights I go back to the hotel room from the track late, order room service or bring home some

Top: Skaifey joined me in the commentary box after his retirement from full-time racing. This is in Adelaide, 2009. *AN1 Images/Justin Deeley*
Above: Jess Yates.

THE TIGHTROPE OF TV

takeaway, and process everything I have learned that day for discussion on air the next day.

I don't like having a giant meal or multiple beers or a late night; I want to bring my A-game to every broadcast. To get the most out of myself, I'm largely invisible from a social perspective on race weekends. If I feel I'm going into the next day disorganised and underprepared, even if no one else notices it, I will – and that's unacceptable to me.

I enjoy great relationships with the vast majority of Supercar drivers and the broader industry. I try to catch as many in person each weekend as possible, and we chat and I jot down notes. Developing a level of trust is vital. Over the years, I've been entrusted with all kinds of highly sensitive information, but I know that betraying that confidence would spell the end of my access. Often these relationships allow me to call or text after hours, and I'll typically get a response and a valuable update. I'm very fortunate in that regard.

Although I take my job very seriously, I try to convey the fun and joy of motorsport as best I can. We're not saving lives, and racing can be a funny business at times.

In the broadcast team, we always work backwards from a list of key commandments and must-dos, which we drum into ourselves constantly. Where are we? Who are the players? What are the key rivalries, and what's happening in the locker room?

I have one key point I always try to hammer home to myself and my colleagues, and that is to ensure that nobody at home ever has to ask after a telecast: 'What happened to so and so?' If we do our jobs properly, there should be no mysteries left behind when we go off air. At least, that's the aim.

People shake their heads when, on occasion, I show them what it looks like inside the television commentary box. It's a busy and crazy place. There are multiple TV screens in front of Mark and I, one showing the live feed with the pictures viewers are seeing at home, detailed timing information and a live 'tracker' so we can see where each car is on the circuit, plus two screens containing more than 30 columns of complex strategy information. These include stuff like when a car last stopped in the pits, how long it stopped for, how much fuel it took on board, when it will next run out of fuel, how many tyres were fitted, and so on.

Then there's the audio thunder in my head. In my headphones, the racket is extreme. I hear myself and the wider commentary feed, occasionally the director and production talkback, constant live scanning of all 24 driver radios, while Oscar, our commentary box engineer, chips in with tech or strategy input. Often all at once.

It's not uncommon for Mark to look at me to raise a key point that I should respond to, for Oscar to light up the back channel, directing my attention to column 17 on his strategy feed, for Nathan to chime in with an overarching point or question, for Director Brian Forshaw to point us to a replay about to appear, and for Producer David Tunnicliffe to give us the heads-up that Larko needs to chip in from the pit lane – and all while a driver starts barking on his or her radio about a bad pit stop. It can be eye-crossing chaos! Any time I bring a colleague in to listen to this frenzy, they walk away thinking we're all insane.

At Bathurst, I plaster the wall and table in front of us with sheets of paper featuring all sorts of trigger notes for

THE TIGHTROPE OF TV

myself. Lists of previous race winners, pertinent data relating to the circuit, technical and strategy detail and information on competitors that's handy for me to have at eyeline rather than buried in a folder of papers.

It takes me roughly a month to prepare for Bathurst, and just over a week for each regular broadcast. Plus I constantly update my files on a daily trickle in between. I have a copy of the Supercars Operations Manual at my fingertips, with pertinent sections tagged and highlighted, ready to refer to as the need arises. There are also reams of statistics and background info on each driver and team. The great challenge is to pluck one of these elements and embed it within the commentary and try to do it in a seamless manner, making sure it's relevant to the discussion and to what's happening on the track.

Since Fox Sports signed up to take the Supercars rights in 2015, the Supercars Media broadcasts have been 'all you can eat', and the people and resources on offer are amazing. Bathurst is the peak where more than 300 talented people are devoted to making Mount Panorama come to life. We cover every practice and qualifying session and every race, all with no advertisements within the sessions or races.

To meet this requirement, our telecasts have many more layers. In 1985 at Bathurst, there was one outside broadcast van at the bottom of the Mountain and one at the top. In 2020 I counted five giant vans in the TV compound.

I hate it when television makes racing look slow or mundane, and I push – probably too much sometimes – to break the mould. Racing is anything but mundane, so rather than just putting out a 'coverage', I'm all about bringing the show to life so it roars into your lounge room.

I'm extremely hard on myself for any mistakes I make, especially as a broadcaster. I usually know when I've made a mistake, and it rattles me. If I accidentally call the wrong driver's name or fail to identify which driver is in which car during a race like the Bathurst 1000 where two drivers share a car, it annoys me greatly. Sometimes you can check yourself on air and fix it up, sometimes not. Mistakes like that make me uncomfortable, hot and sweaty, so I debrief my commentary work and make exit notes, just as I did as a driver.

Too much sporting and motorsport commentary is cliché-ridden, singsong, lightweight fluff, and I find that approach seriously annoying as both a fan and devotee.

I always aim to adhere to a simple four-step commentary formula. My aim is to transport every single viewer with a virtual 'access all areas' pass to everything, so each person feels as though they're right in the middle of the action and fully informed.

My formula is: entertain with passion and inform with facts; break down technical and strategic complexity with easy-to-grasp simplicity; explain what cannot be seen; and avoid leaving questions unanswered.

It may seem odd, but rather than imagining I am hollering away to a large audience, I like to picture I'm having a warm and personal conversation with each individual watching.

For someone who didn't want to continue to work in television in 2003, I now love what I do. We have a great on-air team, led by the extremely talented and hardworking Jess Yates, while our backstage Supercars Media production team, originally led by Simon Fordham and now by the gifted but crazy Nathan Prendergast, is simply world class. I'm proud to play a role in what we produce.

Reflections

Jess Yates – Fox Sports Supercars Championship TV host

I grew up watching and hearing Neil as the face and voice of motor racing in Australia, so the immense privilege I have to work alongside him is not lost on me. I really have a front row seat to the best in the business.

Neil is the consummate professional; he is world class. His incredible work ethic inspires our entire team. The sheer number of hours and the level of detail he applies in his preparation is unparalleled. I have learned so much from him. It goes a long way to explaining Neil's longevity in broadcasting. Through all the iterations of the ATCC/Supercars television broadcast, all the network rights changes, all the CEOs who have come and gone, Neil has been a constant and that's not by mistake. It is simply because his passion and expertise make him one of a kind.

Crompo can be a pretty serious bloke; he likes to play by the rules most of the time. That's not to say we don't have a heap of fun. I like to tease Neil by calling him George – after Steve Martin's character in the movie *Father of the Bride*. We joke Neil also comes from a long line of overreactors. Over the last decade working together we've become great mates, and above all else it's Neil's friendship that I value most.

36

THE TAKE OFF FOR AIRTIME

BY 2009 I FREQUENTLY felt as though I knew enough about broadcasting and creating motorsport content to make a change. To avoid being a one-trick talent pony, I decided I wanted to be more diverse in business. AirTime Media was born.

I am a huge believer in youth, reinvention and development, so one of the by-products of the creation of AirTime that I'm proud of is that it's become a platform for a range of talented creatives, including camera operators, editors, on-air talent, production staff, graphics and audio gurus, to ply their trade, hone their craft or learn the ropes.

Our first project was *V8Xtra*, a weekly magazine V8 Supercars show, which was a joint venture production between the Seven Network and V8 Supercars. The original show was a basket case, and I was stuck hosting what was in fact a crook program. Both Tony Cochrane and Saul Shtein (at the time the head of Seven Sport) wanted to kill it off.

I stepped in and proposed a different idea. Why give up a weekly Saturday timeslot promoting V8 Supercars on free-to-air TV? Why not fix the issues? We discussed making a revamped show, and somehow got the nod. Nathan Prendergast headed up the behind-the-camera side, and I co-produced, managed and presented the show. It was 'Neil & Nath Motors'. We did everything, even including assembling our own set furniture! We rescued the show from being put down.

Saul and Tony were not known for their tolerance of below par outcomes. In fact, Saul suggested we had four episodes to get it right, or the show was gone. My response: 'If I haven't fixed it in four episodes, please go ahead and pull the trigger.' We made 90 shows, before the next broadcast contract moved the category's rights to Fox Sports.

This portion of my broadcasting journey has been a great learning and growing experience. Pikes Peak, in Colorado, was a standout place to make a program. We made a one-hour doco in 2013, called *The Race to the Clouds*, for Peugeot, and it aired on Channel Seven and Fox Sports. The mission was to showcase the Pikes Peak International Hill Climb, a truly extreme event, and Sébastien Loeb's record-breaking attempt to conquer the 4300-metre mountain.

The Pikes Peak event is nuts. Imagine cars, bikes, truck and automotive devices of all shapes and sizes being driven and ridden flat-out. The course includes a 20-kilometre climb, 156 turns, variable weather and very little in the way of guardrails. Pikes had crazy risk written all over it, and bringing that to life was a fun gig.

Again, we were the raiders. It was a guerrilla production. We had a very small budget, just Nathan and I teaming up with a local camera operator, who struggled even to find the record button on the camera. It was hard work before, during and after, but we had the doco on-air within a month of our return.

Another US production group tackled the same project with an army of people, a massive budget and spent six months in post-production. Clearly I'm biased, but they missed the target by a mile – and airing it six months too late meant it lacked relevance anyway.

We also loved making the *Shannons Legends of Motorsport* series in 2014 and 2015. As the name implies, we made feature programs about the hero drivers, cars and events of yesteryear. These programs will forever serve as special markers, paying homage to the foundation members of Australian Touring Car Championship racing and what we now know as Supercars.

We featured as many heroes as possible. Aaron Noonan was dragged in to research the project, and we raided the vast Seven archive and shot interviews and content all around Australia. Our subjects included Peter Brock, Allan Moffat, Colin Bond, Larry Perkins, Bob Morris, Allan Grice, Fred Gibson, George Fury, Brad Jones, Kevin Bartlett, Mike Raymond, Garry Wilkinson, Tomas Mezera, Graham Moore, Bill Buckle, John Bowe and Mount Panorama.

There have been so many racing and corporate projects over the last dozen years that the hard drives in my office are jammed with terabytes of content, but one project really

Roger Penske, the Chairman of the Penske Corporation and an incredible figure in the automotive world. Producing a documentary on his amazing racing story was a great experience. He's the racer's racer. *Penske Corporation*

stands out. When Roger Penske decided to tackle Supercars with Marcos Ambrose in 2015, we all sat up straight. I regard Roger Penske as a living legend of motorsport. He is right up there with Henry Ford and Enzo Ferrari as one of the key automotive and motorsport figures of the last century, and here he was wanting to play in Supercars racing.

I'd met Roger many times before his arrival in Supercars. Our paths had crossed in 1997 when I was in the IndyCar paddock. Often Team Penske were our paddock neighbours, and I had the good fortune to interview Roger many times over the years. It struck me that while I was well aware of the depth and breadth of the Penske story, many Australian fans would not be aware of his extraordinary background in North American motorsport.

In a twist of fate, my old HRT boss, John Crennan, was consulting to Penske's new Supercars team, and I had met Tim Cindric, the President of Team Penske, several times ahead of the team's arrival down under. Tim previously worked for Steve Horne at the Truesports IndyCar team, and stayed on when Truesports became Team Rahal in my old temporary US hometown of Columbus, Ohio. So there was a loose connection.

Boldly, I thought I'd pitch the idea in 2016 of a Team Penske documentary, and convened a meeting at Bathurst. John and Tim listened, but initially there wasn't huge enthusiasm. Roger had knocked back every other single approach for similar projects.

My original thinking was based on attracting some sponsor funding to make this idea fly, so John and I met with several prospective backers, but the effort came to nought.

THE TAKE OFF FOR AIRTIME

I'm not sure how but I managed to convince them to let me proceed. It might have been the offer to give them veto rights over all content, or maybe they felt it was going to help grow Penske's mainstream business interests in Australia. But whatever the reason, they agreed to let me visit them in the United States and interview Roger and explain the history of Team Penske.

Now the problem was funding. I had zero. My travel deadline was getting closer, so I took a punt and made the whole thing unfunded. I won't disclose the cost, but it was a lot of my own money – enough to make my wife, Sarah, more than raise her eyebrows about what the hell I was doing.

The first interview was to be shot at Scottsdale, outside Phoenix in Arizona. The shoot coincided with the NASCAR round. Roger owned a giant auto mall in Scottsdale, with nine different franchises on site. His racing museum sits as the shining centrepiece of the car dealerships.

Jonathan Gibson was then the Vice President of Team Penske, and Jeremy Troiano was the Senior Communications Manager. Making arrangements via Jonathan and Jeremy was a pleasure. Initially, the time frames we agreed were intended to ensure that Roger's time was protected, but he quickly waved them away. All in all, the experience was tremendous and the interview went very well. He and I clicked and he invited me to the race as his guest.

On race day we had breakfast in his private suite, watching the Formula 1 feed and listening to my little mate Leigh Diffey doing the call.

In all my conversations with Roger, I understood first and foremost that he's a racer's racer. He loves racing, and lives it. Racing powers Roger and his business empire. Our visit to the United States also involved a trip to the Team Penske shop in Mooresville, North Carolina. It's not really a typical workshop. It's a glistening corporation that employs over 600 people that happens to make and operate race cars. And that's just a tiny fraction of his vast automotive empire.

The second key point that echoed across everything I discovered onsite was that every man and woman I met who worked for Roger revered him. I'd never witnessed anything like it in my life, and certainly not in motorsport.

I threw as many resources as I could afford to tell Roger Penske's story. The documentary aired on Fox Sports in Australia, and drew praise from Roger and his senior management team, Bud Denker, Walter Czarnecki, Tim Cindric and Jonathan Gibson. Roger sent a heartfelt personal letter of thanks, which sits framed on the wall of my office to this day.

*

The next time I saw Roger was in Perth in April 2017. He told me I should come to Indianapolis for the Indy 500, and he'd take care of the rest. Initially I hedged, as I had other bookings around those dates. Steve Horne happened to be in Perth that weekend and he pulled me up.

'What the hell are you thinking?' he said. 'Roger Penske has asked you to go to Indy with him. Clear your diary and do it now!'

As usual, Steve was right. Indy 2017 was an incredible personal and professional experience. My office base was Roger's personal trailer. I spent the weekend by his side, enjoying a police escort to the venue, a private family banquet in the pre-race lead-up, time in the team garage (where I was reacquainted with old friends Hélio Castroneves and Will Power), being introduced to racing royalty in pit lane, and watching the race with Roger's wife, Kathy, in their private suite. I'm not ashamed to say this was pure fanboy stuff.

I've subsequently visited Roger's operation a bunch of times. I've been to Phoenix and to Detroit multiple times, and spent time at head office in Michigan. Telling Penske's story is one of the things I'm proudest of in my broadcasting and production career, and certainly one of the best investments I've ever made.

The project unlocked a wonderful friendship, created a raft of new relationships, and afforded me a rare privilege to witness something and someone special from a vantage point I could never have imagined.

Reflections

Nathan Prendergast – Supercars General Manager of Television and Content 2017 – present

The best way to understand Neil Crompton is to go flying in an aeroplane with him. It's a combination of strict professionalism, the pure skill and genius to fly an aircraft and the passion and enjoyment of what he gets out of flying. It captures the very broad set of elements that make him up as a person.

In my younger days I was intimidated by him, but I first met him properly around the time of his wedding to his wife, Sarah, in 2008. I somehow ended up being the guy who edited his wedding video and we formed a relationship from there.

Our working relationship kicked off on a flight to New Zealand for a round of the V8 Supercars Championship. The *V8Xtra* television program of the time on Channel Seven was unloved and in doubt to continue, and he requested to the Head of Sport, Saul Shtein, that he be permitted to keep it alive. He walked across the aisle of the plane and asked me if I reckoned if we could make the show for a pretty cheap amount per episode. I said, 'Sure, let's do it' – and we did it for three or four seasons and have made a lot of great television together ever since.

As a person, you'll not meet anyone with higher integrity. He is a friend for life and someone who will do absolutely anything for you at the drop of a hat. He's always been there for me on a professional and personal level.

As on-air talent, he's one of the best in the business. His world-class commentary is the unmistakable sound of Supercars, yet he's just as comfortable in front of camera. His respect with the competitor group in pit lane gives him access to people and information that few in the game ever could get, and his extended vocabulary is original and educated without isolating the audience. Combine that with his time racing with some of the best drivers globally for 15 years and that makes Neil one of the best in the world at his craft.

It must be said too that he can be the most annoying, hyper-organised nerd you've ever met who has to follow process and order in everything in his life! He's always an A to B to C guy, who can't skip a step along the way. It's one of the reasons why he's so good at what he does, and we love him for it.

Neil is all about passion and perfection. His integrity is the key word, though; it shines through at every level.

Nathan Prendergast. *AirTime Media*

37

THE GREATEST GREAT RACE

I'M OFTEN ASKED WHETHER I have a favourite race, or what was the best race I've called. There have been so many high points along the way that it's near impossible for me to isolate a single race. If I dig deeply, though, I can pick out one that had every imaginable entertainment ingredient. It unfolded like a carefully crafted drama, and was a race that delivered the ultimate crescendo. The commentary box hummed as the unbelievable storyline played out, and my voice struggled to keep up.

The 2014 race was the longest Bathurst 1000 in the race's storied history. It typified all that we've come to love about the Bathurst 1000 – and this one had an additional twist, with a mid-race stoppage that really did turn the whole shebang into an enduro event – for everybody.

There was one lap remaining to determine the victor. On this day, Sunday, 12 October 2014, victory in Australia's most revered motorsport event came down to two men: Jamie Whincup and Chaz Mostert. Both had started at the tail of the field nearly eight hours earlier, and now found themselves in a one-on-one battle for victory over the last 6.213 kilometres of the famous Mount Panorama circuit.

Whincup's Red Bull Commodore held the lead, though an emerging problem was threatening to deny him his fifth Bathurst 1000 victory: his fuel tank was nearly dry. Lap after lap he'd received radio messages from his team, which we broadcast to millions watching at home, pleading with him to back off and conserve fuel in order to make it to the finish.

But conserving fuel and racing fast enough to hold off a challenger at the same time is just about impossible. You can't do one without affecting the other. Jamie ignored all the warnings about low fuel and voted for pace.

Behind Whincup sat Mostert, his Pepsi Max blue Falcon loaded with enough fuel to make it to the finish line, which meant he could attack the leader without fear of running dry. At age 22, he was in just his second Bathurst 1000. Heading up the long climb towards the top of the Mountain, he had the #1 Holden in his sights.

That Whincup and Mostert could be fighting for victory in the closing laps seemed improbable at the start of the day. The former had started 23rd on the grid after a crash in qualifying on the Friday afternoon, while the latter started 25th, having had his qualifying time removed for passing a car under a red flag during the session.

In the commentary box, I mustered my all for a grandstand finish as viewers watching on Channel Seven around Australia and the world sat and watched this unbelievable finish. A monumental climax was building.

'Mostert is going to throw everything he's got at it, but he has got to be careful not to throw it in the weeds,' I exclaimed as the two cars rounded the second corner of the final lap, Mostert locking onto the rear of the leading car.

Over the following moments Whincup was able to keep his nose in front across the narrow section at the top of the famous circuit, where passing is virtually impossible unless one driver moves aside – or runs out of fuel.

'He's got to be in trouble – can he redeem this? I very much doubt it,' I followed up with as the two cars zipped past the roaring crowd at the top of Mount Panorama. The fans were going nuts, waving their Holden and Ford flags, roaring at the top of their lungs. My voice was broken; I couldn't match the racket of the crowd. It was clear that Whincup was cooked.

'This is off the scale, off the scale,' I boomed as Mostert looked to attack the wounded Commodore at Forrest's Elbow, the corner that takes the cars onto Conrod Straight.

He rattled the rear bumper bar of Whincup's car. It was faltering and spluttering, and then came the moment the young gun stormed by the now defenceless five-time Supercars champion, set off down Conrod Straight and swept to an incredible victory, complete with a sideways slide at the final corner before greeting the chequered flag.

It delivered Chaz his first Bathurst win, and his co-driver Paul Morris a victory in his 22nd and last attempt at the Great Race. Morris had been stuck in the fence at Griffins

Bend at turn two, one of a bunch of drivers caught out when the track surface broke up early in the race. The fact that he and Mostert had won was simply astonishing.

I said on-air I was out of breath. In fact I was totally and utterly stuffed.

The layers of the story of that race were plentiful. Perhaps the biggest was the fact the race came to a grinding stop on lap 60 when the bitumen at Griffins Bend began to break up in the worst place possible – on the racing line in the inside of the corner. Debris and chunks from the road forced a range of cars to spear straight off and into the tyre wall.

In unprecedented scenes, the race was red-flagged and the whole field sat parked up on Pit Straight for an hour, waiting for the track to be patched up and the race to resume. It was like a half-time break for oranges!

At one stage I thought we might lose the race completely and it wouldn't be restarted. When the officials are trying to jam quick-drying resin into the gaps in the road to get the race back on track, you know things aren't looking too good!

I remember seeing the faces of Saul Shtein and Col Southey, the executive team from Channel Seven, in the TV compound afterwards. They're blokes who had seen it all in sport and on TV, and they were shaking their heads, speechless.

I'd been up since 4.30 am in meetings and sorting the final preparations. The 'yapping' started on air at 7 am, and there we were, still going, 12 hours later. The race itself ran for nearly eight hours that day, making it the longest Bathurst 1000 on the clock in history.

*

In recent times, so many of the Great Races at Bathurst have been decided by less than a second. That's amazing – and I love it. It's incredible because the 60 men and women who create these race cars all go about it in a completely different way. If you peer inside, say, a Dick Johnson Racing Mustang Supercar or a Tickford Mustang, there might be outward similarities but really they will have taken hugely different approaches beneath the skin.

The cars are adjusted and fettled in completely different ways. The two drivers have their own physical and mental skill sets. And then there's the random nuances of the day at Bathurst – the wind, temperature changes, rain and the random acts of weirdness including kangaroos, errant rocks, runaway tyres and more.

The Great Race delivers like no other. It epitomises everything I love about motorsport, and it eventually builds to that final moment where everyone in the industry has delivered their absolute maximum. It doesn't matter whether you're an administrator, a mechanic, a team owner, a race driver or anyone else involved, Bathurst draws the best out of everyone. You can sense that from the minute you drive into the place at the start of race week.

And that's massively powerful. It's made my hair stand on end annually since 1977, and especially in 2014!

Reflections

Scott McLaughlin – Supercars Champion 2018, 2019 and 2020, Team Penske IndyCar driver

Neil Crompton is the guy I grew up listening to on television, the Murray Walker of Supercars, the voice that is instantly connected to Australia's unique form of motorsport as Murray was to Formula 1.

When you think of Supercars, you think of 'Crompo'. I'm honoured that he's called every Supercars Championship race that I've ever competed in. His voice has provided the soundtrack to my Supercars career, all of the highs and all of the lows.

I still get shivers up my spine watching my 2017 pole position lap at Bathurst. It was a special moment in my career to become the first Supercars driver to lap Mount Panorama in the two-minute-three-second bracket and Neil's call made it even more special.

'He's got it two wheels in the dirt at McPhillamy, does that give him an invoice?' he said as I drifted the right-side wheels out onto the dirt verge on the side of the track at well over 200 kilometres per hour. 'Is there a price to pay for that one?'

I'll remember it for years to come, a typical Crompton call. Measured, accurate, professional, very special. He has an incredible ability as a broadcaster to simplify everything that is initially hard to understand and always hits the right mix of light and shade with his on-air delivery.

Neil is world-class, he could call any form of racing around the world with authority, and he'd do it with his typical trademark professionalism, but he's the signature voice of Supercars and that's very, very special. He's a phenomenal operator. I remember being in a Supercars Development Series meeting earlier in my career and he walked into the room to speak to the young drivers. No one was really paying much attention to what was going on until he walked into the room. His entrance lit a spark and he walked in with an aura of professionalism and an amazing story of where he's been, who he's seen and who he's done it with across his career.

I'll never forget that day, the first day I met Neil. Ever since then I've respected his opinions on everything.

Scott McLaughlin. *AN1 Images/Dirk Klynsmith*

38

SIDETRACKED

I'D JUST FINISHED A quick lunch with Will Davison in the tent beside the Dick Johnson Racing transporter, and I wandered towards the garages for a sit-down interview with Jamie Whincup. It was the early afternoon of Friday, 16 April 2021 at Symmons Plains Raceway, near Launceston in Tasmania.

The phone rang: it was the call I'd been expecting from the specialist. I gestured to Jamie that I needed to break away from what should have been a normal greeting. I found a nearby wheelie bin to lean on in front of the Triple Eight transporter and propped in the sunshine.

The doctor confirmed the news I didn't want to hear. Bad news.

I had cancer.

Prostate cancer, to be precise.

For more than 40 years I had been something of a specialist at wriggling out of tight spaces, finding ways to ward off bad news or difficulties and still move forward. Not this time.

I went quiet. Race events are always a passing parade of friends, colleagues and associates. We smile, gesture, nod, greet, stop and chat. The extended motor racing community are all members of a giant religion, and even when it's dysfunctional I can't help but love the congregation.

But when I received this news, my world went oddly silent. Friendly faces walking to and from the administration centre became opaque. I couldn't see, hear or think.

I called Nathan Prendergast. Nath is more a brother than a boss. We'd worked very closely for over a decade. He immediately said I should come to his office in the production trailer. I vaguely recall Larko shooting a gag my way as I passed by, but nothing registered.

Once inside, I shared the news and fell apart. Nath bundled me into his car and we vanished from sight for a few hours.

My first decision was whether to go home to Sydney or keep working. This was a difficult call. I agonised over it. Part of me thought the best thing I could do was to get out of there; I was worried that the shock of the diagnosis and leaving the race meeting in such circumstances would make the situation much worse. Once the initial shock subsided, I decided to keep doing what I loved. Sitting at home with negative thoughts swirling around me wasn't for me. Jess Yates was away on maternity leave, so the hosting duties for this race had fallen to me, on top of my regular commentary act. I felt no hardship at sharing a desk with Mark Skaife and Marcos Ambrose – in fact, it was good fun with great mates – but I had to fend off the negative emotion that threatened to overwhelm me. However, once I was off camera, away from the host desk and the gaze of others, the feeling of dread was almost too much. Maintaining composure on that weekend was the hardest thing I've ever done in broadcasting.

Staying focused wasn't easy. In truth, I had badly underestimated the lingering discomfort I would feel from the hospital procedure conducted earlier in the week, and mentally I was extremely fragile. After delivering the final words in each segment across Saturday and Sunday, I felt as though I was going to burst.

It wasn't meant to be that way. The procedure was originally intended to follow the Tasmanian race, but the event date was shifted a week due to another COVID-19 scare.

*

The circumstances that led to my diagnosis are bizarre.

I had a life insurance policy that was getting too costly, and my broker found an alternative product. Launching any new policy of this nature required the usual medical checks before they take your cash. In the analysis, a small anomaly was discovered, but it was not considered a big deal and a follow-up test was suggested.

At the exact same time, Andrew Wiles, the Walkinshaw Andretti United Communications Manager called. 'Don't yell at me and call me names,' he said, 'but would you be interested in driving for us at Sandown on the Monday drive day after the race meeting? We've got a third car and 180 guests and could use an extra driving hand, and we thought you might like a run.'

Apart from racing for the team back in the stone age when it was known as the Holden Racing Team, I'd done thousands of kilometres for the HRT drive day programs, so I understood the routine and the expectation and knew a bunch of the crew.

Normally I'd have said no, but I was keen to have another run, knowing that, at 60 years of age, I was much closer to the time when I'd no longer be able to take this sort of opportunity. I'd had a run in a Brad Jones Racing Supercar a year earlier and thoroughly enjoyed the experience.

The WAU drive required me to re-activate my Motorsport Australia (MA) National Competition Licence – and, as I was by now a senior citizen, this required another medical. This meant contacting an old friend, Dr Anton Mechtler. Anton, a former production car racer, had been handling my racing licence medical renewals for years.

'Yeah, mate, no problem,' he said. 'Fill out your forms, get your blood and other tests and the ECG done, and then come and see me and we'll do the paperwork. Are you feeling healthy?'

'One hundred per cent,' I said. 'I feel great. Been riding my mountain bike, the odd water ski. I'm busy as hell but everything is fine.'

I then told Anton about the insurance medical and the fact they'd spotted a tiny trace of blood in my urine. He didn't like the sound of that, and told me the exact day he wanted the follow-up test done. The outcome from test two was both good and bad. There was no evidence of a blood trace, but in the space of just 14 days my PSA (prostate-specific antigen) levels had jumped significantly.

This discovery sent me off to a specialist, then an MRI scan, followed by a biopsy procedure under a general anaesthetic in hospital, where they plucked out 21 sushi-like bits of me for analysis. I was now on the slippery slope, with very little control. All of this came just a few days before the Symmons Plains event in Tasmania.

The potential life insurance policy change started the process, and the MA licence renewal had brought what became a serious issue sharply into focus. I could have just ditched the life insurance policy change and been none the wiser. As fate, passion or serendipity would have it, I wanted to drive a Supercar again, and this desire may well have saved my life, or at least extended it.

*

The drive day was awesome. I shared the car with Kurt Kostecki. I drove at my own comfortable pace, enough to satisfy my thirst and give the guests an insight into the amazing world of Supercars. I was nowhere near the pace at which the real players operate, however it was enough for me to feel the car, reignite that special feeling and observe the drivers at close quarters on a great track.

Hanging out, having fun and sharing war stories in the front of the team transporter with Chaz Mostert, Bryce Fullwood, Lee Holdsworth and Warren Luff reminded me of the wonderful camaraderie I'd experienced with teammates and friends over the years. Driving any top-level racing car as a profession is beyond a privilege.

We even spun a goofy April Fool's Day gag: that team co-owner Michael Andretti and I were coming out of retirement to race together at Bathurst. The whole thing was damn good fun.

Team Principal Bruce Stewart issued me an open invitation to drive some more hot laps anytime I felt up to it in the future. But the grim medical news was yet to be delivered. I knew deep down inside that something was wrong, and I may have been in trouble, which made the drive at Sandown all the more special.

*

The surgical intervention was swift. By early June I was in a Sydney hospital for major surgery. Inbound to the operating theatre I was asked if I wanted to glimpse the machinery involved in the robotic surgery. It was an offer I politely declined. I have huge respect for the incredible skills of the talented people involved and the amazing technology at their fingertips but, frankly, if I could have escaped with my open-backed gown flailing in the breeze, I certainly would have.

Once we came to a halt in the middle of their version of the workshop, the anaesthetist took one look at me and said, 'You don't want to be here, do you?' By the time I tried to articulate an answer my world had faded to black.

The surgery took over four hours. At about the five- or six-hour mark I woke, sensing I was being pushed in a bed to a room. I could hear a nurse merrily chatting away and my responses were nothing more than disconnected gibberish. I do recall she said there was a lovely girl awaiting my arrival in the room, to which I crudely responded by asking, 'Is she a hottie?' As a matter of fact, she was: Sarah was there to survey the wreckage.

Several recollections stand out from the morphine-induced fog. Sarah had departed when I gleefully spotted my phone. I dialled both Nathan Prendergast and Brad Jones and then tried to systemically call everyone in my favourites list. Word got back to Sarah, the 'Leader of the Opposition', and on urgent instruction from my doctor, she called the hospital. The staff politely asked me to put the phone down and rest. Their actions spared various family members and mates like Skaifey and Larko, and VIPs and various others from my idiotic chat.

On the very serious matter of cancer, the specialist was confident he and his team had removed the cancerous organ and the spread was contained. The recovery at home was initially painful and slower than my restless demeanour was prepared to endure, but in the end I surrendered to a regime of proper rest and sleep and zero work. As the weeks unfolded, my health improvement accelerated dramatically.

Three months after the diagnosis and seven weeks after the operation the subsequent blood test confirmed I was out of the woods.

There will be an ongoing watching brief and management plan but, for the most part, life will return to normal, all thanks to the genius and skills of the specialist Dr Graham Coombes and my dear friend Dr Anton Mechtler.

*

I've had no shortage of sporting and political battles in my life, however I'd be a liar if I said I wasn't worried about the implications of facing off against cancer. I'll deal with that challenge in my own quiet and focused way.

Although I have a public role in my day job, I like to remain out of sight as much as possible, so I don't follow or contribute to social media, and I don't seek public attention or validation. However, I've been made aware (by my girls) of the surprising, amazing and overwhelming support offered by so many people from all over since my health announcement. I'm humbled by this, and deeply grateful – it's really helped. I more than appreciate that so many have taken time to offer me support and lift my spirits. It's certainly been a tough time, but this aspect has been extremely uplifting. Thank you all.

I didn't attain any educational qualifications at school. I don't possess any special training or skills, and any success I've had can be attributed to me just 'having a go'. For more than 40 years I've followed a simple mantra, and it starts with loving what you do. I love car racing and I set about becoming part of the culture. I pride myself on working hard, being fully prepared, being detailed and going the extra mile. That's it. There is no secret sauce.

The last 20-odd years of personal and professional growth have been especially amazing. I'm fortunate to enjoy a wonderful marriage with Sarah. I would have crashed and burned years ago without her. Sarah is simply my best friend, and I can't believe we tripped over each other. She has taught me so much about life, and thank goodness she's a completely different person to me.

The headline from our union is Sienna, a.k.a. Sis. Sis is from another planet, a strange concoction of the two of us. She has her mum's creative and passionate flair, with a

My gorgeous girls, Sienna and Emma. *Crompton collection*

bucketload of emotional intelligence, while my contribution is her can-do approach and the fact that she likes a chat – fancy that! She has twice the confidence I had at her age. Sarah and I are so looking forward to encouraging and witnessing her evolution.

My first-born daughter, Emma, is very special to me. Always aspiring to be a responsible and the best possible parent, I worried whether there would be any lingering damage after my divorce from Emma's mum. I need not have worried. Watching her grow into a beautiful, wonderful, busy young woman has been pretty cool. Today Emma is Junior Communications Manager for a public relations agency in Sydney. This means she's all over social media, unlike her dad! That's the universe paying me back. I'm very proud of her.

None of this would have been possible without the extraordinary support provided by my mum and dad, for which I'm eternally thankful. Dad passed away in 2016, and Mum is still accelerating her way through life.

It's impossible to identify all the special memories – they are beyond mega.

Cheering for Peter Brock in 1972, when he rolled out the freshly painted now red and white Holden Torana XU-1 complete with Globe mag wheels at Calder, and then driving for him 15 years later in 1987.

Bumping into one of Mike Raymond's old mates, the famed American motor racing commentator and journalist Chris Economaki, at the Long Beach Grand Prix in 1990, and again in the media centre at Indianapolis in 2002. Chris's yarns were priceless.

Spending time with Mark Webber during the Belgian Grand Prix at Spa in 2012. The weather was bad – no shock – when MW leapt out of the car in the Red Bull garage during the second practice session and said, 'Get in!' I initially refused, fearing I would die of embarrassment, but eventually yielded. Cameras came from everywhere. When a journo asked Mark, 'Who is this guy?' he told the mob I was a porn star from Australia! Being plugged into the Red Bull operation that weekend was a special highlight.

The private tour of Bernie Ecclestone's racing car collection with Mark Webber and his dad, Alan. Sitting in Alberto Ascari's Ferrari, crouching by James Hunt's World Championship-winning McLaren. Leaning on Nelson Piquet's Brabham. I've never seen anything like it – and never will again.

In the 1980s, 1990s and early 2000s, racing results meant everything. Winning, or trying to win, was a ruthless pursuit. Now, when I consider my time racing against my mates and peers, Glenn Seton, Mark Skaife, Brad Jones and Mark Larkham, I'm just so grateful I was there. The value is the relationships, the comradery, the fun and the nonsense war stories, which have grown out of all proportion – of course! We love it.

Calling a Formula 1 Grand Prix with the wonderful Murray Walker, and remaining in contact with him for many years afterwards. Wow!

Standing on the yard of bricks at Indianapolis with Steve Horne, and being employed to drive for his touring car project seven years later, and moving to America.

Building an enterprise and employing many good people, including the talented Craig Nayda. I'm extremely proud of the Toyota GAZOO Racing Australia 86 Series, and the growth of our content production business.

Perching on the TV host desk with Jessica Yates and Mark Skaife, untangling the events of the day in Supercars and having a good time doing it.

Looking around on a starting grid to see Alan Jones, Larry Perkins, Jim Richards, Peter Brock and Colin Bond in front of me, or behind or alongside me. Breathtaking.

Commanding an aircraft. Every trip makes my heart soar. I've got close to 2000 hours logged now.

Flying in Ross Palmer's private jet from Detroit to Chicago while trying to hustle an IndyCar deal with Ross.

Calling the Bathurst 1000 23 times.

Rolling onto the track at Winton in 1985, sharing my first race car with my good friend Peter McKay.

Flying through the air, oblivious to risk, on any number of motocross bikes for years.

Sharing a motor racing passion with drummer Nigel Olsson backstage at an Elton John concert – twice.

Chairing the Supercars Commission, and serving as an Independent Commissioner for six years. Making a contribution – making a difference – matters.

Saturday morning radio, 'The Stick Shift', on Triple M with Mark Skaife. Utter madness most weeks, and tremendous fun.

Calling the very first Singapore Grand Prix on location, and subsequently being asked to return for the next eight years by the organisers. I love Singapore.

Racing and winning in the Honda at Laguna Seca, in California, in 1997.

Proudly representing Holden and Ford as a factory driver in touring car and V8 Supercars racing.

Goofing off on *The Telstra BigPond Panel Beaters Show*

with my mate Brad Jones, long before everybody discovered podcasting.

Being with my gorgeous, funny, wise and incredibly supportive wife, Sarah. She should be given a medal for putting up with all the endless madness.

Convincing Tony Cochrane that another rock concert could wait, and that touring car racing had an entertainment future and he should be part of it.

Sleeping under the commentary box bench while jointly calling the 1990 Le Mans 24 Hour race with James Allen, then barely being able to remain awake. Interviewing my then race team boss, Tom Walkinshaw, and his number one driver, Martin Brundle, on the podium after their famous win with the Jaguar.

Proudly representing great brands like Mobil, Telecom Mobile, Coca Cola, Labatt and Ford Credit as a driver, and now Hino, Pirtek, Toyota, Mobil and Pedders as an ambassador.

Counting Roger Penske as a colleague and friend. Crazy.

The only time I can recall being totally starstruck. Barry Sheene was being … well, being Barry Sheene, and he introduced me to George Harrison. In response to Barry's cheeky offering, George turned to me said, 'Ee's a cheeky munkee, isn't ee?' – to which I responded with a nervous sound akin to the bleat of a billy goat. Not a single intelligent syllable passed my lips. Idiot!

Racing at Bathurst – 16 times in the Bathurst 1000, plus six Bathurst 12 Hour races and a 24 Hour.

Presenting and calling for the Network Ten, SBS, the ABC, Channel Seven (in multiple eras), ESPN, Triple M, Telstra BigPond and Fox Sports.

My kids, Emma and Sienna. Beautiful, vibrant girls full of good grace and lots of zing.

My life has been a giant mosaic with thousands and thousands of fond memories. Of course there have been ugly spots too, but I wouldn't change a minute of it.

I have no idea what comes next. I have no intention of retiring from anything in life. The throttle will remain pegged at 100 per cent, and I'll be open to every opportunity.

I'm reminded of a line from one of my mates, the former Formula 1 and IndyCar driver Derek Daly. We were discussing the right moment to retire from driving, and when we'd know it had come along. 'Oh, that's easy,' he said. 'When your heart no longer skips a beat as you drive through the front gate, it's time to stop.'

Good advice, I reckon. For the record, my heart still flutters at the front gate, especially at Bathurst. I love what I do, and I'll do as I've always done – my best. If it's good enough, then opportunity abounds. If not, I'll try something different. I fully intend to approach my illness as a pit stop, not a DNF. There's too much to do!

I began my journey as a kid in country Victoria with an obsession for motor racing, and I'll face whatever comes next, personally and professionally, eternally grateful for the amazing life I've enjoyed to date.

I have observed motor racing as a devoted fan, I've driven some of the most amazing racing cars as a professional, with and against some of the sport's biggest names, and I've talked passionately about this fabulous caper in all of its wonder and glory for decades.

I've enjoyed the best seat in the house.